The Icelandic Adventures

Of Pike Ward

Edited by
K.J. Findlay

Amphora Press

Published in the UK by Amphora Press
Imprint Academic Ltd., PO Box 200, Exeter EX5 5YX, UK

Distributed in the USA by
Ingram Book Company,
One Ingram Blvd., La Vergne, TN 37086, USA

ISBN 9781845409869 (hardcover)
978185409906 (paperback)

A CIP catalogue record for this book is available from the
British Library and US Library of Congress

Cover design by Joe Chisholm (joechisholm.co.uk)

All photographs, unless otherwise stated, are from Pike Ward's Icelandic
Scrapbook Volumes 1–8, reproduced with permission of the South West
Heritage Trust

Contents

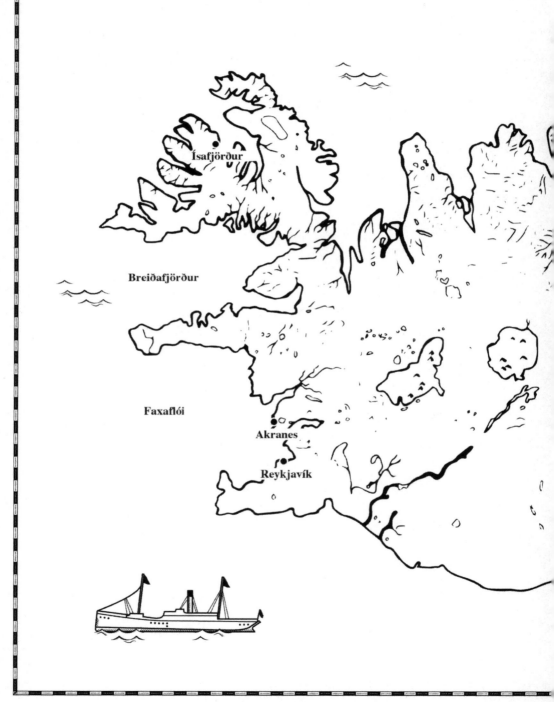

Húsavík

Akureyri

Bakkafjörður

Vopnafjörður

Seyðisfjörður

Egilsstaðir

Eskifjörður

Berufjörður

Vatnajökull

To the
Faroe Islands

To Mr Pike Ward

We remember you here, Mr. Ward!
For many years
you put gold on the farmer's table,
your words and deeds have truly been blessed.
You saved us from hardship
and we salute you for it.

You're leaving this ice-capped country
and heading back home
where you will enjoy honour and wealth
but you will not be forgotten
by those who love you,
our dear Mr. Ward.

Bjólfur wishes that your beloved country
will celebrate you on your return
and that you will have a good life
over there. — With us
your name will never be forgotten
but written in gold.

— Presented to Pike Ward by Fjelagið Bjólfur
  Translated by Hallgrímur Jökull Ámundason
  With thanks to Andrea Ward

Introduction

'*...a sea-farer, an adventurer, a trader in high latitudes, whose story, if it came to be written, would seem to belong to other times than ours...*'
—May Morris, An Appreciation of Pike Ward, 1937

Pike Ward was a fish merchant from Devon who became a Knight of the Grand Cross of the Icelandic Falcon, the nation's highest honour. According to an affectionate cartoon of 1901, he was 'the best-known man in Iceland', yet his role in the nation's remarkable rise has been largely forgotten. For more than twenty years he lived between England and Iceland until he was as Icelandic as he was English. He wrote this entertaining and evocative diary in 1906, when he was 49. In middle-age he was an imposing figure, tall and generously built, with a sturdy, waxed moustache. He was gregarious, jovial and canny, and had a talent for making friends, but his family life was marred by sadness.

The diary is his account of one working year in Iceland, from March to November. He wrote it by hand, recording events almost daily in three notebooks that went everywhere with him. They travelled in the luggage racks of the *Flying Scotsman* and on steamships that pitched and plunged across the North Atlantic. They sat on his desk and overheard the latest talk of Reykjavík society. They were packed into saddlebags and carried by tough little horses over mountains and cliffs and through the vast, empty grandeur of the Icelandic landscape. Eventually, the three battered books found their way into a storage box in the Bristol home of Pike's great-grandson, Steven, where they were rediscovered in 2016.

More than a century after it was written, the fresh and unaffected style of Pike's writing is striking. It is peppered with comical anecdotes and vivid descriptions, along with some moving accounts of tragedy and moments of exasperation and worry. It is, without doubt, a diary that was meant to be read rather than an outlet for private reflections. What was included and what was left out, what was explained and what was assumed to be understood, were decisions shaped by the audience in Pike's mind. The frequent comparisons to south Devon suggest that he was writing for loved ones or acquaintances in his home town, Teignmouth. The need for a certain amount of self-censorship when writing for others is perhaps behind his original choice of title: *The Book of Lies*. There is nothing in the writing itself that speaks of deliberate deception; indeed, the diary's significance is its authenticity as a contemporary, eye-witness account of a pivotal period in Iceland's history, told from Pike's unusual viewpoint as both insider and outsider.

As well as a notebook, he usually carried a camera. He was a prolific photographer, shooting in standard and stereo formats, and he developed his own images in a DIY darkroom or the studios of professional photographer friends. In both his writing and photography, it is Pike's rare ability to connect with people at all levels of society, from officials and intellectuals to servants and fishermen, that elevates his work from diverting travelogue to something much more valuable. He created a rich and unique record of Iceland at the turn of the 20th century, a window through which we can glimpse everyday life in a country transforming itself from an isolated and impoverished outpost to an affluent, independent nation.

***

Pike Ward was born in the seaside town of Teignmouth in 1856, the first of four children born to Eliza and George Perkins Ward. As the eldest son, he was given his mother's maiden name, Pike, as his first name. Teignmouth was a busy port close to the clay mines around Newton Abbot and George was a ship broker, merchant and shipping insurance agent. The business did well and the Wards were a prominent, middle-class family.

Two episodes from 1861, when Pike was five years old, give us clues to George's character. Encouraged by his friends, he ran for election to the Teignmouth Local Board on a single-issue campaign. His aim was to stop the building of a sea wall, not because it was a bad idea but because he felt taxpayers' money was being used unfairly to benefit the landed gentry. He argued that the Earl of Devon, who owned the site, would have a new asset built free of charge on land that he could close to ordinary people on a whim. George was a popular candidate and was duly elected. A few months later, he was brought before the local court for disobeying the orders of a coastguard in a dispute over aiding a grounded vessel, threatening to strike the man and refusing to apologise. George's status as a pillar of the community evidently did not stop him challenging authority when he saw fit. Like his father, Pike combined a self-confident sociability with a wide streak of nonconformity.

When George died in 1881, 25-year-old Pike became a director of the company, but it was Pike's mother, Eliza, who took over the day-to-day business of shipbroking. She was clever and tenacious, and Pike adored her. Her old friend and client Charles Davey Blake, of the clay mining company Watts, Blake, Bearne & Co., described her as 'the most intelligent and experienced of the citizens of Teignmouth'. The port handled around 100,000 tonnes of imports and exports per year and Eliza worked hard to maintain the company's share of the trade, directing ships all over Britain and Europe. In 1905, Charles wrote to her:

> 'What a lively little place Teignmouth will be with all these steamers etc coming — and how proud you will be at seeing nearly all the captains coming to your office and taking off their caps to you. I am very glad for the sake of your dear little self that so much grist comes to your mill. You deserve it all.'

In the diary, it is clear that Pike enjoys the company of women and values their friendship. The Wards were not fervently religious or sectarian, but they had ties to the Congregationalist Church and to a tradition of religious dissent that promoted equality between the sexes as well as between social classes, a background that helps to explain Pike's egalitarian outlook.

With Eliza capably running the family business, Pike was free to explore other avenues. In 1887, he became one of the directors of a new company, the Teignmouth Quay Company Ltd, which aimed to extend the town's quay and wharf capacity. Worthy though this scheme may have been, it cannot have provided much excitement, and it is easy to imagine that middle-class life in a small Victorian town was limiting, if not stifling, to a man with energy and curiosity. Like many Devon merchants, George had been involved in importing cod from New-foundland and Labrador, and even lived there for a while, but the stocks were declining and it did not seem to Pike that the old trade was worth pursuing. If he wanted adventure, new business opportunities and a name for himself out of the shadow of his family, he would have to go elsewhere.

In his mid-thirties, Pike looked a thousand miles to the north and decided to investigate the opportunities in Iceland. He arrived on a large island of magnificent, savage beauty, utterly unlike green and gentle Devon. A scattered population of just 80,000 souls battled a harsh climate, poor land and the weight of six centuries of misfortune and foreign rule. But the seas were rich and change was everywhere in the air. It was here that Pike found his place in the world.

To understand his role in Iceland's 20th-century transformation, we need to go back to the start of the nation's story. Iceland was settled in the 9th century by Viking pioneers, men of mainly Norwegian descent and women of more mixed heritage: wives, servants and slaves including many from Ireland and Britain. This fascinating group of people carved farmsteads from the new land and organised their society around a confederacy of chieftains. They had no overall ruler, and made decisions through a complex legal system based around the Alþingi, the annual outdoor assembly. The tales of these times, of blood-feuds and rivalries, feats of courage and the everyday struggles of life in an unforgiving land, were later recorded in the Icelandic Sagas, the extraordinary body of work that underpins Iceland's literary culture. Over time, power became concentrated in the hands of fewer families, until in-fighting led the Icelanders to submit to the Norwegian king in 1262. The Kalmar Union of 1397 brought the kingdoms of Norway, Denmark and Sweden together under a single monarch, including Norway's overseas territories. Denmark emerged as the dominant power in the union, and thus Iceland found itself under Danish rule. Over the centuries, climate change, famine, disease, natural disasters and the imposition by Denmark of trade monopoly laws all contributed to Iceland's decline into abject poverty, reaching a miserable low point in the 18th century.

As the 19th century progressed, the climate improved slightly, the population began to recover from the catastrophes of the previous century and trade restrictions were lifted, although the economy remained under the control of Danish merchants. Although life for most Icelanders was still wretched, a sense of national pride began to grow, inspired by nationalist and folklorist movements in mainland Europe. By the 1830s, pressure was building throughout the Danish territories and Icelanders demanded a new national assembly. The cause was taken up by a small group of Icelandic students in Copenhagen who published political articles and poems of praise to the motherland. They were motivated by pride in their ancient language and culture on one hand, and a desire to modernise their country on the other. The calls for greater autonomy soon developed into a struggle for full independence. The Danish government conceded slowly, in stages, starting with the re-establishment of the Alþingi at Reykjavík in 1845.

In his 2000 work *The History of Iceland*, Gunnar Karlsson raises the question of why the Danes bothered to hang on to Iceland at all. It was a military liability in the North Atlantic, being almost impossible to defend, and by this time the financial support Iceland received from the Danish treasury outweighed the revenue it contributed. He suggests that the reason was more sentimental than pragmatic. The 19th-century romanticisation of the Viking Age cast Iceland as a repository of the 'true' Norse culture, an idea that had appeal not just in Iceland but throughout northern Europe. Gunnar Karlsson suggests this nostalgia was behind Denmark's reluctance to let Iceland go, just as in Iceland it was fuelling the passion for independence.

Eventually, following years of negotiations and disputes, the Alþingi accepted a new constitution in 1874 as a sort of birthday present from the Danish king to mark the millennium of Iceland's settlement. It did not go as far as many people wanted, but it established a distinct status for Iceland under the Danish crown. In the years between Pike arriving in Iceland in 1891 and writing this diary in 1906, he witnessed further steps towards independence, including a significant expansion of Home Rule in 1904, when the role of governor was abolished and replaced with a minister for Iceland, a native Icelander based in Reykjavík.

Despite the mood of national ambition, Pike arrived in a country where the majority of people still lived in appalling poverty. Villages and towns had never developed as in other parts of Europe, and isolated farmsteads were the basic unit of society. Anyone who did not own farmland was tied by law to working for someone who did. The work was hard and people were equipped with only the most rudimentary tools. Farmhouses were made of turf and were usually cold, damp and infested with lice. In his 2010 social history *Wasteland With Words*, Sigurður Gylfi Magnússon reveals that it was common practice for hands, clothes and sheets to be washed in urine when they were washed at all, for people to spit on the floor and for food bowls to be licked clean by dogs. Disease was rife and children often died before they reached adulthood. In a traditional farmhouse, everyone lived in a single room called the baðstofa, often built on an upper level with livestock below to take advantage of the meagre warmth rising from the animals. Rooms were boarded with wood in better-off homes, or else the walls were bare turf. There was often no outhouse, so human and animal waste was piled in middens close to the living quarters. However, Pike's years in Iceland coincided with a period of great change, as urbanisation on the coasts accelerated, Reykjavík grew and transformed into a capital, and sanitation improved. By the time this diary was written, doctors and social reformers were campaigning for better public health and housing, and gradually sickness, suffering and death were becoming less ubiquitous in Icelanders' everyday lives.

Around this time, Iceland was becoming increasingly popular with more adventurous British tourists, although a trip there was still considered exotic enough to merit reports to local newspapers and lectures on return. The Reverend R.F. Ashley Spencer told his audience at the Tylers Green Mutual Improvement Society in Buckinghamshire in 1901 that Iceland was a place where, 'the snowfields look in bright sunshine like dazzling fairy-lands'. He asserted that, 'no Briton, fagged with hard work, who sought restoration to health and energy would regret spending a holiday among its geysers and volcanoes'. Guides took tourists on ponies to see the main sites at Þingvellir, Geysir, Hekla and Gullfoss. There was an interest in what was perceived as a shared Germanic heritage and intellectuals such as the designer and poet William Morris were captivated by the country and its Sagas. However, most people in Britain remained largely ignorant of their northerly neighbour. In 1906, *The Exeter and Plymouth Gazette* expressed a patronising degree of surprise on being told that there was a theatre in Reykjavík, 'on the outer-most fringe of civilisation', where drama 'lingers on, shivering like a delicate mental edelweiss, on the brink of the abyss beyond which there is an intellectual void'.

In fact, despite the hardships and lack of formal infrastructure, Iceland was an educated society with almost universal literacy, an astonishing achievement when compared with more developed countries in the same period. Children learned at home by reading with their families in the evenings after work, their progress checked periodically by the local clergy. At a time when most people owned next to nothing, nearly every home had at least one book and literature was highly valued. The Sagas, religious texts and poetry, along with a rich oral tradition of folk tales, provided an architecture of the imagination that helped people to both understand and escape their everyday lives. Sigurður Gylfi Magnússon has shown that enormous effort went in to disseminating written material in rural society, as people he terms 'barefoot historians' tirelessly copied out texts by hand and shared them. This love of learning was, he argues, a 'peasant mechanism for survival', an intellectual other-world that made life bearable. As well as reading, people took great pride in writing. Many people from humble backgrounds wrote diaries and autobiographies. Diaries were hugely popular in Victorian Britain too, and diarists usually wrote with an audience of friends and family in mind. In this regard, Pike's diary followed a British convention, although it is tempting to wonder to what extent he was also inspired by the Icelandic urge towards self-expression and the validation of ordinary experiences through writing.

In the early Middle Ages, the stories of Iceland and Britain intertwined as people sailed around the Viking world, fighting, trading, settling, and marrying. Over time the links broke, and in later centuries Iceland's relationship with Britain, and England in particular, came to be defined by fish. English boats began sailing to Iceland to fish soon after the turn of the 15th century. The English soon dominated the trade in Icelandic fish, much to the annoyance of the Danish monarchs who tried to prohibit their boats. The English resisted and the conflict sometimes turned to violence in the cold Atlantic seas. English fishermen made the journey to Iceland so frequently that Gunnar Karlsson even suggests that the expertise they gained helped to lay the foundations of the maritime supremacy that made the British Empire possible. By the 16th century, German merchants were muscling in on the trade, leading to skirmishes between crews. Eventually the Danish crown tightened its grip on Iceland to benefit Danish merchants, and the English and Germans went elsewhere to fish. Just as the modern age dawned, Iceland became disconnected from the great trading powers of Europe and increasingly isolated as a Danish outpost.

Icelandic fish remained of little commercial interest to Britain until the mid-19th century, when Icelandic waters began to look tempting once again. The cod stocks in Newfoundland and Labrador were in decline, Danish trade restrictions in Iceland were being relaxed and mechanised trawling was rapidly developing out of British ports. By the end of the century, at least 40 trawlers from Hull and Grimsby were working off the coast of Iceland annually, with many more from Aberdeen, Lerwick and other ports. It was reported in the British press that a steam trawler could obtain a full cargo of the best quality mixed fish in 24 hours and could make over £1,000 in two trips. British crews were known to poach Danish waters, damage breeding grounds and encroach into estuaries and shallow banks fished by Icelanders. British steam trawlers were frequently seized and their skippers fined by Danish authorities. In 1895, the British government sent four naval ships to keep order. Their commander negotiated an agreement on fishing limits, only to be infuriated when the British trawlermen promptly reneged on it. He sympathised with the 'miserably poor' Icelandic fishermen who had to watch their livelihoods being taken from them. He noted the 'very bitter mood' of the Icelanders and the likelihood of reprisals against the British. In general, however, the British position was to pressure the less powerful Danish government to reduce Icelandic territorial waters as far as possible, and in 1901 the

Icelandic limit was set at just three nautical miles. The previous year, three Icelanders had drowned while attempting to arrest the captain of the Hull trawler *Royalist* who responded by capsizing their rowing boat. *Royalist* was seized a month later while fishing illegally in Danish waters. Laws which restricted foreign trawlers from approaching Icelandic ports may have done more harm than good in this situation, since they ensured the trawlers stayed at sea, drifting in the fish banks even in perilous weather. On his retirement in 1903, the captain of a Danish government cruiser noted in *The Scotsman* that trawler owners, safely counting their profits back in Britain, 'could not easily find better help than laws that keep their fishermen frightened'.

Against this fractious backdrop, how was it that Pike Ward, an English fish merchant, became one of the most widely respected and well-loved people in Iceland? The answer lies in his ability to understand the trade not just from a British, or even Danish, perspective but from an Icelandic viewpoint, something that few other foreigners managed.

The centuries-old system of bondage that obliged Icelanders to work on farms effectively outlawed fishing as a full-time occupation. It was a seasonal activity, undertaken by farm workers as part of their duties. They used small, open rowing boats that were limited to day-long trips and could only exploit shallow waters close to shore. Despite the radicalism of the independence movement, Icelandic lawmakers were socially conservative, but changes in attitudes, pressure from Denmark and a growing population made it increasingly difficult to enforce the restrictions. By the time Pike arrived in the 1890s, growing numbers of workers were leaving the land and moving to the fishing stations that were springing up along the coast. Enterprising Icelanders could at last run larger, sail-powered vessels, employ specialised fishermen and follow the fish to deeper waters. Processing the catch employed even more people, especially women. A native, commercial fishing industry was being born, but it needed investment if it was to survive.

When he first visited Iceland, Pike Ward bought fish from British traders in the east, but he soon had two important realisations. Firstly, that while the Danes and the British bickered over the spoils of the deep sea, Icelanders were fishing in-shore and needed new customers.

They might not have steam trawlers, but they were bringing in decent catches in rowing boats and, increasingly, sail boats. The trade was weighted against the Icelanders however, as it was still mainly carried out by barter with Danish merchants who inflated the value of their goods. Few Icelanders had access to money and they were trapped in iniquitous tick arrangements. Pike understood that what they needed was cash. Secondly, he saw that the Danes and other foreigners would only buy large cod, and the smaller fish, the type that the British markets wanted, were going to waste. Salt-fish was a popular staple in Britain in the days before fresh fish could be frozen at sea. In Devon it was crudely known as 'toe rag', and was served fried in batter or made into fish pie. If the smaller fish could be processed, salted and soft-dried in the way that British consumers liked, he could corner the market in a product that no-one else was buying.

Pike knew that if he could trade directly with the Icelandic fishermen, he could benefit himself and them. He had befriended the photographer and bookseller Sigfús Eymundsson in Reykjavík, so in 1893 he tried buying from fishermen in Akranes with Sigfús acting as interlocutor. The merchants attempted to dissuade the fishermen from selling to Pike but the offer to buy otherwise unwanted fish was too good to ignore and the experiment was a success. Pike learned Icelandic and was soon able to deal with the fishermen himself. In 1898, he moved to Hafnarfjörður, just south of Reykjavík, and set up a fish curing station there. Over time he expanded his trade from the south-west to the fjords of the north-west, and eventually to the east coast.

By the time he wrote this diary, he had established three bases, at Reykjavík, Ísafjörður and Seyðisfjörður. He spent his winters in Devon, returning to Iceland every spring. As there were no roads to speak of, he reached his bases by steamship, and from there made trips to the remote fishing stations using pack ponies and small boats. Everywhere he or his agents went, they stipulated exactly what type of fish he wanted and how it was to be prepared. He only wanted 'smáfiskur', small fish, no bigger than 16 inches. It was to be salted in good, pure salt for ten days, washed, pressed and soft-dried in the open. Fish that was too tender, overly dry or broken would not be accepted. Pike taught people how to carry out the process and imported the salt they needed. The product became known universally as 'Wardsfiskur', Ward's Fish. It was a new product for a new market, one that could not be controlled by Danish merchants and, most importantly, Pike paid for it up front, in cash.

When the bank in Reykjavík ran out of Danish banknotes in 1896, the fishermen trusted him to take his cargoes and send gold from England. From then on, he always paid in gold (which he carried with him in a leather bag) until Íslandsbanki started issuing banknotes in 1904.

In the mid-19th century, a tiny quantity, just over 30 tonnes, of Icelandic salt-fish was exported directly to Britain annually. By 1906, Pike alone was buying around 500 tonnes per year and he was no longer the only British buyer. The Scottish company Copeland and Berrie had become well established and also paid in cash. Pike's money transformed the fortunes of Icelandic fishing communities, and their growing industry changed Icelandic society beyond all recognition. People could now go to Danish merchants for goods that they could pay for there and then, and demand better prices. They could invest in bigger boats, motors and nets. They could buy timber to construct fish stores. They could form co-operatives and control their business collectively. In time, Icelanders would develop the ports, buy the mechanised vessels and learn the skills to build a trawling industry, and with it a wealthy, modern nation.

Pike himself had experimented with trawling in 1899 but had given it up after just a year. He was the first person to run a trawler from an Icelandic port, the *Utopia* at Hafnarfjörður. The venture seemed to go well at first, but the British crew was unreliable and drunken, and could not be replaced from an Icelandic population with no experience of mechanised fishing. Pike lost £6,000 and never tried trawling again.

While living in Hafnarfjörður, Pike was known for his generosity and for the innovations he brought, such as the horse-drawn cart he built himself, the first in Iceland. People did not believe that he could get two horses to pull such a thing, but they were delighted when not only did he succeed but he offered lifts to Reykjavík in it. He made it known in Hafnarfjörður and everywhere he went that he wanted to purchase Icelandic objects, things to remind him of the country and its people. Over the years he built an unrivalled collection of Icelandic folk craft that filled his home.

For 22 years, Pike travelled back and forth between Devon and Iceland, between two existences. In 1896, when he was 40, he married Grace Agnes Wollacott in London and their first child, Edward, was born two years later. Agnes and Edward lived with Eliza in Teignmouth, where Pike would return each winter. Agnes died giving birth to their second son in 1901, while Pike was away. The tragedy was doubled 10 days later, when their baby died. Pike chose to give the child an anglicised Icelandic name: Thorarin. Edward, aged three, was sent to live with a maternal aunt near Exeter.

Thorarin Ward may have been named after Pike's friend, the painter Þórarinn B. Þorláksson, who painted a portrait of him around this time. It is a revealing image, taken from a photograph of Pike with the background changed from a nondescript building to the mountains near Reykjavík. Þórarinn was part of a small group of artists who were consciously creating a new visual language for the emerging nation. By choosing to be represented by him in this setting, seated on his Icelandic horse and dressed for a life in Iceland, Pike made it clear that he was no longer simply an Englishman abroad. As he put it years later, Iceland had become 'something in the blood'.

One

Voyage to Reykjavík

I left Teignmouth on Saturday March 3rd for London, where I spent the weekend with my friend H.W. Perry. On Monday March 5th, we went from Euston Station to Edinburgh by the ten o'clock Flying Scotsman, and on arrival there took a cab to Leith and put up at the Commercial Hotel. After having had tea, went to the docks to see if the steamer *Vesta* had arrived and was informed she would dock in the morning as she had already arrived in Leith Roads.

On Tuesday March 6th, after ascertaining if the boat was in, I got my baggage taken aboard and saw the captain, who was an old friend of mine and was delighted to see me again. He informed me that the boat would sail at six o'clock that evening, so after sending off several farewell telegrams I went on board and took up my quarters in a cabin as far forward from the crew as possible. As I was then the only passenger except a young Norwegian named Kruger, I had a good choice of bunks but, as it turned out later, not a happy choice. At the time appointed, we cast off from the quay and wended our way through the shipping to the dock entrance and, after a lot of hauling and shouting and hooting of steam whistles, got out into Leith Roads and said farewell to the pilot and full speed ahead. It was blowing a smart gale from the north-west, which is a fair wind out of the Firth of Forth, and after supper I retired to my bunk and had a good night's sleep.

On Wednesday morning, I awoke in good time and went on deck and found it still blowing a gale but as it was from the land, the sea was comparatively smoother, although the vessel had a strong list to the starboard owing to the force of the wind. I was not uncomfortable and was able to get a good breakfast. All that day we got along fairly well until we opened up the Moray Firth which gave a longer drift for the sea we began to pitch a bit but nothing got to inconvenience me.

As night drew on, we approached the Orkney Islands and at 11 o'clock got fairly in the west fjord opposite to Kirkwall. Here the captain decided to remain until daylight as it was still blowing hard and had every appearance of a heavy sea when we should get out into the Atlantic, and as he had three large motor boats lashed on his fore deck for conveyance to Iceland, he did not like to face the sea as he might injure the boats.

At 6am on Thursday morning, March 8th, we made another start and we had only been out an hour before whack! A great sea dashed on board and knocked the motor boats adrift, so Captain had to put the steamer before the sea in order to re-secure them. We then made another start. She rolled and pitched and took a bigger list to starboard every plunge until at last I was standing on my head, as it were, in my bunk. I got some more pillows and cushions and wedged myself fast as well as I could but the continued rolling was very uncomfortable, especially as I am so fat that I would not remain wedged fast, and so I wobbled up and down at every roll. About 6pm, she gave one extra roll and bang came open the door of the washstand, and out came the water can full of water and the tin with the waste water, and crash it all went over the floor, and me hanging out over the side of my bunk making a grab at my stockings, boots, slippers, books etc. that had all got loose. My slippers got full of water and the now empty cans got slinging up and down the floor as she rolled and a pretty old dido it kicked up. Swish, swash, went the water and rattle, rattle went the cans. I slung these out of the door into the saloon and my things up on the sofa and collapsed into my bunk again, but the water had got onto the heated steam pipes running along the side of the vessel and inside the cabin, so a great vapour arose and such a horrid smell so that the stewardess came to see what the matter was. It was a sort of impromptu Turkish bath, so I told her what had happened and she slipped away into the next stateroom and made up a bed there for me. So I changed houses in pretty quick time and soon fell asleep.

9th **March**

I looked out of the porthole and saw Little Diamond Island[1] and there I got up and began to wash and dress and get on to the deck. I found we were just off the island of Nalsoe, which means the Needle Island as there is a hole in one cove of it which they say is like the eye of a needle. This island runs alongside the island of Stromoe, which means Tide Island, and thus forms the harbour of Tórshavn, for which port we were bound.

We let go anchor at six o'clock and by this time the steward had got me a good dish of fried eggs (four) and bacon and a cup of coffee and I sat down with great gusto to enjoy myself after two days' fast. There came on board to me two men I know very well so we had a long chat and did some little business. Then two other of my friends, Captain Jens Andresen and Captain Hans Jacobsen came on board and also did business as to future prospects of fishing in Iceland, as the first is the owner of some nine or ten smacks and the latter is his admiral, as I call him. They are in the habit in May of proceeding to Iceland and fishing off the coast there and landing and selling their catch to the Danish and Icelandic merchants who reside on the Westfjords, but the last three or four years I have bought from them, and when not buying I have assisted them to cure their fish and generally made myself useful to them, so that we are fast friends and I hope someday that I or the company[2] will be able to make something out of these connections. However, we could not make anything definite but shall meet again in May at Ísafjörður, but the foundation is laid and so must await events later.

They hove up anchor at 10pm after landing the mails. As this is only a mail boat to Faroe and brings no cargo for the islands, we were not detained long and so we slipped out through the islands, through Kalsoy, and once more into the Northern Atlantic, and I slipped once more into my bunk. I fell asleep pretty quickly and did not wake up until late in the morning when I felt a tremendous bump to the ship and heard noises of crashing and banging, and I half out of the bunk. I

---

[1]   Lítla Dímun, the smallest of the main Faroe Islands.
[2]   At this stage, Pike appears to be working on behalf of the Newfoundland and Labrador Fish and Oil Company Ltd, based in Exeter, rather than the family company.

found out later on that a big sea had hit the ship forwards and had disturbed those plaguing boats again, and this time they were nearly overboard the rail guards. The deck of the ship was smashed and the iron stanchions had pierced the bottoms of the boats, and one of them had a great hole a man could crawl into in her side. It was only the broken stanchions that had saved them from being washed clean over-board, so the vessel had to be put before the sea again and it took them 12 hours to re-secure them. Then away north again against a bitter north gale, and so it went on from Friday night 10 o'clock March 9th until Tuesday morning 10am March 13th, rolling, plunging, staggering and heaving when we should have done the distance in ordinary weather in 38 hours.

The captain has given me a look in once or twice a day just to see how I was getting on, and how he was getting on, and I had asked him if there was any ice on deck.

'Ice! You had better come and see.'

I asked him if he would give me a call before we got into port so I could have a look at it and take a photo if worthwhile, as I suspected there would be a good lot there, as the glass in my porthole was covered with about two inches of ice and a long icicle as big as one's arm was hanging down over the washstand. So he called me in the morning of the 13th and said there was a good light, so I dressed and put on my overcoat and scarf and fur hat and got my camera and up I went. I opened the side door and whiff! In came the strong cold air and nearly took my breath away, so I quickly closed that door and had a gulp or two and then sneaked out of the leeward door and had a crawl up the windward and looked forward as well as I possibly could in such bitter weather. There was the vessel all on one side, curving and tossing and rolling, then the side just levels with the sea, and on the weather side the great, angry, grey waves lashing at the sides and flinging the spray all over the ship, at times as high as the funnels, the sloping deck all a mass of ice and everything wet or frozen, so I thought, 'Well here goes, I must have that photo.' I got the camera ready and crawled along the deck. It was impossible to stand, at least for me, and I grasped everything I could lay my hands on, which of course wetted my mittens, and then cold wind getting into my lungs after four days and nights in the heated cabin made me gasp for breath. Anyhow, I managed to get a couple of shots and then something went wrong with the pneumatic apparatus of the camera so I had to use the trigger, which necessitated my taking my mittens off and then my troubles began.

I snapped a couple more photos but I was so cold that the shivering of my hands shook up the camera and gave a very poor result. By this time, the air inside the camera had made a steam over the lens and this froze before I discovered it, so out of the number I only got one really decent photo. Captain now called me to come on the bridge but that was more than I could manage. One of the men gave me a hand and I got two or three snaps up there but things were no good, so he gave me a man to get me back to the cabin. I got there properly done up, which was only to be expected after being cooped up in a foetid atmosphere for four days and then getting out suddenly into 30 degrees of frost and facing a gale-force wind and spray lashing like a whip, so when the sailor opened the door and put me inside, I collapsed on the mat and got off my overcoat and scarf and hat and broke into a profuse perspiration. Eventually I got my breath back and crawled down to the cabin.

My fingers had got frost bitten and the steward saw it and got a bucket of ice water and a lump of snow and rubbed and rubbed until circulation began to come into them, and then the pain was just like being hit with a hammer. The difference is that when you hit your finger with a hammer, you sling it down and say something and then put your finger or thumb in your mouth, but in this case the hammer is there all the time. I fairly cried with the pain and squirmed and wriggled like a worm, but there was no getting away from this pain and the steward would not let go and I said things and stamped and yelled with the pain and my nails got quite black and lasted for three or four days afterwards. Captain said I was lucky not to lose them and I daresay I should have done so, only the steward would not let me go but rubbed like a man. But everything must have an end and the pain began to abate and my fingers began to turn red instead of ghastly white, and I lay down all standing and was soon in a sound sleep.

I awoke to find the ship steadier and I knew then we had got near to somewhere, so I went on deck and found we were approaching Berufjörður, our first place of call. I asked the steward to get me my usual pick-up of ham and eggs and coffee and I was soon over head and ears in comfort, and after it a pipe, and so ended my worst of passages after some 30 voyages up and down at all times of the year.

I found out afterwards, when it was too late, that the pneumatic arrangement had got wet and become frozen and would not work. In developing the photos, I found that after the first two the steam caused by the condensed air and the cold on the lens made a mist over all.

After landing our mails and goods at Berufjörður, we sailed on March 13th for Fáskrúðsfjörður and arrived there during the evening. Very dark and cloudy with occasional snowstorms but hardly any wind. We remained there until daylight and sailed again for Eskifjörður, arriving just at breakfast time on March 14th. Both of these fjords are grand natural harbours some four or five miles from entrance to end and surrounded by high mountains but very few houses. This time of the year the whole is buried in snow.

Sailed again about 1pm for Norðfjörður, which is also a good harbour, the weather very cold and occasional snowstorms but not much wind. I wanted much to go on shore here to see my friends the priest and his wife, as I often stay with them buying fish, but as the measles were prevalent in the Faroes we were under quarantine. We were not allowed onshore, neither were the people from onshore allowed on board, so we had to content ourselves by shouting our greetings as the priest came off in a boat to see me.

We remained there all night but left again in the early morning and arrived at Seyðisfjörður on March 15th. This is a very long fjord and has a good pier erected at the end by a firm of Englishmen who were going to do a large fishing business but through mismanagement failed, and the Icelanders got, for a nice song, a capital pier to which our vessel was moored. Here the doctor came on board and after questioning if we were sick or had had the measles we were allowed to walk on shore, so I went around and saw my friends and had a yarn with them all.

We left Sunday morning early, March 18th, and had a rather fine passage to Húsavík, rounding the cape of Langanes which is the north coast corner and just inside the Arctic Circle. Langanes is a long low point of rocks and is exceedingly dangerous unless a wide berth is given to it. It was a pretty sight to see the sun shining on the snow and ice-covered mountains, clearly seen 40 or 50 miles away in the clear, bright atmosphere and standing out sharp against a clear, blue sky. We passed Lundey Island and darkness gradually set in, when in the clear sky away to the north a brilliant display of the Aurora or Northern Lights was dancing and flickering about, which Icelanders call the Valkyrie dance. We arrived at Húsavík about 12 midnight and waited until the morning. This is a bad harbour, quite open to the Arctic Ocean.

Left Húsavík on Monday morning about ten o'clock, March 19th, after picking up a good number of passengers, as we were the first mail boat for the year. We had previously got a few from the other places, nearly all of whom I knew, so that the state rooms began to be over full but I, up to this time, had succeeded in not being disturbed by a stable companion. The most of these passengers went on shore at our next stopping place, Akureyri, where we arrived at 9 o'clock. We found the inner harbour, as it is called, full of fjord ice but it was not very thick so we crashed through this and got to the quay all right and moored for the night.

There are two towns here, if one might call them towns, one called Oddeyri which is right on a tongue of gravel which forms the inner harbour, and the other one another small tongue called Akureyri. A road has been made connecting the two places and houses are beginning to spring up all along the road so making one long straggling place of it. This Akureyri is the capital of the north and in both places there are about 1,500 inhabitants, and it is accounted a very beautiful place by the Icelanders. Well, perhaps it is on bright summer's evening as I have seen it, in the placid water of the magnificent fjord and the high mountains on each side, and at the back a wide open valley with a broad river running between vast stretches of grassland, and the midnight sun shining over all. It certainly is a picture of wildness, not beauty, but to see it now in March, a drear, dark, washed out, bleak, blizzardly hole, it is impossible to find a more miserable prospect. The quay here is formed by an old French vessel filled with stones and sank in deep water, and a bridge to connect it with the shore. Very useful but very primitive.

Here lives the poet laureate of Iceland, an old priest called Matthías Jochumsson, known all over the learned world, speaks nine languages and has translated Shakespeare into Icelandic and a lot more wonderful things. Here I know a lot of people so spent the day in going around visiting and drinking sundry cups of coffee and today our quarantine is finished so we are free to go where we like. On visiting my friends the Stephensens, who is a brother to the late governor Magnús Stephensen of Iceland,[3] I find that Mrs Stephensen is going with us to Reykjavík. Had a look at my pony which Mrs Stephensen is keeping for me and found it was all right and good.

Left Akureyri Wednesday morning, March 21st, at 6am and called at Hvalbakseyri to land some goods. Only two houses here and both are shops. It is situated about halfway out of the fjord at the end of which Akureyri is situated. In these fjords, there are a number of tongues of gravel which form out of the sides of the mountains and project out into the fjords, just the same as the tongue or spit grows out on which Teignmouth is built. These tongues or points are all called 'eyri' and the names of each are attached, for instance, Akur-eyri, Hvalbaks-eyri, Odd-eyri. It is said Akureyri takes its name from a colony of Irish peasants who migrated to Iceland in the early days of Christianity. Some went to the Westman Islands on the south coast, Patreksfjörður (Patrick's fjord) on the west and Papey (Pope's island) on the east. One Irish name for green space is akur, from which they say we get our word acre, a land measure. How far that is true I don't know; I give it as I am told. Hvalbaks is whale's back and odd is otter, although there are no otters here now, there may have been in old times when these names were given.[4]

---

3   Magnús Stephensen (1836–1917) served the Danish government as the last Governor of Iceland until 1904, when the first Minister of Iceland took office under Home Rule.

4   While correct that *eyri* means spit, Pike's place name explanations for Akureyri and Oddeyri are highly unlikely. The presence of Irish monks in Iceland before the Norse settlers of the ninth century is much debated, but the Irish word *acra*

We now have a good few passengers on board but I still had my berth to myself, although the other cabins were packed two, three and four in them which is very uncomfortable. We came to Siglufjörður about 10am, March 21st and left again about 3pm. This is a very important place in the autumn as it is the resort of a number of Norwegian herring fishers. I have counted as many as 160 vessels in here of all sorts and rigs but now in the spring there is nothing doing and it looks a dead and alive sort of place, but it's a good harbour and easily got at from the Arctic Ocean which is alive with herrings from July to October.

The Icelandic passengers pass much of time by singing their own national songs, of which they are very proud and some of them have rather nice voices. They sing glees and part songs but it's all in the Old Hundredth Hymn sort of tune, all mournful and sad. One old chap, who is a priest in Öxarfjörður near Húsavík, sings after the style of the old Vikings, making up as he goes along. It's a sort of Hickey Dickey, Derby Ram tune such as one used to hear on winter nights 40 years ago around the fire on the hearth in the old farmhouses, where one old chap would sing the doings of a certain highwayman or a celebrated farmer like Uncle Tom Cobley.[5] This old priest stands up and blows himself out like a pouter pigeon. He has large protruding eyes, an aquiline nose, an untrimmed beard of the colour and substance of the ancient stuffing of armchairs, and his hair stands up straight on end on an egg-shaped forehead. He first looks all around, then fixes his stare on one of the audience, and then bellows forth his strain at the top of his voice and keeps time with one foot, the same tune over and over again. Sometimes sad, sometimes humorous, voices are used, and at the latter a burst of laughter from the Icelanders. This goes on for

---

(acre) is a later loan word from English. *Akur* is thought to be from a Norse root meaning crop field, while *odd* means pointy. Papey is conventionally thought to have some connection to Irish Papar monks who may have lived there. However, more recent scholarship has suggested the name is connected to puffins or to breast-shaped topography. Pike is correct that *hvalsbak* means whale's back, and that Patreksfjörður may have been named after St Patrick.

5   The comparisons to English musical traditions in this passage refer to *The Old Hundredth*, a well-known hymn tune, and to the folk songs *Derby Ram* and *Widecombe Fair*.

perhaps half an hour and then suddenly stops and he collapses on the smoking room sofa and has a pint bottle of beer.

We arrived at Sauðárkrókur about 11pm in a strong wind and a blinding snowstorm and found the steamer *Kong Inge* which left Leith with us the same evening. She had beaten us and she left the same night for her return voyage. She belongs to the Thore line of opposition steamers and are not subsidised to carry the mail as the United Steamship Company boats are, of which the *Vesta* is one.[6] We now got very bad weather and had to leave again in the morning and get shelter across the bay. The passengers amuse themselves of playing cards and as we had another priest on board the two worthies were always playing picquet. It generally ended up in a quarrel and the cards thrown about and the bit of paper on which the score was kept torn into shreds, but after a little while they made friends and started again.

In Sauðárkrókur but could not get into communication with the shore until next morning. During the night, after supper, the wind came off the land and cleared the sky and we were treated to a most magnificent display of Aurora. The heavens were lit up and the Lights played about in most fantastic shapes. We got one very fine effect called by the scientists the 'corona' which is, as well as I can describe it, a sort of button right overhead and streaming out in every direction are long plaits of light until the whole heavens are covered and it's all straight lines. Well, something like one used to see on the front of old fashioned pianos, the silk in plaits to each corner and a button or tassel in the centre and this taking up the whole sky. It was very grand and seldom seen. Then it all died away, only to reform in another shape, circles, streamers, torches, waving and quivering all across the heavens. The light and appearance is just like when one rubs a sulphur match on the hand, smoke and fire and light without burning, or that peculiar sulphurous blue light which casts a shadow just like a strong moonlight.

On the morning of the 23rd, the sea was moderate so the cargo was discharged and all, or nearly all, our passengers went on shore to visit their friends. We had on board several distinguished passengers: two

---

[6]   The Thore line was operated by Þór E. Tulinius, and Pike also refers to it as the Tulinius line. The United Steamship Company is Denmark's DFDS.

MPs, two priests, a bank director, two or three factors or managers of business, some students and a doctor. They came on board about 4pm. I called it the Battle of Sauðárkrókur, there were so many dead and wounded and I was told that on shore it was just as bad. So the steward and stewardess had their work cut out to put them to bed and the steward to keep them there. At 6pm, hove up anchor and got out of the fjord, passing on the way the island of Drangey which is a flat topped mass of rock standing straight up from the sea and on which dwelt in the old days a man called Grettir the Strong.[7] It is said in the old sagas that he swam to the mainland about two miles after he was wounded by some men sent out to the island to kill him. It's rather a good story, the life and doings of this man, and you can find it in W. Howell's *Icelandic Pictures*.[8]

We rounded the point of Skagatá during the night and the next morning (March 24th) at daylight we came to Skagaströnd, a bad harbour and only a very few houses there. At 8am got under way again and after an hour's steaming came to Blönduós which is accounted one of the worst harbours in Iceland. All these places from Siglufjörður are not fishing villages but are traders' stations for the back country which is very well favoured by nice open grass and valleys where the richest farmers live. Many of them have 300 to 500 sheep and 100 to 150 ponies which they export in the month of September together with the wool and tallow, hides, and salt muttons in casks, most of which finds its way to Norway (I mean the salt muttons; the live sheep or ponies go to England, Leith or Newcastle).

I omitted to say that at Sauðárkrókur, or rather the river that flows into the bay, here was the scene of W. Howell's drowning. He would cross in a difficult place and got sucked down in quicksands and was overwhelmed. His body was found two days after and was buried in a lonely churchyard. Dr Lunn of the Polytechnic London sent up a very nice marble tombstone which is actually there. From the steamer, one can see the mountain at the foot of which he lies, whilst away on the right-hand amongst another group of mountains is the church of Hólar,

---

[7] *Grettir's Saga*, one of the great Sagas of Icelanders (Íslendingasögur), available in several translations.

[8] *Icelandic Pictures Drawn With Pen And Pencil* by Frederick W.W. Howell (1893).

one of the two bishoprics of Catholic Iceland. There the printing of the first Icelandic bible was done and much of the carving, the patterns of which exist to this day and is general on the boxes and bed boards. This carving was introduced by a German who was brought up to Iceland by the bishop to carve the marble reredos which is still now in the Reykjavík museum. The bishop learnt the carving and style of drawing from him and from that source comes nearly all the patterns of Icelandic carving.

We remained at Blönduós all that day and early next morning left for Hvammstangi. This is a very difficult place to get into and it necessitated our going a long way out to sea in order to come in amongst the submerged rocks. It's a difficult piece of navigation as there are no regular charts of this bay, Húnaflói (Young Bear's Bay), and the captain has to go by certain marks on the high mountains in the distance for his guidance. Last year he struck on a rock quite unknown to any navigator and he called it 'Vista' and so marked it on his chart.

Hvammstangi is quite a new trading place, only having been established last year, and there is only one house and one store here but we landed quite a lot of goods which kept us here all day. We left again in the early morning and arrived at Borðeyri, a very old trading centre although some half a dozen houses. There are merchants here, as there is a large (for Iceland) country at the back and numerous sheep farms which draw their supplies from this place and in the autumn ship their produce of mutton, tallow, hides and wool. Here we landed one of our motor boats and were glad enough to get rid of it. At Blönduós, we got an old doctor on board and he at once fell out with our one priest, as they are opposite in politics. Our friend decided he would go no further in the same ship but would prefer to go across country to Reykjavík and he, together with the missionary Lárus who is here trying to get converts to the Plymouth Brethren and came on board at Sauðárkrókur, went on shore here at Borðeyri to walk to Reykjavík. If one looks at the map of Iceland one will see that it is a short distance to Reykjavík and the journey would take about three days.

March 26th

We left Borðeyri and as we were going out of the harbour our old priest was seen standing on a cliff overlooking the fjord, so nearly all the passengers congregated in the stern of the vessel and sang one of the glees he had composed and then gave him three cheers. He waved his handkerchief and our people did the same and the steamer hooted; quite an exciting scene. We got to Steingrímsfjörður in about four hours and landed another of our motor boats. As we were to remain here for the night, many of our passengers went onshore and there was another drinking bout, many drunk and carried aboard in the small hours of the night. Here we got a great number of passengers, young men with their sweethearts and wives bound to Patreksfjörður for the fishing and fish curing. We now had close on 300 passengers on board so I could not hold my berth any longer but got an Alþingismaður, or MP, named Guðjón[9] for my berth mate. I know him very well but he has a nasty cough and spits continually in the wash basin but does not get drunk, which is one mercy.

Many of the younger men amuse themselves on deck by wrestling, or as it is called in Icelandic, glíma. As this is a wrestling part of the island, there are many clever at it. In Rider Haggard's book of *Eric Brighteyes*,[10] mention is made of a man called Óspak who came from the north to wrestle with Eric, and in this fjord there is an eyrie called Óspakseyri where he was supposed to have lived but is now occupied by the sýslumaður, or sheriff, of the county. Left early morning and arrived at Reykjarfjörður where, as its name signifies ('reykja', to smoke), there are some hot springs at the end of it. A wild, desolate place, only one store and surrounded by very high, pointed mountains but as good a harbour and good fishing place if there were people to fish.

Left Reykjarfjörður March 27th about noon and got out into the Arctic Ocean. Blowing very strong off the land, which put our vessel much on one side but no sea as it was off the land. We passed the north

---

9   Likely to be Guðjón Guðlaugsson (1857–1939), member of parliament at this time for this district.

10 *Eric Brighteyes* by H. Rider Haggard (1890) is a novel in the style of the Icelandic Sagas.

cape about 6pm when we were treated to a most wonderful sunset. Overhead it was clouded with very heavy dark clouds, but where the sun set into the sea away to the north-west it was quite clear, and a very fresh wind and the smells plainly of the polar ice. We had been on the lookout for this for two or three days but luckily for us the wind was from south-east and so kept off the ice, although the very next day we heard that it had drifted in and quite blocked the passage. If it had caught us in the Húnaflói, it was uncertain when we should have got out again so we just escaped that danger.

As the sun sank beneath the waves, a slight snowstorm came on and suddenly everything was tinged with blood-red fire, all the ship, the falling snow, men's faces and away in the distance the great, grim north cape, seen dimly through the falling snow, was all lit up. It only lasted about five minutes but everyone turned out to see it. It was past description but very wonderful, grand and awe-inspiring.

Arrived at Ísafjörður, March 27th, about midnight and found a lot of fjord ice, about a foot thick, coming out with the tide from the inner harbour which crashed and banged against our bows and sides. The pilot for the inner harbour came on board but the night was too dark to allow of our going in, so remained at anchor all night. The pilot told me here that my man Jóhannes Pétursson had had a fire and that his house and shop had been burned to the ground and all its contents, but as it was an old house and all fully insured it was a good job. On the morning of the 28th March, the steamer got into the inner harbour and came alongside the pier of Ásgeir Ásgeirsson who is one of the largest businesses in Iceland but he lives in Copenhagen best part of the year. Jóhannes and Sigurður Haflidason, my other man, came on board and had breakfast with me and gave particulars of the fire.

On the evening of the 5th March, they locked up the shop and went upstairs to prepare for a ball which was to be held opening a new Good Templars Hall. Whilst so engaged, the fire broke out (they think in a small store at the back of the house in which there were two or three barrels of petroleum stored) and the flames so quickly spread that they could hardly save what they stood upright in. The contents of the office and a lot of my things were destroyed but the fireproof safe they got out containing all the books. I had always kept this close to a window so they broke down the woodwork and got that out all right but all my knick-knacks, armchair, reading books, a lot of tinned foods, my sea-going clothes and, the worst of all, my sea-going feather bed and down quilt were all gone. They had migrated to another place and were living in two rooms with whatever furniture they could scrape up.

I paid a visit to Jóhannes and found his wife looking very well and well-clad, and his daughter Gunna[11] was engaged to the brother of Sigurður, a smart young fellow called Jón, and he was at that time at sea in a motor boat fishing and was expected in that night. There was nothing to do here and so after dinner, 4pm, the steamer left again for Önundarfjörður and now we began to get down the west coast quickly.

We left again that night and got to Dýrafjörður, March 28th. Quickly cleared there and left our remaining motor boat there, and so on to Patreksfjörður where we landed a lot of our passengers. Left again March 29th and after a rough passage across Breiðafjörður and *Faxa Bay*, finally arrived at Reykjavík on March 30th at 7am. I remained on board to breakfast and then got a boat to take me and my luggage on shore, and up to my snug and comfortable rooms and found a fire had been lit and we cleaned up. Wrote some letters, went to the post office and got my home mail and papers and glad to find all well at home. Went to my usual boarding house had my dinner and supper, and to bed and slept like a top until the morning.

---

11 Short for Guðrún, as she appears elsewhere in the diary.

Two

Reykjavík

March 31st

Went around visiting my various friends.

April 1st, Sunday

Several of my friends visited me and in the evening spent a few hours with Ásgeir Sigurðsson, Copland and Berrie's[1] factor. Talked over all the news and the doings of various people. Found that a contract had been made with a diamond boring company in England to come and bore for gold. He also gave me a list of English people which they expected to be in their business this summer, so that there will be soon a regular colony of Britons up here: a man for their grocery department, his wife and five children; another for the drapery, wife and two children; a young fellow in an office; another for Ísafjörður branch. There is also a man for the Marconi wireless telegraphy called Newman who has been here all the winter and had become engaged to the hotel-keeper's daughter, Sigga Zoega. I don't know him yet but Ásgeir says he is a nice fellow but from his description, and as he has been aboard the Atlantic lines operating, he is half a sailor.

Tuesday April 3rd

Spent all day writing letters but it was bitter weather, wind, rain and snow. Wednesday the same, April 4th, but still colder so that the snow became very deep.

---

[1] Scottish trading company based in Leith and one of the biggest companies in Iceland at this time.

Thursday April 5th

Paid a visit to the governor's family, had coffee and a talk, of course all about Hall Caine and *The Prodigal Son*.[2] Paid a visit to Dr Guðmundur Björnsson[3] who has returned from his travels in Europe. He got back in *Laura* March 13th, leaving Leith the next day after the *Vesta* and got bad weather up the sound as we did. The fishing smacks have now been out since 14th February and it's usual for them to return every six weeks. They are turning up now one by one with an average fishery.

The greatest gossip and excitement now in Reykjavík is 'spiritualism'. Some young fellow has been in Denmark and learnt the trick and now he is up here practising on the credulity of the Reykjavíks, and two of the leading papers have taken it up. He is supposed to be able to call up the spirits of the dead, great Icelanders, especially the poets, which tickles the fancy of many superstitious people and it's grand to be able to talk with those great men of which the Icelanders are so proud. He combines faith healing as well and the bishop (!) is under his care for the cure of dyspepsia and fully sucks it all in. Just at the present there are no politics to discuss and so the papers are glad of something to fill up and cause interest in order to sell their papers.

I find that a Captain Gad, who is a naval man and who is to have command next voyage of the mail boat *Ceres*, has arrived. Helga H (the girl which Hall Caine took his Helga from in *The Prodigal Son* — Captain Gad met her two summers ago when he was here in the Danish man-of-war) got engaged to everyone's surprise, as she is a girl that drinks and smokes and is altogether a rough character, but a very smart girl to look at: tall, well-formed, good carriage and a perfect lady speaking five or six languages, but…

---

2   *The Prodigal Son* by Sir Thomas Henry Hall Caine, 1904. Hall Caine visited Iceland to research the novel and was on friendly terms with Pike. Several characters are based on real members of Reykjavík society, including the former governor. It was dramatised in 1905 with productions in Washington, New York and London.

3   Dr Guðmundur Björnsson (1864–1937), physician and MP. He became medical director and head of the medical school in Reykjavík in this year.

Friday and Saturday April 6th and 7th

A furious south-west gale waged both days and the fishing smacks came crowding in under very small canvasses. About 12 o'clock on Saturday, one was seen approaching the harbour with only mizzen and forestay sail set and evidently in trouble. Instead of coming direct into the harbour, she passed outside of one of the protecting islands and was apparently making for the winter harbour, about six miles and within the fjord, instead of which she suddenly luffed or came side-ways to the wind and endeavoured to get into a cove on the windward side of a large island called Viðey. She was observed to lower the fore-stay sail and (it was thought) let go her anchor, which did not hold if they did, and she drifted on a reef of rocks about 150 fathoms from the cliffs of the islands. Then it was all excitement from the onlookers from Reykjavík, who by this time had become interested in the movements of the vessel. Huge seas began to break over the ship which lay broad-side to the waves and the crew could be seen climbing up the rigging of the foremast. 23 men could be counted but as the seas thundered on the sides, the vessel gradually lay more and more on one side, and in between the driving snow squalls the poor fellows could be seen one after the other dropping into the angry waves to their deaths. The horror of it all and nothing could be done to save their lives. They were too far from the shore to swim even if they could have, and there is no lifeboat here. The governor did all he could, dispatched a boat to the two or three steamers and steam trawlers which were in the harbour, asking them to try and save the men and he would pay for it, but of course the steamers had all their work cut out to hold on in safety, nor could he expect them to steam in amongst the dangerous reef rocks and when they got there, enable to get at the men on the vessel. So by 3 o'clock the whole tragedy was over and 23 men met their deaths, I regret before our eyes or at least a mile from us.[4]

On Sunday April 8th, the winds shifted a little and abated a little. A boat was enabled to visit the island, on which there was one house and only two men and their families live, and found that these two men had

---

[4] The wrecking of the cutter *Ingvar* described here, along with other vessels, is still considered Iceland's worst maritime disaster. 70 sailors are known to have died in the storm.

not known of it until nearly all had been drowned, as the house lay in a hollow and the vessel could not be seen from the windows. Even if they had, they could do nothing but what they did do, and that was to get the bodies as they drifted on shore. They had got 11 bodies, which they carried to the house on pony backs.

Three of the smacks that have come in have lost each a man over-board so that in all there are 26 souls gone in this gale. At three o'clock, from the mail boat *Skalholt* were signals and she came in four days later and reported having taken six days to come from the Westman Islands, which usually occupies 12 hours. She comes direct from Copenhagen and consequently does not bring me any letters. Spent Sunday evening with Ásgeir Sigurðsson and his wife who is a Scottish lady. Ásgeir is manager for the Copland and Berrie business, which in 11 years has grown to be the largest business in Iceland having a turnover of 2,500,000 krónur (£138,000), which is rather a large concern even if in England.

Monday April 9th

Rather a better day although raw and cold and towards evening, heavy snow. Have had several people to see me today from various parts of the coast to make arrangements for business the coming summer, amongst them Jón Guðmundsson from Álftafjörður in Ísafjörður fjord. He has brought his wife here to undergo a serious operation which is to take place this afternoon in the French hospital. I hope it will turn out well as she is a nice woman and always does her best for me when I am staying at her house, which I very often do in the summer.

Tuesday April 10th

A nice, fine, bright day so after breakfast I went off for a walk and got so far as the salmon river. Then I went off to the right along the banks and again to the right towards the Hafnarfjörður road, over the moor, but found it very hard walking as the ground was frozen underneath and over that the melted snow remained. The peat and gravel was saturated like a sponge but the water could not soak through the frozen ground beneath so that one's foot sank down two or three inches, and some places a foot, in this and so made it a difficult way to walk. It took it out of me fine, for I perspired freely, and after being away about four hours, walking all the time, I returned to my rooms and changed all my clothes for fear of taking a chill, but it did me a lot of good and I was able to have a good dinner.

Wednesday April 11th

I had intended riding to Hafnarfjörður today if it had been as fine as yesterday but it snowed the whole day, more or less. The dead bodies of the men drowned on the island of Viðey were brought over in two lighters and were carried up to the graveyard and deposited in the chapel there. Many of the inhabitants congregated at the pier, quite a thousand, and accompanied the hand barrows from pier to graveyard and all flags flown at half mast, but there was no great show of sorrow like one would have imagined or what would have been shown in a fishing town in England. They, the Icelanders, show very little sorrow or joy in their faces.

Thursday April 12th is observed here as one of the most holy days in the Lutheran liturgy and is called the 'Christening day' so all stores, shops and hotels are closed and everyone, or at least many of the people, go to church but it's a very rough day blowing from the north and snowing all the time. A young fellow called Smith from Goole is here in Reykjavík on business; his father has sold several fishing smacks to the Icelanders and he is here collecting the money, which he finds rather difficult. He is staying at the Hotel Reykjavík and there met another young Englishman who has been here all the winter attending to the Marconi telegraph.[5] He is called Newman and is about 25 years

---

[5] Several telegraphy companies were anxious to establish stations in Iceland due to its location between Europe and North America, the main rivals being Marconi and the Great Northern Telegraph Company. There was fierce debate among the Icelandic MPs and the Danish authorities over whether wireless or cable technology should be supported. The Marconi Company was invited by those who favoured wireless to demonstrate the technology in Iceland. To this end, engineer A.G. Newman was sent in 1905 to set up a mast near Reykjavík and to show that news could be successfully received from Marconi's wireless station at Poldhu in Cornwall. Great Northern, meanwhile, was laying cable from the Shetland Islands with a subsidy from the Danish and Icelandic governments. British trawler owners had lobbied their own government to contribute funding to the initiative, but without success.

of age and comes from Dover. He is a telegraphist operator and has
served his time with the Marconi Company and has been on board the
Atlantic liners working the instruments until October last when he was
sent up here. He has become engaged to the hotelkeeper's daughter
Sigga Zoega; she is rather a nice-looking girl of about 18 years of age,
speaks English fairly well. These two young fellows asked me in to
dinner so I spent the afternoon with them, it was a sort of merry
Christmas with so much snow about. The *Skalholt* left again for the west
coast so now we are looking forward to the next arrivals from the *Holar*
which comes from Leith and ought to arrive here on Sunday.

Good Friday, April 13th

A bitter night blowing and snowing so that the streets are now about
five or six feet deep in snow. After breakfast went to Dr Guðmundur
Björnsson and had a yarn with him. He tells me that full authority has
been sent to Mr Depree in Exeter to carry on the negotiations with Mr
Payne of London for the city of Reykjavík to obtain possession of the
salmon river[6] so as to carry out the water scheme and that it was all
going satisfactorily.

All the fishing smacks have been accounted for, with the exception
of two, but there are grave doubts of their safety as a lot of wreckage
has been driven on shore about 12 miles further north of this and it is
feared that at least one of these smacks have been lost there. I wonder
where the *Rose* is? By my calculations she should have been near the
Icelandic coast about this time, but my letters will show her position
when I get them on Sunday.

Last night a meeting of the heads of the various trades was called to
consider ways and means of getting a lifeboat for the harbour of
Reykjavík. Of course I recommended an English lifeboat but this was
considered too expensive and the boat too heavy and cumbersome.

---

[6] The river Elliðaár, on the outskirts of Reykjavík. For some years Guðmundur
Björnsson had been advocating the need for a clean, piped water supply to
tackle disease in the city. Pike became involved in the scheme in 1903 at the
behest of the city council and brought in Mr Depree, of the Exeter engineering
firm Willey & Co., to investigate. Their preferred choice of water supply, the
Elliðaár, was owned by Mr Payne, who sold it to the city later in 1906.

Some who had seen them inclined to the Bornholm, Denmark class. Of course, I did not know these but I pointed out to them they were not so safe as the English boats for, from their description, they were merely open surf boats similar to the Broadstairs or Great Yarmouth beach-combers and were only safe when used by competent men (and men who were accustomed to get their living day by day in these boats), but a Royal National Lifeboat was acknowledged to be the most efficient boat in the world. Anyhow, it was decided to send around and see if they could collect £100 towards the fund and there I expect it will end.[7]

Saturday April 14th

Very bad day again, much snow and wind. News has come in that is certain the other two smacks have gone with all hands so that there has now been lost 78 to 80 men, which is a terrible calamity for so small a population. Very cold and a bitter north wind blowing so I have to fire up pretty considerably to keep my rooms warm.

Sunday April 15th, Easter Sunday

A very fine day of bright sunshine and although a strong frost is on, some 15 or 16 degrees, still one can walk out without a greatcoat as there is no wind. All people go to church 8am, 12noon and 5pm. When I say all, a great number of women and old men. The others moon about the streets, or rather in roads around the business landing places, and as all the hotels are closed there is little or no drunkenness. These days are really holy days and not holidays. Today quite a procession of steamers came in, one after the other, with coal and goods from England. Four steamers of 500 tons each and three English trawlers to land sick men, one of whom had got broken up pretty badly in the steam winch, both arms broken in two places each with thumbs torn off, and four or five ribs broken and badly bruised all over, but the doctor says he will get all right. One French trawler with his bridge cut

---

7   An appeal was launched and Ásgeir Sigurðsson started the donations with 100 krónur, but nothing came of it. Pike wrote to the secretary of the RNLI station in Teignmouth to request that an old lifeboat be donated for use in Iceland, but none was found.

off to the deck by heavy sea, and a German trawler with a broken-legged man.

I entertained several visitors today and had a constant stream of men in to see me and consequently many bottles of soda water used and cigars smoked. We had Easter eggs for breakfast, which were ordinary eggs with the shells coloured red.

Monday April 16th

Also a very fine day, all hands in church, but after 6pm Easter is all over and the theatre is open, and the concert room, and everyone gives themselves up to merriment although 80 men have lost their lives and 12 of them are in the dead house waiting burial. At noon today, two more steamers came in, one the mail boat *Holar*, but only one letter for me and one packet of newspapers so suppose they have been sent (the others I mean) by the *Kong Inge*, Tulinius liner, which left Leith 24 hours before the *Holar*. She has to call in the Faroes, so must wait patiently until tomorrow when she is expected in, and also the *Laura* mail boat.

Jón Guðmundsson was amongst the callers yesterday. His wife has not yet been operated on and he was very anxious and wished it could all be done soon as the anxiety was very trying. Tried to get a walk today but the frozen snow was so slippery had to give it up.

Tuesday April 17th

Laura and *Kong Inge* mail boats came in this morning and I got all my home letters and the remainder of my newspapers and was glad to know that all was well at home, so had a good time reading all home news; a very fine day.

Wednesday April 18th

Also a fine day so got my pony and rode to Hafnarfjörður, which is about six miles south of Reykjavík and where I lived two years, 1899–1900. The road was very wet, owing to the melting snows, but the weather was one of those spring days we get here in the north: clear air so that 40 miles distant hills look as if only three or four miles away. As one rides over the undulating road, the scene rises very grand indeed. The long, stretching, snow-covered plains and the distant, white, sharp mountains on the left hand, and the blue sea with shining mirror-like surfaces on the right hand, and the clear, still appearance and the restful, peaceful, quietness of it all was a picture for poetry, the cloudless bright sky and the glistening snow over all. It's difficult to describe the loveliness and the loneliness of it all.

I paid a visit to my one friend Þorsteinn Egilsson who, together with his wife, gave me a hearty welcome and a good dinner of roast ptarmigans and egg flip after, then coffee to finish up and the ride back in the evening with a sharp frost, and it was altogether a very nice enjoyable day's outing.

Here I heard about the rescue of two trawler crews who were wrecked on the south coast. Some two years ago a German trawler[8] was driven on shore at a very dangerous spot on the south coast called Leirur, where for two hundred miles of glacier mountains there are no inhabitants, and the poor fellows wandered along the sands westwards hoping to find a house, but it was not until four of them died with exposure and want of food, and the remainder badly frost-bitten, that they came to a farm. Out of a crew of 14, only two men came through without loss of limbs or fingers: four dead and two lost both feet; three lost a leg each and three lost an arm each. The German emperor sent a decoration to the farmer who took them in and the doctor who operated on the survivors. Just fancy having one's leg off in a turf farmhouse. No nurse, no antiseptics, no appliances of any sort.

The German consul here in Reykjavík, who is an Icelandic merchant named Ditlev Thomsen,[9] then had a house of refuge built at his own expenses at this desolate shore and put with it provisions and clothes and a notice in German, English and French, instructing shipwrecked men to use the house and to hoist a flag to let the nearest farmer know they were there. So these two crews, a German and an English trawler, came onshore and found the house (owing to a chart having been sent

---

8   The *Friedrich Albert*, stranded in 1903.
9   Ditlev Thomsen (1867–1935) was a successful Reykjavík department store owner who travelled in Europe to promote Icelandic exports and became German consul in 1896. He had the cabin for shipwrecked sailors built at Skeiðarársandi.

to all trawlers, all nations trading and fishing in Icelandic waters) and were saved, every man of them, and sent to Reykjavík from where they returned to their homes in March last. I expect this consul will get a German decoration for his goodness and liberality in erecting this house.

Today the men that were drowned at Viðey were buried. All the shops and places of business were closed for two hours whilst the interment was taking place.

Thursday April 19th

Very cold and miserable day, snowing and sleeting but no wind, consequently all the streets are one sloppy mess. Coast steamer *Holar* leaves for the east coast.

Friday April 20th

Fine in the morning but a strong north-west gale afternoon and evening, bitter cold. Jón Guðmundsson's wife operated on today at the hospital. He came in to tell me that it all went well and the doctors were sanguine of a speedy recovery. A grand supper and presentation of a plate to the chief engineer of the SS *Laura* as he had completed his 100th voyage to Iceland. He is very well-liked and he and the captain of the *Laura* are like two brothers. I was not bid to the feast, for which I was thankful; they kept it up until the small hours of the morning. Mr Newman of Marconi has just shown me his messages for the week, including the San Francisco account of the earthquake there and losses.[10] So at last we are in touch with the outer world, but so disinterested are the Icelanders that the newspapers, of which there are 14 published here, not one will send for the copy, but he has to make out three or four copies and take them around to the principal papers for publication and then they cut out most of it, so a lot of good a telegraph is to the natives. Mr Newman is of course anxious to get his news

---

[10] The San Francisco earthquake had occurred two days previously, igniting fires that would burn for three days. The final death toll was not known at this stage but was eventually estimated at 3,000.

published and I should not be surprised if he has to <u>pay</u> the news-papers to put his news in instead of the editors paying him.

Had dinner with Mr Newman and Mr Smith and a very good dinner it was. I must see about changing my boarding house to this hotel as the food is much better and one meets more English people. At my boarding house there are only some Danish shop assistants. It is quite changed from formerly as there were Icelanders and all friends of mine, but they are all gone and all were congenial. I often have my meals without exchanging a word. This Hotel Reykjavík is a new build-ing and the proprietors try and make English food and really do it well so I think I must change diggings. In Reykjavík they are beginning to aim at some idea of aggrandisement and some pretentions to archi-tectural beauty, as the Joiners' Society and the new bank and several other large buildings. The bank is of stone and looks more like a prison, but the Joiners' house is wood galvanised with clad. Opposite to my windows are the doctor's house, Dr Guðmundur Björnsson, and the house of the government surveyor Knud Zimsen; the latter is concrete built.

Saturday April 21st

Still bad weather. Had a visit from my missionary friend Lárus. He had got a free passage to England in a Norwegian steamer but had suddenly discovered that the Aliens Act was in force, so he could not land unless he paid £5 of ready money. As he was going to England on a gleaning expedition, the £5 was in prospect and not in hand, so he had to be helped. Had a visit from the Salvation Army for their annual and a visit from two ladies collecting for the lottery in aid of the drowned seamen, so altogether had quite a nice day, sort of, 'casting bread (or money) on many waters'.

Laura left today, Saturday, for the west coast. Jón Guðmundsson went with her, his wife being now considered out of danger.

Sunday April 22nd

Rather better day today but raw and cold with snow and rain. Smith came in and spent the afternoon with me.

Monday April 23rd

Another bad day and I was poorly all day. I think I must have taken cold yesterday with having thin boots on. Bad head and did not eat anything all day, but strangely enough I had a constant stream of visitors and I wished them all a long distance, for I could hardly hold up my head.

Tuesday April 24th

All right today and the weather bright and clear, so I went and called on Smith and Newman and got them to go for a good long walk and got back to dinner well tired.

Wednesday April 25th

Very fine and bright day, so got my pony and went to Hafnarfjörður to visit Mr Egilsson, who made me very welcome. I returned to Reykjavík in the evening about 9pm, very nice day and a nice outing.

Thursday April 26th

Very rough, bad day, so I had to keep indoors the whole day. A very miserable day indeed, as being entirely alone could not help thinking of 10 years ago this day.[11]

Friday April 27th

Blew a gale from the north all night and this morning two vessels drifted from their anchors and stranded on the rocks under the town: one a nearly new Danish three mast schooner called *Ursa* loaded with 400 tons of coal (she only came in yesterday, being the first sailing vessel to arrive up), and the other was a French fishing schooner. They both stranded near to each other. The bottom in Reykjavík harbour is very bad holding ground and when once a vessel begins to drag, she nearly always gets on the rocks. No-one was drowned as they went on

[11]   It is 10 years and six days since Pike's wedding to Grace Agnes Woollacott. It is 10 years and four days since the birth of Margaret Anne Sarah Vening (see epilogue).

shore at high water and at low water the crew came off by a ladder, bringing their clothes and other belongings. Both vessels will become ﹒﹒tal wrecks as they are on rocks and this breaks up a vessel very ckly, and at high water in the evening they both filled with water.

Saturday April 28th

ə gale still continues and it's bitterly cold. It finds its way into every ﹒vice of the house and it takes me all my time to stoke up the stove to t 40 degrees of heat in the place. A large old wooden hulk in the ﹒rbour belonging to Copland and Berrie in which was stored 300 tons ﹒ coal sank this morning, the weather having been so bad for the last ﹒ree days that is was impossible for the men to get aboard and pump ﹒er out, so she gradually filled until the sea broke over her and down ﹒he went.

News came in this morning that one of the best fishermen, called Guðmundur Einarsson, had been drowned on Thursday night. He had been fishing on the south side of Faxa Bay all the winter since January. He lives on a point near Reykjavík about 30 miles from the place where he had been fishing. He had hired a large lighter in which there was a motor to bring his fish in salt from his fishing place to his home but got caught in the north gale about halfway up and the boat sank with the fish, and Guðmundur and another man who had charge of the motor got drowned. The rudder, which was about the only floatable thing in the lighter, came on shore so it was known then that the accident had happened. He was one of the best-known fishermen in the Faxa Bay and a great friend of mine and I have done a great deal of business with him in former days.

The *Laura* came back today from the west coast but as there are no letters from my man in Ísafjörður I conclude that the *Rose* had not yet arrived there, although she sailed from Torquay April 1st so she must be getting a hard time of it. It is reported that the north coast of Ísafjörður is full of polar ice owing to this north gale. Towards evening it eased off so that the maids and passengers from *Laura* were enabled to get ashore.

Sunday April 29th

Still bad weather so did not go out except to meals. Smith came in and spent nearly the whole day with me.

Monday April 30th

Finished off my home letters and posted them and, it being a fine, bright day, went for a long walk. *Laura* was to have sailed tonight but she had to go to Hafnarfjörður and take in about 20 tons of fish and that delayed her.

Tuesday May 1st

Fine day but cold, six degrees of frost. The Tulinius line mail boat came in and brought letters from England. Got mine from post office and was glad to hear that all was well at home. Got news of the earthquake in San Francisco but we had already heard of that through the Marconi telegraph. It is stated here that there was a slight earthquake on the same night, but I did not feel it.

I hear today that Karitas, the wife of Jón Guðmundsson, died last night in the hospital so poor Jón, who left in the *Laura* and was expecting his wife to come back home all well in the *Ceres*, will only meet her dead body which will be sent up today in the Tulinius boat *Kong Inge*. Very sad indeed for him as she was such a good woman and such a good wife and good housekeeper.

Wednesday May 2nd

Still fine weather, bright and clear. Went for a ride to the salmon river but it is cold, four degrees of frost. Attended to the auction of coals from the Danish wreck. They fetched about two shillings per ton more than if the cargo had been ordered up from England.

I got a 'lump fish' today and photographed it as it is such a curious fish but very ugly and is boneless, a lump of hard jelly, but much esteemed by the Icelanders, either fried or boiled. It is very rich and similar in taste to eels. It is about the size of a vegetable marrow and is about three pounds weight. The male fish is tinged red and the female a dark blue. They come up from the sea in vast shoals in the spring to lay their eggs and are taken in small, moored nets of fine worsted which are set amongst the rocks and in which the fish entangle themselves. The fish is split open and hung up in the wind to dry and are sold to the countrymen in that state at about four a penny. When used in the dry state it is boiled as a soup, a sort of turtle soup one might say, but the taste and smell, ugh! I believe they are found at times in the north of Scotland and I once heard of one being taken and exhibited at Exmouth.

Thursday May 3rd

A gale sprang up last night from the north and continued all day with heavy snow so we are all white again but only one degree of frost. That does not say much, as the wind penetrates so that it seems infinitely more cold today indoors than yesterday out of doors. Three Danish schooners and one cargo steamer arrived today but have not yet heard of their weather experiences.

News came in of the wreck of the coasting schooner *Agnes* belonging to Thomsen the merchant here and used for delivering goods in the Faxa Bay, but no one drowned. She was about 35 tons, the size vessel that the company wish me to use in lieu of the *Rose* which they consider too large, too <u>expensive</u>.

This afternoon, my washerwoman Stína, who is lame and has one leg cocked up under her and uses a crutch, came in to sell me a crochet counterpane. I have a large three-fold screen inside my door to keep the draught off and as screens are most unusual here in Iceland, in fact I believe this is the only one ever seen here, she must needs try and support herself by the middle fold and of course capsized the lot, falling backward and putting the sitting half of herself through the centre. There she laid, heels up in the air and squealing like a good 'un. The screen fell on the table so she vanished halfway through the screen, so now I have a job to patch it up again.

Friday May 4th

Nice, fine, bright day. Went for a ride so far as the salmon river.

Saturday May 5th

Another fine, bright day. Went for a ride with Newman the Marconi man and his sweetheart Sigga Zoega to Hafnarfjörður. Had coffee and cake there and returned in time for dinner at four o'clock, most enjoyable day. SS *Kong Inge* sailed for the west coast which should have sailed last Tuesday but was detained by the north winds which prevented the unloading.

Sunday May 6th

Bright, nice day. Went for a walk in the morning and entertained visitors in the afternoon and after supper went for another walk. Bright night and the long twilight made more so with a full moon.

Monday May 7th

Bright but cold. Went for a ride to salmon river. After supper I went out to the Marconi signal station. This consists of a high mast rigged up about 150 feet high and on the top is an arrangement of wires, nine in all, spread in all directions from the very top of the mast to the ground, spreading out like the ribs of an umbrella. Against these wires come the waves of air, agitated from Poldhu in Cornwall about 1,000 miles away. Each of these wires is connected with a single wire leading into the small hut at the foot of the mast and inside the hut are the apparatus. First it leads into a small box about the size of a cigar box containing a clockwork arrangement and through which the waves of air are conducted by the single wire. This sets up a flow of electricity which is then conducted by two wires leading from the clockwork box into another box about two foot square and in this box is an arrangement of wires like the inside of a grand piano. Against these wires the waves are forced, like when one sings or shouts into a sound cone. The sound is then passed by wire into a sort of telephone attached to the ears of the operator and the tickings of the Morse code can be heard and the operator then writes down what he hears.

Mr Newman kindly let me hear the tickings, which I thought very indistinct but he wrote rapidly the messages. Some were press messages of general news and then he said, 'Oh they are going to stop the press messages and will now talk to two steamers', one an English-American liner and one a French-American liner, the *Provence*. He wrote down the messages' meaning, which mostly consisted of congratulating messages and wishes of a good voyage and one was to a young couple from a father and mother, for it said, 'Best of luck, wealth and happiness all your lives with all love from Father and Mother'. All very interesting.

I stayed two hours in the hut and then returned to my lodgings with Mr Newman. I asked him about how, if a dozen stations were sending messages, would they not interfere with each other, but he showed me how it was arranged in the two foot box: a certain time is arranged, for instance Poldhu is A time, and in the Icelandic box and all boxes are a number of plugholes into which one of wires attached to a plug is thrust, so that Poldhu A time/Iceland A plug is attached and so on through a number of letters representing the calling and answering times. When two unknown steamers approach, they each have to find out the time wanted and the plugs are adjusted accordingly. A steamer with, say, D time calls, which rings a bell on number two steamer, the operator begins with plug A and so goes down the time board until he hears the ticks and then takes his message and replies on the same time. He tells me that on the American continent there are a great number of Marconi stations, and when on board a liner the operator has a busy time of it receiving messages, and that they are never out of touch with the land the whole passage, for as soon as they are out of the Cornish call they are in the Cape Cod America call.

Tuesday May 8th

Bright, fine day, went for a walk in the morning and a ride in the afternoon. It is still cold with a north wind, sharp and clear. The SS *Skalholt* should have come in from the coasting voyage but has not yet arrived so we are beginning to think there must be polar ice on the north-west coast. About 60 French fishing schooners are now in the harbour discharging their spring catch of fish into the home carriers who will sail direct to France when loaded. They have only fished about half of their usual quantity: 15,000 fish against 25,000 the average. All the women-folk of the town very busy spring cleaning, which is a great job.

Everything is turned out onto the street, sofas, chairs, beds and clothes, well beaten and polished out, and inside (the walls and ceiling all being of wood) is well scrubbed and washed.

Wednesday May 9th

Bright, fine day. Went for a ride. At 12 o'clock, heard whistling of a steamer and went out and found it was the *Ceres* arrived two days before her time.

Thursday May 10th

Got up early, fine, bright morning. Went to the post office, where I have a post box, and got my letters. Returned to my rooms and had a good read and was glad to find all well at home, but had no letter from the company, nor from Mr I.B. about the lifeboat I wrote to him about. Was rather amused to read about the end of dear Uncle. Had a visit from Captain Gad of the *Ceres* about the mate who had brought me some monthly magazines and the latest newspapers. Rather surprised to see in all the newspapers that we had been having earthquakes and eruptions of Hekla and all that, but we have had nothing of the sort and it was all a gross fabrication.

Friday May 11th

Very fine and bright, brilliant sunshine, no wind and really in the fore-noon quite warm, so I did not have the stove lighted as I was busy in packing up so as to be ready for a start on Monday to Ísafjörður by the *Ceres*. In the afternoon, went around and paid up my debts and got a good bag of feathers and down to replace my seagoing bed which was burnt at Ísafjörður. Strange that no boats have got in from the west coast, these are now four days late. The harbour is now filled with fishing vessels: Icelandic smacks, French schooners, German steam trawlers, Dutch steam trawlers and several coal and salt schooners, French man-of-war, Norwegian schooners and barques. Over 200 vessels in the port and the town streets are crowded with all nationalities more or less intoxicated. A small sloop caught on fire last night but not much danger done as it was found out before it got big.

Saturday May 12th

Dull day and inclined to rain, which it did now and again. In the afternoon, the SS *Vesta* came in and reported she had been on her voyage as far as Siglufjörður and was there stopped by polar ice, so she turned back and came east and south about, landed her mails here and proceeded to the west to take up the continuation of her voyage this side of the ice, wherever that may be. Was very glad to get some letters by her which did not come by *Ceres*. Shortly after the *Vesta* came the east coast boat *Holar* reporting bad weather and snow on the east coast. Then in came the *Kong Inge* from his west coast trip to Ísafjörður, reports the fjord there very full of polar ice but was enabled to fit into the harbour. Consequently, I got a letter from my man there reporting the arrival of our schooner *Rose* at Dýrafjörður, 30 miles south of Ísafjörður. I suppose he put in there because Ísafjörður was blocked. He arrived there May 4th, 34 days from Torquay, a very long voyage. He reports having damaged some of the topsail of his bulwarks, broken the lower topsail yard and split his mainsail. My man went in *Kong Inge* from Ísafjörður to Dýrafjörður to assist the captain of *Rose* to put his damage right. I should know more particulars next week when I go up in the *Ceres*. No news of SS *Skalholt* and it is supposed she is fast in the ice mass at Borðeyri, as that bay is full of ice and she was reported overland as having been there last Saturday.

There has not been as much drunkenness here this 'lock', as it's called. This time of year, engagements are terminated, workmen and workwomen change their employers, servants change their places and all get re-engagements. Consequently this is a meeting place for employers and employees and the streets are crowded with countrymen and women, shops packed, and ponies, hundreds of them, standing loaded or unloaded, or being loaded and unloaded in the open; quite an animated scene. The Good Templars have succeeded in getting a law passed that all hotels and liquor-selling places are to be closed at 9.30pm and not opened before 7am and that came in force yesterday so that the people had no chance to overstep greatly after the shops were closed at 8.30. Groups of men stand talking and snuffing out of their flask-like snuff horns. Here and there meetings of friends and relations, the men kissing each other and embracing; good, long, succulent kisses.

Servant girls assisting one the other to carry their tin boxes and, in a number of cases, a chest of cheap wooden drawers which continually insist to slide out and deposit their contents on the muddy ground. A string of pack ponies came pushing through the crowd and a constant jabber-jabber of voices, but strangely enough no loud shouting or laughter, all sort of quiet noise and bustle.

Sunday May 13th

The streets seem strangely empty today except here and there a pony waggoned with a load of household goods, 'flutningadagur' (May the 14th) being the day to change houses if they are going to do it.[12] Being Sunday, it's a fine opportunity to get help to remove those few sticks from one house to the other. Furniture one can hardly call it, it mostly consists of a few barrels and biscuit boxes, a homemade sofa topped up with a heap of bedding, and squeezed in between the legs of a deal table painted mostly red is a cast-iron crock and an enamelled coffee pot, the cart being followed by the owners of the furniture, with a cheap looking glass under one of the arms and a print of the king of Denmark under the other.

Amongst the curious sights I saw yesterday was the wife of the minister, as the new governor is called, out in the street with a blue, striped, silk dress, a gold belt and gold chains all on her (she is a young, stout, dressy person without hat or jacket), bargaining with a man who had a barrow full of fresh cod. She eventually bought one, put her fingers all bedecked with rings in under its gills and bore it triumphantly into her house, looking awfully pleased with herself.

Monday May 14th

Very wet, dismal day, calm but rain dripping down in big lumps. I spent the morning in clearing up and locking up my two rooms. As I had ordered a man to fetch my baggage at one o'clock, I was quite ready for him, but after waiting until two o'clock and he did not turn

---

[12] Fardagar is the more commonly used term for this day. Under Iceland's restrictive labour practices, it was the only day of the year when ordinary people could change employer.

up, I had to get out to find others. I found two and they went off to get a boat, which took them until four o'clock, and then it began to blow up from the north right on the land, so that made it necessary to get two more men to row the boat out, so that took an hour to arrange and finally I started off with my gear to the *Ceres*. By this time there was a lumpy sea and, on nearing the steamer, I saw the captain on the bridge and he signalled to me to stop. I could see that he was about getting his anchor and moving farther out of the harbour, so the men rowed and rowed for an hour and a half and finally, bobbing about for two hours, we got alongside and, after a lot of jabbering about, got my traps on board. Then came the other passengers, not many as it was so rough and raining heavily. At seven o'clock, the steamer hove up anchor and got outside into a lumpy sea and a steady gale blowing. I thought discretion the better part of valour so I retired to my bunk.

Three

Ísafjörður

Felt the boat stop so got up to find a most glorious sunshine and we had arrived at Ólafsvík. This is an open harbour, or rather landing place, and faces due north and the few scattered houses are situated under a very high mountain called Snæfellsjökull, some 5,000 feet high. It was here that Jules Verne commenced his wonderful underground travel to Stromboli in the Mediterranean.[1] The men that came off stated that yesterday they had a blizzard and snow fell covering everything with six feet of snow, and one could well imagine it as the houses could hardly be discerned from the steamer. We remained here discharging our cargo into the open boats two or three tons at a time, and it was fortunate we had such fine weather as quite a lot was sent on shore: bags of flour, boxes of candy sugar, raisins, etc.

Then we left for Stykkishólmur, further into the Breiðafjörður (or Broad Bay), passing along the high, mountainous coast, with its snow-clad peaks shining and glistening in the bright sunshine and capped by the beautiful, clear, blue sky. There, clearly standing out, are two well-known landmarks, one called the 'Coffin' as it resembles a coffin standing on trestles with a pall over it (but now it was a white pall), and the 'Sugar Top', being a conical point standing straight up like the loaves of sugar in a grocer's shop.[2] We also pass the celebrated Ólafsvíkurenni

---

[1] The protagonists in Jules Verne's 1864 science-fiction novel *A Journey to the Centre of the Earth* descend into the mountain, which is a volcano topped with a glacier.

[2] Coffin and Sugar Top were nicknames given by sailors. The Coffin is called Stöð in Icelandic, meaning a boat landing. Sugar Top mountain is properly called Kirkjufell (Church Mountain), one of the most famous landmarks in Iceland.

which is a cliff standing sheer up from the sea and halfway up is a road only wide enough for a man to stand and to walk. This is the only road between Ólafsvík and Stykkishólmur and all travellers write about it in their books.

We arrive at Stykkishólmur about 8 o'clock in the evening and it has now become quite glassy calm. We anchor opposite to the island which forms a protection to the shore (which makes the harbour), Stykkishólmur or 'Island of Pieces', as the rock is of colonnade basaltic formation like Staffa and Iona in Scotland and the Giant's Causeway. This is rather an important place as regards trading with the country at the back of it and imports salted butters, tallow and wool but very little fish. The approach to the harbour is very intricate as the bay is studded with rocks and small islands but with very deep water in the right channel.

Near to this place is the noted Giants', or Berserkers', Road. The legend is that two giants were given the work to make a straight road over a certain valley and when they had finished their work, which they had undertaken in lieu of payment for their keep of food by the farmers in this district, they demanded a hot bath to cleanse them-selves. This the farmers consented to do, provided the giants would have a vapour bath, so they constructed a sort of cave and retired into it, when the farmers rolled a great stone over the entrance and then poured the boiling water into a crevice and so scalded the giants to death. The road remains to this day and is one of the sights shown to tourists.[3]

We leave this place about midnight and in two hours, on the morning of May 16th, we come to the island of Flatey situated in the centre of Breiðafjörður amongst its minnow islands; only a few are large enough to be inhabited. This bay is full of reefs and small islands. So many are they that, in way of conversation amongst the Icelanders, the simile is used, 'uncountable as the islands of Breiðafjörður'. A few houses and a church and of course stores and shops are on it, and it is also a sort of centre for the back country and deals the same as

---

[3] Pike relates the gist of the story that is told in *Eyrbyggja Saga*, but the two prota-gonists are 'beserkers', fierce Vikings who were said to fight in a trance, not giants.

Stykkishólmur. Very little to do here so we leave very quickly, only one hour's stop, and then out west until we round the most westernmost point of Iceland and Europe, off which point is a well-known race of tide. At times, in gales and spring tides, it is very dangerous, resembling the maelstrom of Norway like a seething pot and the roar could be heard above the noise of the wind, but today all is still and quiet and a small open boat came past in safety.

On the cliffs, the guillemots and puffins nest in vast quantities and the peasants make quite a harvest of eggs and young ones in the nesting times, which they collect by descending from the cliff hung onto a rope. The eggs are placed in a basket and handed up but the young birds are killed and flung into the sea where there are boats stationed to pick them up. A very dangerous undertaking, this birds-nesting, and men frequently lose their lives by the rope breaking and stones falling on their heads.

We arrive in Patreksfjörður May 16th, about one o'clock pm, and find the French man-of-war there. She is sent up every year by the French government to both protect the French fisher rights and to keep order amongst the French fishermen, a sort of policeman. Consequently, when she comes into harbour all the French schooners get out as quickly as possible, as the commander of the warship does not punish the drunken sailors but fines the captains for allowing them to get drunk. As each schooner has from 25 to 40 men on board, the master of the schooner gets out to sea in double-quick time, so there were no French schooners here although I was told that on Saturday over 100 were there. Here I meet our schooner the *Rose*. Having had her repairs done in Dýrafjörður, she had been carrying out my instructions by delivering her cargo of salt to the various fishing stations in this district. Captain Kandis came on board the *Ceres* and reported having been obliged to send his mate to England on Monday by a steam trawler, he having not only proved incompetent but a bit insane, so much so the other men became alarmed and had kept him locked up in the forecastle all day until they were fortunate to meet the trawler and got the captain to take the fellow home.

I gave further instructions and was well pleased to hear Captain Kandis had been able to get so well forward with his deliveries. I got two very nice fox skins here from my agent who had been on the look-out for me, and I got the jaw bones of a blue whale which had been promised me for a long time. Owing to one of the bones being at the bottom of the fjord, I could not get it before, but the old chap that owned them had managed to fish it out, so as we steamed out of the harbour, I saw the boat alongside the *Rose* and the bones being hauled aboard.

We got to Dýrafjörður same evening, beautiful, still, quiet night, if one can call broad daylight night? Not a cloud in the sky. The fjord (which is about 15 miles long) as a looking glass, with the snow cover-ing mountains shaped like pyramids, reflected in the still waters. We came up to the eyri which is called Þingeyri, or 'Parliament Tongue'. Nothing but to take and deliver our mails and we leave again at 2am.

May 17th

Arrived at Önundarfjörður at 5am and leave again at 7am. Arrive at Ísafjörður about 10am in most beautiful sunshine which motions on the rippling sea and all looking so peaceful as if sorry for the bad weather of the winter. One could hardly imagine that only last week the whole fjord was packed with Greenland polar ice. Only a few small pieces, about the size of a railway waggon, were stranded here and there along the shore to show what had been.

After breakfast, all the passengers left and I got my traps together and took up my happy home in the North Polar Hotel, as it is called. They do try their best to make me comfortable and have put a stove in my bedroom, which being a match-boarded room six feet broad and eight feet long and quite devoid of ventilation, I stand a good chance of being suffocated or else roasted like those giants at Stykkishólmur. At dinner we had boiled rice to begin with and stewed salt mutton with potatoes to finish with, so I begin what I call my 'three months hard'. I write a few postcards to England to say I am arrived and so to bed.

May 18th

Very fine, bright day, not a cloud in the sky and really quite warm. Meet many of my friends the fishermen, who report a very good fish-ing all over the fjord since the ice cleared away. Hear that a Norwegian steamer has arrived at Álftafjörður with about 50 fishermen from Norway on board and has commenced fishing after the Newfoundland style in dories and so far has done well. At 5pm, the *Vesta* came in on her return voyage from Reykjavík to Leith around the island. Went on board and there met Captain Gad of the *Ceres* so nothing must do but I am dragged back on board *Ceres* with the two captains and made stay to supper and stopped, chatting until midnight when both boats leave for England.

Saturday May 19th

Still fine, bright weather and quite calm, but at times during the day a sea fog gets up and envelops us and then one discovers how raw and cold the air is. Saw many more fishermen today, things look pretty hopeful. Jóhannes Pétursson's wife left last night in the *Ceres* for Reykjavík to consult a doctor there as she has developed a numbness in her hands and feet. Guðrún, Jóhannes Pétursson's daughter, got married on the 8th of May to Jón, a young fellow that was in the shop owned by Jóhannes and is now in a motor fishing boat. A young fellow brought me in another Baldwin-Ziegler Expedition balloon post-message[4] which was sent up in June 1902 and found near here in April 1906, being nearly four years drifting about the Arctic Ocean from Franz Josef Land to Iceland. Had a talk with young Hastings, who has been sent up here from Edinburgh for 12 months in Copland and Berrie's shop.[5] He is a very fine specimen of an Englishman but I think, from what I can glean, he has been an indulged boy at home and has gone wild, and his parent (who is a Presbyterian minister in Edinburgh) thinks to wean him from bad companions, but I am afraid this is not a good place. The monotony is too great and too much temptation to drink, especially as he likes one. He has been given nothing to do in

---

4   The Baldwin-Ziegler Polar Expedition was a failed American attempt to reach the North Pole, 1901–1902. The expedition party ended up stuck at their base in the Franz Josef Land archipelago, unable to strike further north. They sent up fifteen balloons carrying 300 messages that released automatically, with instructions that they should be taken to the nearest American consul. The attempt was abandoned in July 1902.

5   The department store Edinborg (Edinburgh), which opened in Ísafjörður in 1902.

the shop so he loafs and smokes all day. He is a tall, chubby-faced young fellow, looks a sort of 'mother's darling', and it's a great pity he was not first under a strict master instead of the easy-going lot up here who think drinking a virtue.

I got the missing letter from the company after the boats had left. It seems as if it got into the *Vesta*'s post bag instead of the direct out *Ceres* and had been following all about the coast. Anyhow it has come too late for me to answer but I am glad I got it, as now I have some idea of the state of affairs at the office and I can use my judgement in buying with more confidence.

Sunday May 20th

Still bright and fine. I got a bundle of *Daily Mirrors*, which turns up two days after the post arrives, so spend the day reading back news. At 6 o'clock, *Rose* came sailing in with several passengers from Arnarfjörður, amongst them Jón Hallgrímsson our agent there, so had a conference with him about the business.

Monday May 21st

Still fine and bright. Discharged some salt from *Rose* and got her ready to sail again for Ólafsvík.

Tuesday May 22nd

Still fine. *Rose* should have sailed this afternoon but Captain Kandis got intoxicated. I only left him for an hour and when I found him again he had found the grog shop.

Wednesday May 23rd

Rose sailed about seven o'clock this morning with Jón Hallgrímsson, Jóhannes Pétursson and Sigurður Haflidason for Arnarfjörður and Ólafsvík. Fine and bright weather with a good sailing breeze.

Thursday May 24th

Cloudy and bitterly cold, everyone with overcoats on. It being Ascension Day, all the shops are closed and people go to church, it being a Lutheran holy day.

Friday May 25th until Thursday May 31st

We had fine weather, but Thursday brought a change of wind. The thermometer rose from 33 to 45 degrees and brought in the Faroese fishing smacks who are accustomed to arrive here about this time to get on with their summer fishing around the islands. Busy all day with these men arranging prices etc., and in the evening it commenced to rain heavily.

Friday June 1st

Rain and hard wind.

Saturday June 2nd

Rain and a gale. The *Rose* returned from Ólafsvík.

Whitsunday June 3rd

This is the greatest holy day in the Lutheran church and consequently people are more religiously inclined, not even the coffee houses are open. Everyone meets the other with greetings of 'Gleðilega hátíð!' and shakes hands, and towards the afternoon every nine men out of ten are gloriously drunk, as they have spent the day visiting each other and drinking coffee to which is added what they call útíða, which is either a wine glass of brandy or whisky or some kind of spirit. After Sunday útíða, their legs get a bit too long and drag in the ground.

There was no service in our church here as the dean is gone to the Bolungarvík church, which is a branch of this parish. No rain today but a gale of wind, and it is wonderful to see how the snow has cleared in the two or three days of rain and the very little rise in temperature, and in some places one can actually see a blade or two of green.

Whit Monday, June 4th

This is a cloudy, raw day, gale of wind and occasional showers of rain but being also a holy day all shops and cafes closed. It is confirmation day and about fifty children are confirmed by the dean. When children arrive at the age of 13 years, it is the law of both state and church that the rite of confirmation is carried out and it frequently happens that this is the last time that many of these boys and girls go to church until they are married. Flags are hoisted on every flagstaff and people all have their best clothes on. The fathers and mothers of the confirmees strut proudly churchwards with the boy or girl between them. If a boy, he has a new suit of clothes on looking very stiff and uncomfortable. If a girl, she has on the white confirmation dress, white stockings, white shoes and the handsome headdress with golden crown and flowing veil and looking quite pleased with herself. The service lasts from 11am until 4pm and the church is uncomfortably crowded. The good old Icelandic performance is greatly in evidence; the bulk of the congregation constantly stream in and out of church, go back home and drink coffee and back again, but the children remain all the time. After the service, there is a great visiting of friends and relations to the various houses and handshakes of congratulations, drinking of chocolate and coffee and eating sweet biscuits and all sorts of Icelandic cakes. The útíða is much in evidence and the womenfolk, in between coffees, drink cheap port wine.

After dinner, the young men (piltar, as they are called) play at a sort of rounders, a sort of bat and ball game but the bat is a broomstick. At the place I live, which is called the North Pole Hotel, they were stirring at six o'clock, up and down the stairs, banging and shouting and preparing for the feast which takes place after church time. One of the children, the oldest boy Þorsteinn, is to be confirmed so everyone is greatly excited. These Icelandic children are frightfully indulged and after the confirmation time parents seem to lose all control over them. Boys come home intoxicated and smoking cigars, girls do just what they like, stay out even all night and no questions asked. The latter, after confirmation, adopt the Icelandic national costume and are women in all their ways at once. Consequently 25% of the population are illegitimate,[6] but that is held as no disgrace provided the father acknowledges the parenting of the child which bears the father's name and is named as such-and-such a man's son or daughter, and not as our English style. The father provides for the maintenance of the child and in frequent cases the child is brought home and the man's wife takes it amongst <u>her</u> children and brings it up to save expense. When asking a man how many children he has, it is quite frequent for him to say so-and-so many with my wife and so-and-so many outrounders.[7] Childless married people nearly always have two or three of these outrounders which they take in and adopt and bring them up.

My man Jóhannes Pétursson has proudly shown me today his genealogy which traces his descent from one of the Norwegian kings in AD 700. It is compiled from church registers and other documents and manuscripts by a man here who is a well-known compiler of descents and who has a list of all families and their abodes from old times. It's very interesting to trace it all back and it seems as if there was some truth in it. The Norwegian king was called Harald Finehair.[8]

Tuesday June 5th

Fine weather.

Wednesday June 6th

Fine weather, been on shore busy painting ship. Found our house here all upset this morning. Guðrún, Jóhannes Pétursson's daughter, was confined and presented the happy family with a daughter. Had a busy day interviewing fishermen and on their information decided to charter another vessel. As there was an empty Norwegian cutter in the harbour, I engaged her, so now I have two vessels on my hands.

---

6   Official figures put the percentage of births outside marriage in Iceland 1906–1910 at 13%, compared to approximately 4% in England and Wales.

7   Pike's anglicised version of 'utangarðs' — from outside the gate.

8   Harald Finehair, the first warrior king to claim sovereignty over all of Norway, is thought to have lived c.850–c.932.

Thursday June 7th

Fine days. SS *Skalholt* mail steamer came in with the mails and I was glad to find all well at home. After midday I took a motor boat and went into Álftafjörður to see how it was going there with the fishermen. It apparently was satisfactory. Went to the fishing station of a Norwegian called Johansen of Christiania. He is going it in a large scale; has a large steamer which tows out every morning 20 dories (which are small boats with two men in each) to the fishing grounds and after the fishing is over returns to the station where the fish is cured in various manners for various markets. He has also a steam trawler which does not come in every day and consequently is doing very badly with this. I related my experience of steam trawlers and I think rather frightened him a bit. He has also six motor fishing yawls which all need fitting out. He has a large 1,000 ton barque fort, a store ship, and has bought the remains and pier of the whaling station which has closed down. Altogether he must have a very large capital embarked in this venture. In my opinion, he was treating his fish very badly and will never make good saleable stuff of it. He has his wife with him and both are very nice people, quite a lady and gentleman, both speaking good English.

Friday June 8th

Cloudy day. Fishermen still coming in and I think shall commence loading early next week.

Saturday June 9th

Bright day but a worrying day, for in came a steamer for Copland and Berrie, who buy fish, and they came to try and buy 100 tons of the same sort as I do. Consequently a competition comes up and I shall have to increase my price, which is very annoying.

Sunday June 10th

Rough day, rain and wind.

Monday June 11th

Fine day. Go with motor boat into Álftafjörður and call in at village called Hafnir. Found the people there busy preparing the fish for me and all say that they will not sell to anyone else, which is encouraging. Also at Álftafjörður but it remains to be seen. On getting back to Ísafjörður, found the mail steamer *Laura* had arrived with home letters and was glad to hear all was well. She had also brought news that the Good Templars of Reykjavík[9] had bought the Hotel Ísland there for £5,000 and bought the spirit-selling licence as well, so now there is only one place in Reykjavík where drink is retailed.

Tuesday June 12th

Cloudy and windy, spent the whole day answering letters. Got into a row with my landlady for throwing soup out of the window. Someone saw it and told her and, I suspect, said it was so bad I could not eat it, so it reflected on her excellent cooking and rather got her back up, but I explained it was too much, I could not eat it all. The soup was rye bread soup with raisins in it and it looks, smells and tastes like a very wet linseed meal poultice. To eat it, one serves milk with it, but here there is only sheep's milk and very little of that, so tinned condensed is used. It's a gruesome mess and I cannot eat such a mass of it that is piled on the soup plates. So I had to promise never to do that again.

Wednesday June 13th

Squally day. Wind still south which is against our fish curing. Post all my letters, when the captain of *Laura* came and fetched me to go on board and have dinner with him. We yarned over old times until supper time, and after that I went onshore with the mate who had to fetch the mails, and so passed a very pleasant evening. The chief engineer and the captain are very old friends of mine and have been

---

9   The Good Templar organisation, which began in America and campaigned for teetotalism, had close ties to the Church of Iceland, the independence movement and early labour unions. At the time of Pike's writing, it is estimated that around 8% of the Icelandic population were Good Templar members.

associated with the *Laura* for over 15 years. They told me an amusing story about the confusion of tongues:

An Icelander came on board the *Laura* at Arnarfjörður and got into conversation with the engineer, who of course is a Dane, and told how he was going to Reykjavík to fetch a new motor for his boat, but being one indifferent Danish speaker he described it… But I must first say that in Danish a motor is pronounced mo-toor, a long toor, and is neuter gender, but in Icelandic it's pronounced nearly the same as in English 'motor', but instead of T the sound is D. When spoken thus it sounds to a Dane like 'modder' which is the Danish word for mother (the Icelanders always say Mam-ma when speaking of their mother). So the conversation went:

'I am going to Reykjavík to fetch my new modder. I have painted up my old modder and sold her. She was not strong enough so I got a chance to get rid of her and sent to Denmark for a new modder. I am going to put her into my boat and see if she will not make it go faster than my old modder did. She cost me a lot of money this new modder did, but I think it will pay to have her, if she will work well.'

Engineer (as the statement went along, getting more and more aghast until he could stand it no longer and became very angry): 'You Icelanders have no feeling, you do what no other people would, sell your own mother! You scamp and have another because she is stronger! You ought to be jolly well ashamed of yourself, a great, strong man and you deserve a good, sound thrashing and if you stop here talking to me any longer I will do it too, you blackguard!'

The Icelander's turn now came to be astonished, as the engineer is a very nice man and everyone likes him and could not understand the meaning of his wrath. He kept saying, 'My modder, my modder', and the engineer replying, 'Yes, your modder, your modder'. Then came along a well-learnt Icelander and asked what the row was about. Both tried to explain and then suddenly it dawned upon him the mixing of the two words and so he said, 'Oh! He means his mo-<u>toor</u> not his modder', and then of course wrath turned to laughter and a mutual adjournment to drink the new mo-toor's success. As the engineer said, 'If he had said "it", I might have tumbled to what he meant, but he kept saying "her" and "she", that's what put me out.'

It blew strong nearly all the night but towards the morning of the 14th it fired off a little so I engaged a small steamer to tow the *Rose* out to Bolungarvík to try to commence loading. She got there about eight o'clock. I also sent off two motor boats with messengers to the other places of loading for information. Meanwhile, the chief captain of the Faroe smacks came in to see me and I arranged a price for his and other smacks' cargoes, and in the afternoon he left for the fishing grounds. I am sorry to say my messengers have returned saying the weather was too bad for shipping.

Friday June 15th

Still blowing hard but the clouds are high and sunshine in between so that it's a fish drying day. Too much sea to begin shipping but it enables my competitors to get their steamer discharged with coals so I suspect we shall be fighting hard when the time comes for shipping; who shall induce the fishermen to give their fish, to them or me? It's a bit worrying and a nasty, anxious time.

Saturday June 16th

I was watchful all the night and saw the weather was gradually clearing up. At 5am, I dressed and went out to find my motor boats as I had warned them to be ready if it paid off. Of course not one was ready at that time but I knew where the men lived so I knocked them up and a job it is to wake up an Icelander; he sleeps so sound and so fast that it's quite ten minutes' work to rouse him. I got one fellow first and he got others and at last I got my gang together. I sent two by the boats to Hafnir, a little fishing village, and I went off to Bolungarvík and got there about 8am, just in time to get some breakfast on board *Rose*.

My man Jóhannes of course was on shore. He is too much of a gentleman now to sleep on board a vessel, so I hoisted my loading flag (which is a green one with a white star) as soon as I got on board, but after having breakfast and waiting for Jóhannes to come off, I went on shore and found him still in bed. I roused him out, and these Icelanders are so stupid for an hour after waking they seem quite dazed. He was quite sulky so I went off by myself to find the fishermen and get them to commence shipping, but I could make nothing of it. There seemed to be an undercurrent which I could not understand, and even when I got hold of what I thought was the best man amongst them and asked him straight out what was on, he sort of evaded the questions, so I got to know there was much ready and could see a good bit spread out. I could not see any movement towards getting it into the boats, so I found my man Jóhannes, who by this time was getting over his sulks, and sent him off amongst the men, as I thought they would tell him that which they did not like to tell me.

The sequel was that my opponents had offered the men an increase of price if they would wait until tomorrow evening for their steamer to get ready. As soon as I found out that, I ran around and gathered the men together, as I wished to talk with them and wanted all to hear, and then asked what was the price set by the other merchant. They told me and I then said, 'If you will load my vessel tonight I will give the same.' So they at once said, 'Oh yes Mr Vard, of course we will. Any time you give the same price you shall have the preference, but we cannot afford to lose the extra money.' So off they went and we had a busy time.

All this took until 2pm to arrange but by 9pm I had got the lot on board, about 75 tons, as soon as I saw it was going all right. Oh I forgot to say, my two motors came back to the ship all right with their loads and after discharging into the vessel, I went off with all them to the north side of the fjord and began calling at every house there. It is not a village but a strand and the houses are scattered all along the fjord for about six miles, so I began one end and worked up the shore and took all there was there and got back to the vessel at midnight.

A beautiful, fine night and the midnight sun standing on the horizon at 2.30am on the 17th. Up again at 7am. Sent two motors into Ögurnes and myself went into Álftafjörður and saw my men there. They all promised to stand fast to me, provided I got the vessel into that fjord early next morning. This I thought possible, so I motored off to Bolungarvík and got there at 1pm and had breakfast and dinner all in one, still very fine weather. Gave instructions to Jóhannes what to do as soon as the two motors returned from Ögurnes to tow the vessel into Álftafjörður without unloading so they would be heavier to tow the vessel. I went then to Hnífsdalur, a very pretty (for Iceland) village on the south side. Although this is the stronghold of my opponents, I managed to scrape up a motor boat-load as the fish was all spread, and I induced the men to load my boat instead of putting it into stacks to wait for the opposition steamer. I also weighed and paid for another boatful for removal tomorrow. By this time, the steamer had got discharged and had gone down to Bolungarvík to load, but when she came there the cupboard was bare and she only got that which was stored there belonging to their own firm. I got a cup of coffee in Hnífsdalur at 10pm and at 1am, June 18th, I got back to Ísafjörður and to bed.

At 6am, I was up again and, for a wonder, found my motor men up, so it did not take long to get underway and into Álftafjörður, where I hoped to find the *Rose* as my other two motors were not in Ísafjörður harbour. Got to Álftafjörður 8.30am and found the *Rose* there all right with the two motors alongside and all hands asleep, so went on shore and begged a cup of coffee from one of the fishermen. It being ebb tide, there was no time lost, as they cannot load their boats except on a flood tide. By this time, I saw the smoke coming out of the *Rose*'s gully funnel and went on board and had breakfast. 11am got the motors unloaded and sent them off again on the scrape. Just then a motor came in and I recognised it as belonging to the opposition firm, and in it was Berrie and his Reykjavík manager and his Ísafjörður manager. After staying for an hour, they went off in the same direction as I had sent my boats. I heard from the fishermen who now were coming off with their boats with the fish that B and his lot did not know we were in Álftafjörður but had heard late the previous evening that I had cleared Bolungarvík and was poaching Hnífsdalur. The Ísafjörður manager had ridden out there to stop it but came too late. They knew I had left Bolungarvík and had imagined I had gone to the north side with the vessel and so had sent a very large motor over there to oppose me, but when it got there found I had cleared the beaches the night before. We cleared Álftafjörður that evening and waited for the motors to return with their loads, which they did during the night, and then towed the *Rose* into Ísafjörður, getting there at 6am.

June 19th

I had by this time nearly got my cargo for the *Rose*. The same afternoon, the steamer returned with only a few tons in, which they had got from their own people, and on Wednesday June 20th she took in what was ready in Ísafjörður. They ought to have had a good lot ready, as they had been buying the whole winter, but, Icelander-like, had waited until she arrived and nothing ready, and thinking also to take a rise out of me and get the result of my two months' working without any trouble. But for once I was top dog and they had to fill up their quantity with large, full-dried fish for Barcelona instead of small fish for Genoa as intended. The crew of the *Rose* had worked very well day and night without a grumble and I gave them five shillings each for their trouble. The three of them bought a bottle of whisky each and promptly got glorious and fought all night. Consequently, on Thursday June 21st, instead of getting their water on board for the voyage home, they were in their bunks until the evening.

The weather all this time was beautifully fine, bright sunshine night and day, not a cloud in the sky. Berrie and his steamer and Reykjavík manager left this morning for Reykjavík. I did not wish them goodbye but I hear that they are very annoyed. Young Hastings went with them as he kicked over the traces on Saturday night and punched everyone's head he could get hold of, so Berrie thought it best for him to get back to his father again. It was a senseless thing to have ever sent such a young fellow here, a place of drones, not a place to get rid of super-fluous energy. The monotony and waiting and putting off until tomorrow is enough to either kill or drive to drink any young fellow except a plodder.

The mail steamer *Skalholt* came in on her voyage south and out, so I got my letters posted and sent off and am now, after that burst, waiting for the *Vesta* to arrive with home mails. Mr Jóhannes, Mr Siggi and Mr Jón all live in the house where I have my empty rooms as an office and I hear them as I write, turning up proper. I expect they will not be out of their nests until 12 noon tomorrow.

On Saturday night June 16th, whilst I was away from Bolungarvík, a house on shore took alight and burnt to the ground. By the time I got back, a woman got badly burnt and two children, the latter not so bad as their brother, and the man got singed as well. He lost everything he possessed and about £20 in money, which he had got only an hour before for his fish on board the *Rose*.

Friday June 22nd

Cloudy day and inclined to rain. Crew of *Rose* busy getting the vessel ready for the voyage home. Captain signed bills of loading and settled up his accounts so hope he will sail tomorrow morning. Anyhow, he is clear from me now. Today, as a great treat, we had stewed guillemots for dinner. They were not fishy in taste but it was black flesh and had a sort of fried liver taste; they were very hard to bite. We have had no fresh meat since I came here so it was a bit of a change from salt mutton, which I always imagine looks like a boiled dog would look, all red and carrion-like. Our usual daily food is fried fish for breakfast, boiled fish for dinner and cold scraps of each sort for supper, but I always get a couple of boiled eggs extra for supper. We are now getting eider duck eggs or guillemot eggs, which are both of an unknown quality and the insides are a sort of surprise packet until the shell is broken. Sometimes there is a good whiff of gasworks about them, but when they are really fresh they are delicious.

We have a bit of annoyance with Gunna's baby. It squeals all day long and is in the next room to what we use as an office, and rather puts us out in making up accounts. Jóhannes is busy preparing the Norwegian ketch *Gudrun* for his voyage to the Westfjords, getting salt on board which was asked for at Ólafsvík and generally getting ready for a start, I expect on Monday as she is due there next week to commence loading and he goes in charge of her.

Saturday June 23rd

Fine day, bright and clear and a nice wind from the north. Both *Rose* and *Gudrun* ready for sea, both captains drunk so neither sailed. Both say barometer falling and likely for bad weather, this is their excuse. Siggi, my man, has got all the accounts cleared up and cash balanced. I write my letters and am also cleared up. Jóhannes announces that it will be necessary for another man to go to help him with *Gudrun*'s cargo, so I employ his son-in-law Jón Hafliðason, brother to my Siggi.

Since Jóhannes has discovered he is descended from Norwegian kings, he has put on so much side he cannot work, in fact I think if it were possible he would have a servant eat his food for him. His wife keeps two maids and his second daughter, Hjördís (or short 'Dísa'), has returned from England where she has been for 12 months learning housework. She has brought back a bicycle with her and says in broken English, 'I do not like being servant', so she swells about dressed in English costume and bedecked with cheap servant girl's finery.

Sunday June 24th

Fine day in the morning but evidence of plenty of wind outside. However, *Rose* sailed in this morning all right and I hope will have a good run home. Jóhannes and Jón swell about in their best clothes. Towards evening it clouds over and the wind rises and it rains heavily.

Monday June 25th

Fine here in the fjord but outside in the main fjord it is rough and stormy, but as I am a bit sulky, Jóhannes decides it's best to try it and so goes on board *Gudrun*. They sail off but only get about two or three miles out and then I see them heave to, waiting for the weather to clear. The mail steamer *Perwie* of Thore line comes in and brings business and home letters so I am busy all day answering these letters. She sailed again at 6pm, weather still dirty outside.

The Icelander has a peculiar manner of counting: instead of saying one hundred and fifty or two hundred and fifty and so on, he says half of 200 or half of 300, or half of 500 for 450 and so on, and if he wants to say 253 he says three and half 300, which at times is puzzling. For example, I was talking to a man and he said he had two and a half dozen of children and I asked, 'What! All with one wife?'

'Oh yes and my brother has three and a half dozen.'

This I thought rather much of a joke so I said, 'How do you find names for them all?' I supposed he was like a man called Nilsson here who had 27 children and had exhausted all the family names so the boy before the last was called Karl and he could think of no other name for the very last boy so he called him 'Ditto'. 'Oh no', says my man, 'it's not very many, three boys and five girls. I am a young man yet and have only been married nine years.' Then it dawned upon me that it was two and six he meant, and it was only eight children, instead of 30 as was my first impression when he said two and a half dozen.

June 26th

Edward's birthday so I hoisted my flag up. It's a very cold, raw day, heavy fog half down the mountains and in the harbour are many fishing cutters driven in with the bad weather outside. They report the polar ice only half a mile from the north cape so I expect it will stop *Vesta* from getting around; she is expected here today on her up voyage. The wind is north-east and is a good off-shore wind for both *Rose* and *Gudrun,* so expect they are getting along all right. Siggi and I have nothing to do now the two vessels and mails are gone, except wait. Baby still squealing. As a special treat today for dinner, we had wind-dried mutton, boiled. This is very expensive and costs about one shilling per pound. It is prepared from legs of mutton first hung up with the skin on and smoked over a peat fire, then exposed to the drying wind until every particle of moisture is dried out of it, and kept for 12 months. The boiling of this is a fair treat in the way of smells and in eating. A small piece goes a long way but the natives go for it and stow away enormous quantity at a sitting, therefore it's too expensive to be put upon a common lodging-house table too frequently; quite frequent enough for me though!

To celebrate the Birthday of Edward, I ate the Christmas pudding given me by his grandma and consequently got a fast fit of indigestion.

June 27th

Very nice day. Last night many Norwegian sailors were onshore and got into a noise with the policeman here, who called upon other Icelanders to help him put a man into the lock-up. The others attempted a rescue and there was a pretty dido for a couple of hours, but the Icelanders succeeded in getting seven Norwegians locked up. As the lock-up is only a wooden building, they were confined by leg and arm irons, and, as the sheriff was away holding court and will not be home until late tomorrow, they will get nothing except bread and water all day today. If the Norwegians had not been so intoxicated and had more concentration, they could have rescued all their men but they ran all over the place shouting what they would do instead of combining, and so the worst got captured and run in.

June 28th

Fine but cold and foggy. Policeman went off in a motor boat and captured two more Norwegians and the sheriff took all day trying the men. They were brought out one by one, and each case took about an hour. It ended up in paying fines from £1 to £5 for their spree. The worst two men got a £5 fine each. As the captains refused to pay these heavy fines, they were put back into the lock-up again to work off their fines, which is done by a bread and water diet. £1 per day is got rid of if the prisoner decides on bread and water, but if he wishes for the ordinary prison diet of soup and bread and coffee, he only works off five shillings per day. One of these men decides for bread and water and the other for the prison diet, so we shall see how the bread and water chap holds out, for if he gives in before his time is up, he loses the time he has already served and has to go right through as if he had not begun the bread and water. I expect the number two chap has been through that game before and will not try it the second time.

All the fishing vessels have now cleared off and we have a free harbour.

Friday June 29th

Fine but still foggy which makes it raw and cold. *Vesta* now three days late. She cannot be stopped by polar ice as a whale boat was seen yesterday passing this fjord towing five whales. He must have come around the north cape. The fishing vessels have reported all the week the ice some half a mile off the north cape but room for a steamer to pass clear. Also news comes by the Álftafjörður trawler which came from Siglufjörður that Friðrik Wathne's[10] new steamer had run on shore near that place and become a total wreck. He was trying to pass inside

---

[10] Friðrik Wathne (1852–1924) was one of four brothers who immigrated to Iceland from Norway and became successful ship owners and traders.

the ice and struck on a rock and sunk in half an hour, but no-one was drowned as it was calm.

Saturday June 30th

Fine, bright day. Took a motor boat and went into Álftafjörður to inspect our store there and to make arrangements as to the discharge of the cargo of salt which I expect by the Danish schooner *Veritas*. Returned here about 6pm and found the French man-of-war was here, arrived on her tour around the island. At 9pm, the *Ceres* mail boat arrived with home mails, and I was glad to hear 'all's well' there.

Sunday July 1st

Fine but thick fog overhead. Spent the morning answering letters. Was surprised to have nothing from the company, but a letter from Jóhannes Pétursson from Ólafsvík saying Copland and Berrie have sent a messenger there and had risen the price to such a height that it had exceeded the limit I had given him, and consequently he would get no cargo there and was proceeding to Patreksfjörður. Very annoying after I have taken so much trouble with this out-of-the-way place. It's like a man who digs up a piece of ground and sows potatoes and, after waiting for them to grow, in the middle of the night a thief creeps in and digs them up and decamps with the result of 12 months waiting and planning. Clearly annoying, for if I had not prepared the ground, C&B would not have thought of it, but suppose must not complain as it's called Healthy Competition, which is considered good for all trades.

With the *Ceres* came two men from Bradford with a cinematograph to take living pictures of Icelanders for lecture purposes. Had splendid machines with them but, the weather being so foggy and such, they did not take any pictures in this place. At 9pm, the *Vesta* arrived five days late, but reported no ice to stop the vessel except around the cape of Langanes, the most eastern north-east corner. There she had to go dead slow to fit between the bergs but her stoppage was first at Berufjörður. In getting out two large motor boats, the first mate and carpenter got entangled in the steam winch; the mate lost his arm and all the fingers off the left hand, and the carpenter lost both hands, broken ribs, and (it is supposed) injured his spine. They were both taken on shore to the

French hospital at Fáskrúðsfjörður and are of course there now. Then the next stoppage was at Akureyri. Having so much cargo it delayed them two days discharging, and at Blönduós another day was lost with the same cause. I was very surprised to get no letters from England by this boat. They both left again at midnight.

The two Norwegians stood out their time with bread and water and got liberated today, and their vessels came in and fetched them, so that now was finished.

Monday July 2nd

Fine, bright, clear day. Sent a motor boat to a village called Súgandafjörður for three tons of fish and the boat returned all right in the evening. Had that horrible fish soup for dinner today so preferred to go without and made up for it at supper time with eider duck eggs.

Tuesday July 3rd

Fine, bright day. Beginning to look around previous to packing up.

Wednesday July 4th

Fine, bright day. Spent all day in going through the business with Sigurður Haflidason, my clerk here, and giving him written instructions of what to do when I am gone, and packing up my boxes ready for a start east tomorrow if *Vesta* should come. Baby squealing all day and the old woman grandmother chanting a lullaby.

Portrait of Pike Ward by Þórarinn B. Þorláksson. Circa 1900
With thanks to the National Museum of Iceland

Cartoon (1900) 'The Best-Known Man in Iceland'
With thanks to the National Museum of Iceland

Deck scene onboard S/S "Vesta" March 1/906
on voyage to Iceland. these 2 photos were taken
at-sea 70 miles before sighting the coast.

Guðmundur Björnsson, eminent doctor and Pike's good friend in Reykjavík

Women cleaning fish at Ísafjörður

Pike at Seyðisfjörður

Filling my bed with feathers

Jakob Jónsson, Pike's travelling companion

A coalfish at Nordfjord weighing 55 pounds –

Stone 'vards' or vörður as described in the diary, between Seyðisfjörður and Borgarfjörður

Jakob with the horses on the road to Eskifjörður

Haymaking at Seyðisfjörður

Sigsí   Galle   Olgar

The shoemaker Jón Ludvigsson cuts the retired sheriff's hair in Seyðisfjörður

Pike and Siggi's journey from Eskifjörður to Norðfjörður in 1908, when they got stuck in a snowstorm

View from the mountain pass 2000 ft high
on the road from Eskifjord to Norafjord : The gathering clouds
on the mountains opposite gradually enveloped us & heavy snow
fell =.

Rudarfjord   Eskjfjord

Vidfjord   Hedlisfjord

"Norafjord

Siggie & I got caught in a mountain pass
by a snow storm middle of august 1908 on
the road from Eskifjord to Nordfjord.

The pass

French schooners opposite
the trading station Nordfjord.

Coffee with friends, Pike on far right

A childs funeral at Reykjavik
. 1907 .

"Mid-house" (Midhus) farm (note the barrel for chimney in turf house)
Siggie (Sigurdur Hafladisson) & I enquire for lodgings Steindor the
farmer holds my pony & the wife stands at the door : The
wooden portion is the guest house & in the turf house lives the family

Photograph of Valhalla, Pike Ward's home in Teignmouth (National Museum of Iceland)

Photograph of Pike Ward.
With thanks to the National Museum of Iceland

Four

Seyðisfjörður

Thursday July 5th to Saturday July 7th

Bad weather, rain and wind, cold and raw. Place full of people waiting for *Vesta* and a great deal of drunkenness. Friday evening, 9pm, the *Vesta* came in and we all went on board, as the captain said she would sail again at 4am, instead of which we did not sail until 9am on Saturday morning. Weather still wet, raw and cold, about 300 passengers aboard, no place to be had so I sleep in the first mate's bunk. The second class passengers find places in the hold, which is nearly full with dried fish heads which they are taking from the fishing places to the farming places, together with bags of salted skate and catfish, to be exchanged by the fishermen for butter, which is often mixed with tallow. In the first cabin, the state rooms have four passengers sleeping in them, the sofas are full, and even on the floor beds are made up, and in the smoking room the sofas are full of sleepers.

We rounded the north cape about 2pm but it was all clouded with fog and mist, no sea to speak of, so I get my breakfast and dinner but it's colder now than it was in March. The two gentlemen from Bradford are on board with their cinematograph but cannot do anything as it is such dull weather, but they are very anxious to take our deck passengers, who are all about the decks in groups with their luggage and eating their rye bread and stock fish, drinking corn brandy and Danish beer. One fellow got so drunk that the captain had to put handcuffs on him and lash him up to the foremast and kept him there for one and a half hours until he became sober. It's not a nice sight to see men and women huddled together in the hold like a lot of pigs in a sty.

We get in to Steingrímsfjörður about 7pm on Sunday July 8th and find the Danish gunboat *Islands Falk* there, surveying the fjord. Weather still raw and cold. We put out many passengers here, also fish heads, and sail again for Blönduós on Monday July 9th at noon. Smooth sea but still clouded, raw and cold. This is a big glacier river, broad but shallow, and we anchor outside the basin. The white water colours the sea to the distance of about two miles from the mouth of the river. Here is one of the termini of the telegraph line and one can see the posts leading from the station into the country. Norwegians are employed to set up these posts and complete the line from Seyðisfjörður to Akureyri to Blönduós and thence to Reykjavík and it had to be completed by the end of October. We have the chief engineer on board who has the management of the line along to make his survey of how it is going. The Icelanders are too proud to dig so Norwegian labour has to be imported to do the work. I expected to have had news before I left Ísafjörður of Jóhannes Pétursson and the vessel *Gudrun*, but nothing came. The captain of *Vesta* and passengers whom I know had seen nothing of her in the Westfjords. Conclude she is still at Ólafsvík so I leave Sigurður Hafliðason behind and he will come east to meet me in August, so until that time I shall have no news of how that part of the business will go.

We leave Blönduós during the night and arrive at Skagaströnd about 7am, July 10th. This is an open harbour, if it can be called a harbour, two or three homes perched on a cliff with a little cove of sandy beach beneath. Remain here until 9am and then go out to a fishing place called Kálfshamarsvík. Here is a fishing station springing up and growing rapidly, and many boats sail from here to the fishing grounds. It is similar to Skagaströnd, cliffs and sandy coves. The cliffs here are beautiful specimens of columnar basalt, some square in shape and others six-cornered and some octagonal, and one place there is a cave right in the middle of the cove. I think I could have gone on shore to take a few photos but the wind is on the shore and a good sea, on which makes the landing difficult, beside the risk of not being able to get back again. We left here about noon and arrived at Sauðárkrókur about 5pm. It was very bad weather, a gale and biting cold. We passed a German steamer in the bay but it was too rough for him to fish so he was 'hove to', waiting for better weather.

At Sauðárkrókur we met the steamer *Kong Inge* of Thore line of boats. This is his terminus and he returns to Copenhagen via the east coast. At midnight we left and saw a most magnificent display of midnight sun. It was just perched on the horizon, a big, blood-red ball of fire, peeping below the thick, heavy clouds, a round of fire reaching on the dull, leaden sea from horizon to ship (which was also clothed in fire), whilst all around was clothed in dull, silver grey. The contrast from fire to full parrot-grey was very great and made a most beautiful picture. The cinematograph people were delighted with it but of course it was impossible to reproduce such wonderful colouring. It calmed off now and during the night it seemed to roll up the clouds, so that when we arrived at Akureyri, 10am, July 11th, it was a lovely specimen of an Icelandic summer day: clear sky, clear air, clear sunshine, just enough wind to make the fjord sparkle, and just warm enough to be quite pleasant.

After breakfast, went on shore to see Mr Stefán Stefánsson to know about my ponies which he had been keeping for the winter for me. Found them all right and made the necessary arrangements to ship them on board *Vesta* to Seyðisfjörður. Bought a very curious carved chair, said to have come from Hólar church and supposed to be over 200 years old, anyhow it's old and shaky enough.

Here the cinematograph people took a series of pictures of shipping ponies. I think I am in that set of pictures 'helping', so hope to figure at many a Mothers' Meeting, as Mr Hibbert, the proprietor, has a lot of engagements for the coming winter amongst Temperance and Chapel. He is a great Temperance man and first began this lantern business like our friend Mr Norton, and took such an interest in the work that he has travelled in many lands to obtain pictures and uses his summer holidays for this purpose. He is a fishmonger by trade in Bradford. He pays a professional photographer a yearly salary to travel about with him, in the summer taking pictures and developing and preparing slides, and in the winter attending religious meetings and showing his lantern. He travels all over the country: London, Bristol, Southampton, Newcastle and all these large towns. He promises to let me know when he is in London or Bristol with his show.[1]

At midnight, July 12th, we leave Akureyri. On the way out of the fjord, we pass a place called Hjalteyri, which is a tongue of sand and has been purchased by a Scotch man called Boyle from Glasgow, and he has erected a station there for herring curing. He has come with four steam herring boats and one cargo boat to take back to Scotland his catches, but up to the present he has done nothing except build his houses and pier. Last year he tried with one boat and made a good thing of it, so that if he is successful this year many others will come.[2] It is computed that this year there are over 500 Norwegian steam fishers here in Iceland to fish for herrings when the time comes, and it's just about now when the fishing begins and continues until the end of September. Vast shoals of very fine herrings are always swimming about in the Arctic. I have so often told the herring concerns in England of this but until now no-one has had the heart to venture. The Norwegians have been at it for four or five years and now the Scotch will try their luck.

Mr Boyle brought about 20 Scotch lassies to cure the herrings, and on landing at Akureyri they all promptly got drunk and fought like cats, to the great edification of the Icelanders. We are taking back two of the best of them. One has a most beautiful black eye and is scratched all over the face and arms, and the other is lame and has her hand bandaged up with a dirty, blood-stained rag. They are continually badgering the English passengers for a drink but the captain has given orders they are to have none whatsoever. I saw one in the middle of the night with nothing on but a petticoat and chemise, trying to pump up some water into a bottle, which she could not succeed in doing, and she was swearing about the 'blank blank' ship, couldn't even get a drink of water, wished she would sink so all hands could get more water than they wanted.

---

[1]   Henry Hibbert went on to work for the Captain Kettle Film Company and owned several cinemas in Bradford. Mr Norton is likely to be Charles Goodwin Norton, a lanternist and filmmaker operating from Bloomsbury.

[2]   John Boyle returned to Scotland two months later reporting a very successful season with profits up on the year before.

In coming out of the fjord, we passed the steamer *Botnia* which was going into Akureyri. She had been sent up by the King of Denmark to collect up the Icelandic parliament men and take them to Copenhagen for a free visit to him. On arrival there, they have a full programme and, much to the disgust of the members, not one free hour will they have, every minute being taken up in festivities. They naturally want to take advantage of the free passage and food to do a bit of business on their own. I expect they will be asking for their pay when they come back, like the men in Reykjavík who, when they saw the sailors drowning, asked if they went out to save them who was going to pay!

The weather changed again by now and it was a strong, cold wind but a smooth sea and we rounded the cape of Langanes once more and saw no ice. We arrived at Vopnafjörður at 2pm. Here I went on shore and had a running visit to all my friends and found my Bakkafjörður man, Halldór Runólfsson. Gave him some money to buy fish and made other business arrangements and sailed again at 5pm. Cold, cloudy weather and arrived at Seyðisfjörður at 2am, July 13th.

Went to bed and got up again at 7am. Got my baggage and ponies on shore and took up my quarters at the hotel, which I am glad to say has lost its spirit-selling licence, so I hope it will not be so rowdy as formerly. The landlord has given me my usual room. I was glad to find here a man called Jakob Jónsson who has been employed by me several times before. He is a bit of a rover, sometimes a merchant, sometimes a fisherman, sometimes a farmer. It so happened last winter he was burnt out of house and shop and so has nothing to do, so I engage him to accompany me about. He is a most curious-looking man and we English call him 'Monkey Brand',[3] as he is exactly like those pictures, but as he is perfectly bald, the Icelanders call him 'Jakob Skalli' which means 'Jakob bald head'. I have always found him a very honest fellow, a flyaway and a rover but he knows everyone in this district and their visitors and friends, and so is very useful to me.

At 3pm the *Vesta* sailed. I find I have caught a fine cold now I have come on shore and although it's a beautiful, fine day in the fjord and very warm, I am sneezing like a good one, so after supper I go to bed

---

[3] A household polishing soap, advertised with pictures of a monkey dressed as a servant.

take a good dose of *ammoniated quinine* and snuggle down with the bed. I awake again in the middle of the night in a great perspiration and fever, toss about for an hour or two, and awake in the morning with a fat head and all the discomfort of catarrh. I have breakfast: boiled fish and coffee. That sounds all right but to see the mess is another thing. A great plate of whale but I am not hungry enough for that yet.

The *Botnia* came in here, her last place of call before leaving the island, and collects up the last stragglers and sails for Copenhagen at 6pm. It has now come in cold again with showers of rain after supper, 8pm. I go to bed again and sleep soundly until 8am.

Sunday July 15th

On looking out of the window, see the hills all covered with new snows and a gale of wind blowing, but glad to find my cold is better. Have the usual breakfast of boiled fish and coffee and sit in the room afterward shivering from the cold and try to think it's good fun. Had a visit from my little friend from Norðfjörður yesterday; he came in a motor boat. I gave him some money but the prospects are very bad for any business. The pricing too high and at present the fishing is far from good, in fact no fishing at all, so it's very dear and very scarce. Get a postcard and a business letter from Exeter, both having come here by Thore Line.

At dinner, for a wonder, we had new beef (very hard and dry but new beef all the same), boiled potatoes, and curds with milk afterwards. These curds are called 'skyr' and is accounted a very fine dish of the Icelanders, but it is very sour and much sugar and milk has to be added before it can be eatable by foreigners. Bitterly cold and snowing, a very strong gale is blowing and it comes whizzing down from the mountains and fairly shakes the house. Several panes of glass get disturbed and fall out with a crash. Some two or three years ago, several houses got blown over here by these whirlwinds, so it makes one look up when an extra puff strikes the house!

Monday July 16th

Still cold and blowy. Sent for my horses and had them shod, ready for a start when the weather clears. The telegraph poles and wires are up here, and telephone messages come along the line from the men working far up the country. News brought here today of the loss of another of Wathne's steamers, the *Eagle,* in Norway.

Have for breakfast today, as a great treat, one eider duck egg and for dinner some more boiled fish and potatoes and boiled rice with ground cinnamon with milk. I shall soon be hungry enough to tackle the whale beef, of which there is a huge dish on the table. It's strange, the mixture of table manners we have here: always serviettes; iron, three-prong forks and knives (very dirty); thick, cheap common glasses and, for coffee, cheap cups and saucers, all cracked and handed round on a tin tray with an embroidered cloth on it. The men eat the fish and spit the bones all over the table, lick their knife clean and dab it straight into the butter.

Cold gone from the head into my throat and it tickles and tickles, and cough, cough, all the time. Had a long confab with Jón Stefánsson, who is the merchant here and was my agent until the company discontinued buying. He then became agent for a Grimsby man and is buying salt-fish for him and sending it in packages by steamer to Grimsby. It's a great mystery to me, as the price the Grimsby man is paying is more than the company say they can buy delivered in Exeter from Grimsby, and yet the Grimsby man has to pay the carriage from here to Grimsby. I am very puzzled and would much like to have the problem solved.

Tuesday July 17th

Better weather today so take the horses for a trial trip, about an hour's ride, to a little village called Vestdalseyri and have an interview with a man there over business, which seems satisfactory. Horses went very well but one of them is a bit wild and spirited and jumps about all over the place quite circus-like, but still a very nice pony. At supper tonight (I knew it had to come), I wolfed a big lump of whale, so I am getting into tune. I hope tomorrow will see me getting packed up for a start.

July 18th

Rain and cold and all overcast. Vessels that are coming in say it's fine weather at sea, bright and sunshining. Nothing to do today except see about getting ready for a start but really I am waiting for the *Kong Inge* to see if there are any letters that require answering before I move. As I do not expect any more home mails until *Vesta* returns on August 5th, I have nothing to think about, so my trip north will just fill up the time. Little or no fishing in this fjord but hear they are doing well at Norðfjörður.

July 19th

Rain and cold gale from east, just like a cold December day in England. Today at breakfast, an old story came to my mind of a tailor who used to live in Teign Street, called Symons. He spent a deal of his time drinking in the publics and one day his little child came to fetch him for dinner. On his enquiring what was for dinner, she said, 'Sprats!' On the way home, he remonstrated with her and bid her say something larger next time. So the following day, she fetched him and in answer to his question, 'What's for dinner?' she said, 'Whales, Father!'

'Is it possible?!' he answered.

A laugh went up from his companions and he was called Possible Symons from that day until he died, but little did I think in my boyhood that I should be actually eating whale from sheer hunger. We have two Norwegian evangelists here, and they have jibbed from our food and go out and buy tins in the shops and have their food in their bedrooms. SS *Kong Inge* came in today to take our letters for England.

July 20th

Cold but no rain. Still very cloudy and thick, heavy masses of fog hang about the mountainside. An unexpected pleasure came today in the shape of a business letter from the company by one of the Thore Line boats, the *Mjolnir*, contents of which were very satisfactory indeed and gave me better heart to go and write, although if it really turns out as I would like it, to do it will mean my staying here all the winter, but of this more later.

July 21st

Still heavy fog overhead and cold but otherwise fine, so determined to make a move, being already packed up. Yesterday afternoon, in getting ready, discovered it was impossible to get a pack saddle to take my 'koffort', as the pack boxes are called here. This is very annoying as I have a good one at Reykjavík, but it never entered my mind that there was any place in Iceland where such a necessary article was unobtainable, but so it is up here. The place is full of surprises and disappointments. I seem to carry about with me a whole cargo of things but I do not take the whole kit about. That very thing is unobtainable whilst all the rest there is plenty of. It appears in this neighbourhood, the custom, instead of boxes, is to use a 'ferðataska', which is saddle bag made of leather or seal skin. The latter is best, being waterproof, but of course there was not one to be bought, borrowed or stolen. After a search amongst all the inhabitants, I got hold of a miserable specimen made of canvas for which I had to pay £2, the original first cost (it really was worth about three shillings and sixpence), and then found all the straps rotten so they had to be removed, so after fussing about for hours, at last got the thing usable.

Had to sort out my boxes again and pick out and make do with a very few things and pack into the taska. Found I had about double so much as would go in, and sorted again until, at last, I was reduced to a very limited kit. It reminded me of a yarn of an old gentleman who used to travel a great deal and a young fellow asking him his advice of what to take on a certain tour. The old fellow advised making a list of all his possessions and then striking out that which he thought he could do without, make a fresh list and revise that, and when he had reduced it to its lowest limits, lose the list and throw the things into a box, blind-eyes. And so it was about that with my little lot: one change of under-clothes; two pairs of socks; two pairs stockings; flannel shirt; sponge bag and contents; half a dozen tins of 'Army Rations'; my letter book and a couple or three books to read, and that was all the bags would hold.

I had ordered my man Jakob Jónsson to bring the ponies at 9am so as to be ready for a start immediately after breakfast but, as usual with Icelandic journeys, it was 11am before we finally set off. Jakob is a man I have known for a long time and was about the first man I met when I got here on the *Vesta*. As he had no employment just then, I engaged him for the trip. But I have got some sort of idea that I mentioned in

Reykjavík to him what my programme was likely to be and he booked ahead and was on the spot at the right moment for getting the job. He had two ponies with him, a brown one, rather aged, and a six year old brown piebald which bore the saddle bags. Jakob changed occasionally from brown to piebald himself and the packs. He is only about 130 pounds weight and is a ridiculous likeness to Monkey Brand soap adverts and does not speak a word of English or Danish.

At the very last moment, the bank manager came and asked if I would oblige him by taking his little son to the farm we should stay at halfway on. Of course, I could not see any objections to that and said like a fool, 'Oh yes' and 'Gladly', thinking the boy would come along on his own pony, when lo and behold out came a big boy, 17 years old, with a saddle which he calmly put on my spare pony. I was in a rage but had to pocket it, and so we set off.

The road leads through the valley at the back of the village for about a mile, past the burying ground and beside the little river, then a gradual ascent to a small farm and from there a zigzag climb about one and a half hours up the side of the mountain, following the course of the river which now becomes a mountain torrent and full of magnificent waterfalls, one after the other. The paths are good, and for Icelandic roads very good, but it's very steep. The pony I was on, the sorrel, was soon in a bath of perspiration and I the same as I was warmly clad, but with the exertion of holding on and being soft to begin with, I had to dispense with the big overcoat.

The fog had lifted a little and the sun began to show dimly through it. The mountain is about 2,000 feet high, in fact most of them range about that here in the east, with one occasionally topped off from 3,000 to 3,500 feet. We stopped for a breather on the top and strapped on greatcoats and waterproofs on the pack pony, and then started off again on a plain called Fjarðarheiði. All high plains in Iceland are called heiði. It is a very wild and rough place, not a blade of grass, only one great desolate heap of stones and gravel with patches of snow and undulating like the waves of a rough sea bed. The road winds in and about the waves with an occasional up and over and down and over a big wave, and so one rides along the track, one after the other, the first pony making the pace and bespattering the following pony and rider with clots of mud with his hooves. The faster they go, the more mud they distribute, and as the rider does not dictate to the pony when to gallop and when to walk, the pace is full of astonishments, for the pony may be just picking his way slowly and you think this is a good opportunity to either fill or light your pipe, or unbutton your coat and get a handkerchief to wipe off the mud collected over yourself in the last sprint, when off sets the animal with a vigorous jerk. You make a grasp for the reins (which you don't get) and whack! comes a clot of mud in your face and eyes (which you do get), and you hold on wildly to saddle, mane, or whatever comes first, and away you go, splish splash, no stopping until the leader considers he has about had enough and then settles down again to a donkey crawl, and by the time you have adjusted yourself and get all straight again, jerk! off you go again, and this goes on for hours.

There was much old snow lying about and much new snow on this, which the ponies did not like and shied and made a great fuss to cross. In the centre of the heiði, a large lake about two miles long by half a mile broad, in which a number of ducks of various sorts were swimming with their young broods, was passed. The heiði seemed never-ending, but away in the far distance one could see the peaks of high, serrated mountains which Jakob said was the edge of the Vatnajökull, the largest glacier in Iceland. The weather had now greatly improved and the clouds and fog were gradually getting higher, thus enabling us to obtain the distant view of these peaks, and here and there a gleam of sunshine began to peep out.

The way along the heath is marked out by pillars of stones piled up with one projecting stone pointing the direction of the track. These heaps are called 'vards'[4] and so like my own name that I am mostly called Vard up here, especially as there is no W in the Icelandic language and W is spoken of as a double V.

Suddenly, after mounting a big wave and as suddenly descending, we saw spread out before us the vast plains of the Lagarfljót, the biggest of the Icelandic rivers, if it can be called a river, for it is more like a long narrow lake than a river, although there is a current towards

---

4   In Icelandic, the singular is varða and the plural is vörður, but Pike creates an anglicised version.

the sea but very slight. We came to about the middle of it and, being 2,000 feet above, could look right and left and see it stretching away for miles and miles until lost in the distance. On the left hand, it resembled the pictures I have seen of Windermere. The big, violet-coloured mountains rising from the bright, white waters of the lake to their sharp, snow-covered peaks made a very beautiful picture, which no photograph could produce. The heavy clouds over all and the gleams here and there of sunshine, and in the foreground the vivid, emerald-green of the new, fresh grass on each side of the waters, dotted here and there with a solitary farmhouse or two; it was all very beautiful, yet sad and wild. Away on the right hand, the fljót was lost in the fog and mist, the land being very flat towards the sea.

The fljót is about 60 miles long and ranging from 100 fathoms to half a mile wide. It is pretty deep but no-one seems to have the curiosity to measure the depth of water in it, nor has it been surveyed, so far as I can find out by enquiries amongst the neighbouring farmers. All they say is it's 'very deep'. About 15 miles from the sea, it's blocked by a waterfall about 50 feet high which forms a sort of weir to the upper waters. This last year, the farmers have clubbed together and bought a small motor boat to ply up and down the waters from one end to the other and have a regular timetable and scale of charges, so it is becoming of some use after so many years of uselessness and really drawback, for it stands right across the most inhabited and best farm district and the farmers, to get at the trading stations, had to cross the water as best they could. They had tried for years to build a bridge over the narrowest part, opposite Egilsstaðir, but every spring the works were carried away by the accumulated ice until they employed a Danish engineer and Danish workmen to build them a bridge. This was completed last year and withstood well the rigours of the spring.

Our road now leads straight down to the plains below and we zigzag down by the side of a deep ravine, black rocks rising sheer upright on each side and the bright, rushing water gushing out from between the rocks laying upon the bright sand. Our ponies go along-side the sheer, upright cliffs of the chasm as fearless as goats. At the bottom of the mountain path, we cross over this torrent by a very decent wooden bridge and then we gallop over the grassy plain to the farmhouse called Egilsstaðir, the destination of our <u>little</u> <u>boy</u>! He is to stay here for a week's holiday, but really to assist the farmer in getting his hay stored, as the grass is now in a fit state to mow. In fact, several men are to be seen out with their little scythes, shaving off the six inch long grass from the curiously-formed round hummocks on the 'tún', or enclosed grass plot, surrounding the farm.

Every Icelandic farm has such a tún, in the centre of which the house and sheep houses stand. It is guarded by a stone or turf wall and carefully preserved, no sheep or horses ever being allowed to graze on it or even people to walk on it, carefully manured in the spring from the sheep houses, carefully mowed in the summer, and then the hay carefully stored away in storehouses adjacent to the sheep houses for winter use. Whilst this is being dried, the men go outside amongst the hills and mow the longest grass they can find. It is borne home on ponies' backs all wet, and dried on the tún. This upland hay is not accounted so good and strong as the tún hay and is only given to the outdoor sheep, whilst the tún hay is given only to the milking ewes, so the number of pony-loads of upland hay obtained gives the farmer an idea of how many outdoor sheep he will be able to retain during the winter. The remainder are slaughtered to save their lives during the winter. So, a farmer who has a flock say of 500 sheep, 60 of which are milking ewes and are kept upon the tún hay, has 440 sheep to look after in the winter. He has only been able to get so-and-so pony loads of upland hay so he slaughters 140 sheep, or more or less as the case might be. He salts them down in casks if too long from the trading station, but if near enough he prefers to drive them in there in September and sell them outright to the merchants there, who slaughter and salt down and export mostly to Norway.

Slaughter time is a great time amongst the womenfolk, who prepare their winter stocks of blood puddings, neck fat, brawn, loin rolls, breast briskets and all sorts of smoked parts, such as hams and legs. Much is heated up into a paste and preserved in stone jars and hermetically sealed with tallow. By the way, the latter is the only fresh meat they get from one slaughter time to the other. Besides the salted meat, the other delicacies are preserved in 'súr', as it's called, which is sour whey and has a sour and faded meat taste clearly beloved by the natives, and whale meat is preserved in the same way, so it all tastes the same. Being brought up from babyhood on such horrible (to us) tasting stuff, all European foods are distasteful to Icelanders and they pity all the rest of the world being obliged to eat such stuff as they do, instead of the delicious Icelandic provender!

Egilsstaðir is a modern house built of concrete, a two-storey, large house with many windows, the farmer being a very well-to-do man and having had the luck to get his old turf farm burnt down about three years ago, well insured. With the bank coming to Seyðisfjörður, he was enabled to build what I should say was the best farmhouse in the land, and as it's right in the way for all travellers to and from the Eastfjords, it is just like our hotel and has accommodation for many people. I should say he makes a good income out of his hotel business, which of course would be very good if it only were in the tourist trade but very seldom indeed does one of this class visit this part of the country.

We have coffee and biscuits, and after saying goodbye to the little boy, we make a start again for our destination, over the meadows (as they may be called here, but in England we should call it a marsh), pass a group of Norwegians who are erecting the telegraph posts, on to the Lagarfljót and cross over the bridge, by which I took a photo. The water of the fljót is of a white, thick churn, being glacier water, 'white muddy water'. Then the way leads towards a farm which we pass without comment, but we should have had a talk there, as events proved after.

The track then struck away to the left instead of the right and Jakob, thinking it was wrong, took an overland route, thinking to strike the correct track on our right hand, but he didn't and so we wandered on and on over morass and mire and got our road. Suddenly in rounding a kopie[5] we struck a lake, which Jakob said was called 'Trout Lake', bright, clear water, and we skirted that for about an hour. We then espied a farm, which we eventually got to after soundly floundering and wandering, and then found that we had come the wrong side of the lake and the road we went from was the correct road, so we hired a

---

[5] A word with no obvious relation in modern Icelandic or Devon dialect that seems to mean a small hill.

boy on a pony to put us straight. Found the road and set off again and finally got to Bót (pronounced 'Boat') at 6pm.

We found the farmer home but his wife away, but he bade us welcome all the same. He was puzzled what to give us to eat, so we produced a tin of 'Army Rations' and whilst that was busy warming, had coffee and pancakes and of course exchanged news and what we were doing and what we were going to do. The farmer was called Pétur and is brother to Jón Stefánsson of Seyðisfjörður, one of my agents there, and of course knew me very well by reports.

Whilst our 'Army Rations' were being warmed, Pétur's wife returned, together with Jón Stefánsson's wife who I knew very well, so we were soon all at home. Pétur's wife, Hilda, soon bustled about and got our supper ready about 9 o'clock, only three hours warming a tin of meat, which is rather quick here. She brought out her preserves as well so we had a good supper, but I noticed that Pétur stuck into my tin as well so I had to fill up with 'svið', which is sheep's head with the hair burnt off and pickled in sour whey and it was at least six months old. Pétur tells me he has about 400 sheep.

At 10pm, Hilda says the beds are ready. As this is a typical farm and is built of turf, we wander through a maze of turf tunnels, quite dark, and eventually, after bumping one's head by the low roof, we emerge into the 'baðstofa', as it's called, where all the people of the farm sleep and eat and live and bathe and die when their time comes. The bed bunks are ranged along the walls on each side, the whole lighted with one two-panelled window in the sloping roof. I thought at first we were to be treated with one of these bunks, but Pétur opened a low door and showed us into an inner chamber in which two beds were made up. The Icelandic bunk is called a 'rúm', but a collapsing bed formed with two cross sticks each end and a piece of bagging stretched between them is called a 'bed', quite the same as an English pronunciation. These 'beds' are quite comfortable, besides the surety that they are clean and free from neighbours, which the bunks are not.

The apartment is about six feet by twelve feet and the roof slopes down to within a foot of the floor, which is composed of beaten or trodden earth. A table in the window (two panes set in the turf wall, which is about six feet thick), a sugar box for a wash stand. A tin basin full of water is the toilet set. Pétur stands chatting and as Jakob proceeds to disrobe, I do the same. Pétur then goes out, but just as we got all our clothes off, in comes Hilda to ask if we want anything and stands chatting, and then Pétur comes again. I get into my pyjamas and am watched with great intent, as this is a new-fangled game to Pétur and Hilda. Jakob turns in with his underclothes on, so after seeing us snuggly in bed, both wish us a good night and retire.

Woke up at 7am, July 22nd, by a cock crowing in the window and picking at the glass. Jakob turns out to see what sort of weather it is and if the horses are all right. He had hobbled them on goose grass the night before, so thought it would be all right. Servant girl comes in with coffee and Jakob drinks both cups, and I have another doze. Hilda comes in and takes away my clothes and boots and returns in half an hour and says that breakfast will be ready in half an hour. Get up and dress. Hilda, meanwhile, buzzes about in and out of the room, getting sundry things out of our walnut chest of drawers which I had not noticed last night. Pass out through the baðstofa, see two men one side in bed and two girls the other side, also in bed. It being Sunday, they have the day to themselves and sleep it out.

Find it's a bright, nice day but heavy clouds overhead. Here being so far from the church, some six hours' ride, they have their own private burying ground. Right opposite the front door is a small, white railing enclosure with a white painted wooden cross over the gate. Here repose the former occupants of the farm, so the inhabitants see where they shall rest every time they go in or out. It was all overgrown and the railing all ramshackle but will be removed, I suppose, when either Pétur or his wife Hilda change houses, for both the living house and the burying place is underground. Hilda, not to be beaten with my tinned 'Army Rations', produces for breakfast one of her own home-made tins of mutton, and very good it was, and with a couple of eggs and some rye bread made a good breakfast, backed up with a couple of cups of coffee. Paid our score, said goodbye, mounted our ponies and rode off at 10am.

The road was somewhat north-east and after leading up to the foot of a kopie, ran alongside it over an undulating plain of grass and scrub, rather wet in places but on the whole a rather decent road, a series of slopes on our left hand and the plain alongside the Lagarfljót on our right hand. It was a pity it was so over-clouded and the fog and mist entirely shut out from our view the magnificent range of mountains which ran parallel to our road and which, on a fine day, must be a very grand pavé of mountain scenery, but one has to imagine it all, for as we went on, the fog gradually rolled towards us from seawards and over the fljót, enveloping all in one great, wet blanket. The utter silence of it all was relieved now and then by the mournful 'peep peep' of the golden plover and the shrill warning cry of the whimbrel in pairs. Over any swampy ground, the wild rush of an alarmed snipe would make our ponies swerve, and then in the scrub an angry clucking would be heard and out would fly a pair of ptarmigans with their brood of young and flutter over the rough grass and flop into it and disappear. They now have their summer grouse-coloured plumage on where once in the scrub they lie as dead as possible.

As we trotted and ambled along, we came to a long plain of fair grassland and in it was a number of ponies visiting and two men in charge. As we rode up, of course the usual formalities of 'Who is this man?' was gone through, and the answer, 'An Englishman', what name and all that, and when they found out who I was and that I was really Ward himself, they shook hands and expressed themselves as having been so lucky to meet and talk with me, for although they were not fishermen still they were glad to meet the man Ward himself. They told me they were going to Mjóifjörður to the whaling station there, to get 20 pony-loads of whale meat (they had 40 ponies with them) and had been travelling 10 days from the interior. The whale steak was so cheap and so nourishing and so good that it paid well to come so long to fetch it, and they could then sell more of their sheep, and wished I could buy sheep as well as fish. So I gave them a pipe of tobacco each, shook hands and left, and we went on our way, they going theirs.

All this time it had been gradually getting colder and colder and more raw and chilly, so that although I had on a Jaeger vest, knitted sweater, flannel shirt, lined flannel waistcoat (double-breasted), serge coat and double-breasted homespun round coat, I began to feel cold, so donned my great waterproof coat, tied my long scarf around my waistcoat to bind it all together, and sat romped up like a cock robin under a gooseberry bush on a winter's day.

We jogged and jogged along, mile after mile, when suddenly the road took a dip and right under our feet, as it were, a tremendous canyon, or ravine, disclosed itself. This was the Jökulsá, or Glacier River (the Icelandic for river is á, pronounced 'ow', and jökull is glacier), one of the most wicked-looking places one could ever see, a great scar in the plain some 80 feet wide and cliffs of black, sinister-looking basaltic rock, and at the bottom, at a depth of some 200 feet, a rushing, mad, angry, clay-coloured, thick, muddy river, hurrying, crashing through the canyon, awaking howling echoes from the perpendicular cliffs. This ravine in winter is quite filled up with ice and snow, and in the spring, in clearing away, the noise it makes is quite deafening and can be heard for miles around. I for my part consider it one of the most wild places in this land, but perhaps it was the bad weather I just saw it in, and I was getting a bad fit of indigestion as well, so that may account for the bad impression I had of this fearful chasm.

We waited here about half an hour and changed horses, and then set off again until we came to the farm at the foot of the mountains over which we had to cross, Fossvellir or 'Cascade Fields'. Rode up amid barking of dogs through the town but saw no-one busy. Sunday, suppose all in bed, especially as it was now raining steadily. Past the farm and the ascent begins alongside of a big waterfall which gushed out of a ravine and doubtless was pretty in sunshine. We went on, higher and higher, until the way became very indistinct and at last could see no track at all. Jakob on ahead, I could see, was wandering, just like he did when he got off the road at Trout Water, but he kept on, kopie after kopie he mounted, trying to see longer ahead, but there was still another kopie a little higher to be mounted, until at last, after two hours of it, I got off my pony and called to him that he had lost the road and he had better return to the farm to get someone to show where it was. He took my red pony and left me, and I told him if he did not return in one and a half hours that I should also go back to the farm and give up going any further that day, and I wish I had done it anyhow, but after waiting for what seemed a very long time, I heard voices approaching and that was Jakob with a farmhand on a pony.

We were the wrong side of the river but not very far from the road, but we had lost about three and a half hours, which was annoying as we had to cross a very high mountain called Smjörfjöll and along and nearing the heiði, which in the best conditions would take five hours at the very best. I wanted to go back but Jakob thought it best to go on, so at last I consented and sorry enough I was afterwards that I did.

The lad took us across the river, which was very rapid and big boulders strewn over the bottom which made it very difficult for the ponies to stand. My sorrel does not like water and refused for some time to go in, and when he did, off he went with a rush which nearly capsized me into the water. We got on to the right road, but could see nothing of our surroundings as it was a thick fog and wet and cold. Guide, a stupid fellow, says nothing but plods along and suddenly stops, says, 'That's far enough; two krónur', which I pay him, and he leaves us without another word.

We go on and find it's rather a good road, nice and dry, and well free from loose stones and the ascent not so steep as I thought it might be. Now strange as it might appear, the higher we went, the drier became the fog, until at last it was still as thick but quite dry and not cold, so could dispense with greatcoat which had become very heavy. Wound my scarf tightly around my waist for support and jog, jog, on. Suddenly, out of the fog come voices and three men appear, walking. They were Norwegians from the telegraph camp further on and they were going to Fossvellir to begin work there on the morrow. Pass on and jog on, nothing to see but one after the other the vards come along, looming in the fog. At first sight they seemed 100 feet high, but in nine or ten steps they diminished to five feet, and so pass out of sight. Hear nothing and see nothing until telegraph post appears so we must have passed the camp long back, and so still get higher and higher, hour after hour, until we came to what Jakob calls the 'Bone Vard' and there, strewn around the foot of it, was a lot of mutton bones. A little cavity in the vard itself with an arch of bones was a place to put notes or letters or messages, as there is a four-cross track here, ours going north to south and the other east to west, and it is halfway across the heath.

Jakob rests here for half hour, give the ponies rye bread, change horses and off again. There was nothing to describe, only the fog. One could only see a vard here and there and a telegraph post here and there, as this is the route of the new telegraph and it is the high road to the north, but one could feel that the descent was gradually coming on. Smjörfjöll, by the way, is nearly 4,000 feet high but being a long, gradual ascent and descent, one does not notice it so much as some of the sheer up and down lesser heights. The fog now begins to rain on our clothes so don our waterproofs again. Ponies by this time had got very tired and there was much snow, both old and new, on this side of the height. The ponies floundered and slipped over it, and in some places we had to get off to lead them over.

We now came to a rather wide mountain torrent called the Stone River, over which we crossed. Although the water was only up to our girths, the ponies slipped and stumbled over the big boulders in the bottom and, being very tired, made it a bit ticklish, but we got over without a wetting. We went on our way, which led now by the side of the river which flowed down the mountainside in a deep ravine. In the fog, one could not see the bottom, only hear the river running and imaging it far deeper than it really was, as the ponies go alongside the cliff as near as possible and one looks out over and does not see the bottom.

Anyhow, we did not slip and we did not find out but kept our way, on and on and on it seemed, never to end, so when it came up to 9 o'clock, I told Jakob that the first farm we came to I should stop at, even if it was only a cottage. I could see we were getting near something, as grass began to show on each side of the road and a sheep or two came out of the fog to gaze at us and leap away again into the mist. At last a bit of level grass out under our feet and the ponies bucked up. They seemed to know there was something near and Jakob said there was a farm about half a mile from us, off the road but he was sure he could find it. The next farm was five miles further on, so I said, 'All right, go ahead', and we crossed a mire and got on a sheep track and struck the farm at 10pm. 12 hours in the saddle, nothing to eat or drink all the time, cold, wet clothes and tired ponies.

The farm, called Guðmundarstaðir, is owned by a widow with two sons and one daughter. When we rode up to the door, the old girl herself came out and knew Jakob, and when he said I was an Englishman, she was rather put out. She asked why for goodness sake had Jakob brought such a man there, she could not do anything for a foreigner, nothing he could eat, nothing at all, but then I chipped in and told her who I was and she sang quite a different tune, for it appears she is the sister of the woman I have often stayed with in Vopnafjörður. Then the daughter came out (she had been busy adorning herself to receive guests).

'Oh good goodness it's meistarinn Vard, get off get off and come right in, what can I get, coffee or what?'

So my troubles were over. We unsaddled and put our gear in the store. Jakob went off and hobbled them on some good grass, and by his return coffee was ready and I had turned out a tin of 'Army Rations', and we were in clover. Meanwhile, the old woman and daughter were busy overhead, banging and sweeping, and the two young men came in and had a chat. We got off our wet boots and overcoats and drank the steaming coffee and felt grateful and at peace with the world. After getting supper at 12 midnight, crawled up the ladder to the attic and found a neat little room with a bunk built in the side of it, and a most inviting looking affair it was, the blue print-covered down bed being flanked with a most elaborately embroidered sheet (open work and a big initial monogram worked on it), and a pillowcase of crochet and frills around. The daughter, Sesselja, said if I wanted anything, I should call out for it. I peeled off and slunk in between the lovely, clean sheets, stretched myself out and in a jiffy I was asleep. Oh the joy and loveliness of a good bed after such a ride, which is no joke but a <u>stern</u> reality.

No wonder I dreamt that night of my schoolboy days when I was at John Kemp's school[6] and he thrashed me with a cane for playing truant. I had quite forgotten all about old Johnny, as we boys used to call him, and quite forgotten the incident of 'mitching'[7] until that dream and it

---

[6] Long Ashton Academy, Bristol. A private school which aimed to 'prepare Young Gentlemen for the Universities, for the learned Professions, and for Mercantile pursuits'.

[7] Devon slang for playing truant.

brought it all back: how I and another boy were tempted by the promise of a ride on old Train's donkey up the cliffs at the Wands; how we stayed away all that day, and next I was afraid to go to school and stayed away a week, and then all was found out; how I had to stand on a stool in school all the morning, gazing at The Cane which had been carefully taken out of the master's desk and laid on top, well in sight; all the boys around making (when they had the chance) pantomimic signs of what I was going to have later on; how I contemplated making a rush for the door whenever it opened; how, after school was over, the boys were ordered to remain in their places and a speech made by old Johnny about the public example he was going to make of me and he hoped all the boys would take warning by this example; how he grasped the cane and took me by the breeches and screwed them up tight; how I kicked him in the ribs in holy terror and oh! how he laid it on and how I yelled. It all came back to me that night and I awoke with a start to find myself in my cosy nest, stiff and sore but at peace and warm and comfortable.

Outside the window was heard the drip, drip of rain and so I laid on and did not stir until Sesselja (can you say this?) came and wanted to know when I would like breakfast, as her brother had been down to the river and had caught a lovely trout and she would like to have it nice when I was ready. Jakob came also and said it was raining hard, so I thought I would have another snooze and asked to be called at 11 o'clock. So the brother came and I got up and dressed and went down to find the breakfast all ready and the trout fried all right, and it was large enough for all hands, that is the two brothers, Jakob and myself.

After breakfast, it being cold in the guest room, I was invited to come into the baðstofa, which is the name of the living room in a farm, and there was a small cooking stove which made it warm and comfortable. It is a very small farm but everything, although small, was neat and clean. A cheap, black, painted harmonium stood at one end in between two bunks, evidently the brother and daughter beds. At the other end was the small window, under which a rickety table stood flanked by two rickety chairs, the roof sloping each side from the ridge in the centre, and a boarded floor, very rickety. Sesselja seated herself at the harmonium and played some Icelandic airs and the two men joined in and sang. One part song, called the 'Elf King', took up the whole household, which consisted of Sesselja, two brothers, a girl about 18 years old (short, thick, very plain, squat face and figure, with toothache and a swollen face which made her look more like an elf) and a little girl about 11 years old with a face like a sheep and about as much expression! As all Icelandic tunes and stories are mournful, this one is one of the best:

A man had been turned out of his farm and he was bearing his two motherless children, one on each arm, over the ice and snow, seeking shelter from the dreadful cold of a winter's night, when the children, gradually losing their senses, thought they heard the Elf King speaking to them. They answered but the father thought they were speaking to him and answered as best he could that he would soon get them warmth and shelter.

So one brother took the Elf King part, the other brother the father part, the 18 year old took the boy's part and the little squeaker took the girl's part. Sesselja played and beat time with her head and nodded to each when they should sing and then when all was over and the children died, they all joined in calling with a mournful wail. Amidst it all the old mother wandered about with a proud expression, picking up little bits from the floor and plucking the down coverlets of the beds and arranging the strip of cheap window curtain and generally making herself a nuisance by distracting the attention of Sesselja, who kept one eye on her mother to see what she was up to and one eye on the score, and consequently, after getting off the road, had to begin over again (after a pair of sort of shots jerked off at her mother).

We had several songs of about the same cheerful description and then the old woman would have a glee called *Good Night*, in which she had also joined in, and had it over twice, after which they started *Home Sweet Home* and that finished me up, so made a move to opt out and see how Jakob was getting on with the horses. Found he was quite ready and all harnessed up, so wished the good people goodbye and made Sesselja a present, as the old woman would not take anything nor make a charge, saying it was a great honour and pleasure for me to come there. Sesselja is a big, raw-boned girl about 30 years old and has a voice like a man and a commandeering manner, and I should say ruled the roost.

So we set off in the mist, as the snow had given over, and splashed out of the tún on to the marshes across which our road wended itself to the Vopna á (river).[8] This is rather wide but we found the right crossing and forded across without incident and arrived at Vopnafjörður about 4pm, the road being rather wet because of the rain, running alongside the river all the way from Guðmundarstaðir to Vopnafjörður trading place. Here I generally stay at the doctor's home but his wife and himself had gone to a place called Þórshöfn in Þistilfjörður, and my other roosting place was quite full (meaning old Mrs Guðmundsson, sister to the widow at Guðmundarstaðir). Luckily, as there is no hotel here, Einar Runólfsson offered to take me in. His wife was also away but expected home that night.

We unrigged the ponies and Jakob took them off to the grazing place and hobbled them for the night. I thought I would look and see how our effects were standing and how they have borne the rub of the journey so far and a pretty fine mess it was. The tins had got loose and ground everything grindable to pieces. All the wraps that I had around my underclothes had gone and all had got loose in the bags but luckily nothing damaged, only wet, so turned the whole lot out and you will see on the binding of this book a big scar, and fortunate it was not more, as the binding of my official letter book was in ribbons.

I took all the contents into the kitchen and found that I knew the woman there; she is a sister to my man Jóhannes Pétursson and has been married to a Dane who has deserted her and left her with four children, so to get a living she has come out to be a servant. She dried my clothes and got a nice supper of fried fish so we did not miss Einar's wife, but she returned just as we had finished supper. A great commotion upstairs and after an hour bed was declared ready, and very nice it was. Nice, large room, wooden bed in the middle of the floor, nice, clean bedding, beautifully embroidered, and a chest of drawers with embroidered cover and knickknacks. Einar's wife is a nice little woman, about seven or eight and 20. Einar is about 30 years old, short and rather plain but Elín, his wife, is a red-haired, pretty,

---

8   The correct name for this river is Hofsá.

little white-skinned woman with laughing blue eyes, and they have such a jolly little kid, about five years old, called Sverrir. He recognised me at once and called, 'Vard er kominn, Vard er kominn'[9] and crawled all over me and was delighted to see me.

Have a good night and sleep well and awake in the morning, July 24th, very fit indeed, but the weather was very distressing. Fog, wet, cold and miserable. After breakfast of fried fish and coffee (very good, all of it), repack our gear. Get some waterproof bags, stuff that is used for packing linen and Manchester goods from the shop, and some oil-cloth stuff used to wrap up cigar boxes for shipment to here from Germany, and make neat packages of my underclothes and stockings. I tie it all with stout cord and wrap all the tins in pieces of bagging. All this makes a very full pack bag, but find room for the surplus by an untied bag tied in the centre of the pack bag. It's rather heaped up and makes a bit of trouble by being top-heavy, and consequently is frequently all on one side of the pony, and occasionally underneath him.

Interview several of my fishermen friends here but fishing is very poor indeed, in fact quite a failure, but I promise to buy what they have to sell and send a vessel to fetch the stuff in September. Get an invitation from Stefán Guðmundsson, the head manager of Ørum and Wulff[10] who have many stations here in the east, to come and have supper with him and a talk of business, which I do, but I don't think under present high prices that anything can be done with these people. Spend the evening with him and play Icelandic whist.

July 25th

Brighter morning but still heavy clouds over all. Jakob comes with the ponies at 10am but, of course, no breakfast ready, and it's not until 11.30 that we make a start northwards. The road leads over the neck at the back of the village and thence down to a fjord called Lónafjörður locally but on the charts Nípsfjörður. The entrance to it is blocked by a sand bar, dry at low spring tides and consequently the fjord is unusable even for boats. This fjord is frozen over in winter and last year a party

---

9   Ward has come.
10   Danish trading company with extensive operations in Iceland.

of men from Vopnafjörður was riding over it when one rider, horse and all, broke through. The man was saved but the horse never came up again and was lost. Not until the spring did the man get his saddle again, of course completely spoilt, but the bridle was lost entirely, saddle and bridle costing nearly as much as the horse.

Skirting this fjord past two farms and then striking inland for about two hours over a level scrub and rough grass plain, we came to Selá. This is a dangerous river, about half a mile broad in the spring, and in consequence a wire ferry has been placed above, about three miles from the regular fording place, but it's only used in spring when the river is very full. Jakob goes on ahead and I follow, and it gets deeper and deeper until it reaches up to my knees and my boots get full of water. There is no turning back, for once these ponies begin to go over a river there is no stopping. One follows the other, and if swimming is wanted, they swim, but over they go so I cling on, expecting every minute to feel the brute start swimming, but just then it shallowed out. We crawl up the bank to dry land and make for a grass flat. Get off and off-saddle and sit down and change our socks, empty the water out of our boots, burn pieces of paper inside to dry them, all unpack the saddle bags and repack to get out dry socks and stockings, and then it began to rain. Anyhow, got it all together again, socks and boots all on and once more comfortable, saddle up and make a start.

We come to bad piece of soft mire land and flounder about and Jakob says we are off the road but I did not think so, as I remembered this soft part two years since I went over it. However, he insisted and so we left it and made a beeline for what Jakob said was the new road, and certainly about a mile on our left there was a line of vards going in the direction we wanted to go. I remembered that last time men were making in places a new road here and there, but I did not imagine they had done so much. We tried to get over to these vards but we sank deeper and deeper into the mire, so I proposed we should bear away to the right again and pick up the old road, but Jakob went on towards the left.

My pony would not budge in the mire so had to get off and stumble back as best I could. In half an hour, I struck the old road again and found it rose up to a hill on which I could get a look around. I remembered the scenery from last time and I could see Jakob still floundering about so shouted to him. He heard me and waved his hand but still kept on towards his new way, so I pegged away along my old way and got on to where a hill rose up with three vards on it. There I could see the New Way but no Jakob, and I could look back and see the way I had come and no Jakob, and as he had said the new way joined the old way about half the distance to Bakkafjörður, I determined to push on there to meet him.

The road gradually rose until the Sandvíkurheiði was reached and here I struck the vards again, so I searched around there to find this new way but I saw no signs of it, nor Jakob. He had unfortunately taken my spare pony with him, consequently I had only one pony to do the whole distance with, but it was the sorrel and he is much stronger than the red. After waiting half an hour, no sign of Jakob, I put a piece of the *Daily Mirror* between two stones right in the road, and a little further on do the same, so he might see I had gone on, mounted and got on my way. I passed two or three rather large ponds on which were a good few ducks of various sorts with their broods. The road being very fair and only wet here and there, I made good headway over the heath, which is not so bare as the Smjörfjöll heath, but occasional patches of rough grass and scrub, out of which a clucking brood of ptarmigan rise and flutter away, and a golden plover too stands up with his black waistcoat on a tuft and peep-peeps at me. Then as the road leads over the brow of the hill, there is Bakkafjörður spread out. The rain having stopped, the clouds risen in the clear evening sky away in the distance on the high-peaked mountains of Finnafjörður, facing me over a hill and a neck, I could see standing out clearly the house of Halldór Runólfsson at Höfn, my destination.

It's a good two hours off yet and pony and I begin our descent to the valley under us. This is steep rather, but the road is good all the way and we get down to the flat, and somehow sorrel, or 'Blackie' as he is called in Icelandic, seems to buck up and ambles along at a good pace and we see the farm Bakki right before us. Blackie goes at it with a rush and imagines his day's work is over, only to meet with disappointment as we skirt alongside the town and get up on the cliffs heading to Höfn. About half an hour further on, Blackie becomes sulky now and dawdles down to his donkey-like joggle and takes no further interest in anything. I bang and bang his sides with my knees after the manner of the natives when riding a single horse but no responsive jerk will he give, but goes along, ears down, as much as to say, 'Oh shut up, why didn't you stop at Bakki? That was far enough.'

Even when the town of Höfn came in sight and we came up to the wall around it, no he would not improve his pace as is customary when arriving at a farm. One dashes up with a rush and a flourish, but Blackie would have nothing of that. He just stalked in and stopped in a sullen sort of way opposite the door and I have no doubt said, 'Get off if you like or stop on, it's all the same to me.' When I got off, he wouldn't look at the grass cut, just stood like a sulky child. Two or three men standing about now came and told me Halldór was not at home but was out herring catching. Then his foreman came and I asked him to put the pony to grass. I said I was come to visit Halldór, so after a lot of chatter with the other men, he came, sulky like, and asked if I had come alone. I told him about Jakob and how I expected him shortly, so he said had better wait for him to look after the horse. I took off the saddle and bridle and just turned him into the tún and the foreman quickly then found someone to take charge of it and go to the outside grazing ground and hobble it.

When I saw that obeyant, I said I should like some coffee as it was eight hours since I had eaten. He said, 'Wait a bit until Jakob comes', so I just went around to the back door where all the women are generally to be found and went into the kitchen and asked of the two or three there who was the housekeeper. One said she was and so I told her who I was and she quickly said, 'Oh, all right, here Gunna, fire up and Mr Ward come with me into the house and take your clothes off.' By the time I had taken leggings, fur skin trousers, etc. off and hung them up and sort of rustled my feathers, she had the coffee ready and I was glad of it.

After coffee, I went out again to see if I could see anything of Jakob, as I was beginning to think he might have turned back altogether, but I saw him passing Bakki tún and in due time he came along, one and a half hours after me. I finely chaffed him about the new road and called him Columbus the Discoverer.

Since I was here last, Halldór has built a very nice two-storey wooden house and, like the manner of these little shopkeepers, he has spent his last shilling to buy a purse. He is an unmannered man, about 32 or 33 years old, and has been exceptionally fortunate the last three or four years in his speculations. He is a fisherman but a very sharp fellow, very slight in build with clean-cut features but not at all strong and looks consumptive. He fished first well and then bought a boat and that did well, then he got engaged to the only daughter of the farmer here and built a sort of shed and made a little shop. There he engaged a boat's crew of Faroesemen and did well with that, and then he heard about me and came to Ísafjörður. I let him have £150 to buy fish but he bought wood with that money and built a store and a shed to keep fish in, and his boats fished more than enough to repay the money he had from me. This was of course fortunate for him, as he had no right to use money entrusted to him to buy fish to buy a house. Anyhow, there it was, and the next year he also did well and seven or eight boats came to fish from his place. His boats fished well, he did well and so did I. The following year, the company did not feel inclined to speculate but Halldór did and got a loan from the Reykjavík bank through me, and he made over £1,000 on that year's work. He then built this house, which cost him £500, and two more houses for his people to live in, and there his sweetheart died from consumption and he was nearly broken-hearted over it. Last year he did very well again and built some more houses, went to Copenhagen, bought some very expensive furniture and fitted his house up very well indeed, but all the money he has made he has laid out in houses etc., and has got no cash in reserve, so that if he should meet with one year's reverse he is a lost man, but so it is with all these merchants, as they call themselves up here; four or five years of prosperity and then the collapse. He must have got here at the very most £3,000 worth of buildings and gear, all got in that short time, and as I look around on it, I sigh. Enough said!

Housekeeper is called Margrét and is a plain old sort, but she got us a nice supper of fried fish and a great jug of milk and coffee after, and then said, 'Your bed is ready'. She shows me up and it's a really nice, little, clean room, papered with pink striped ribbon paper costing four shillings the piece. Iron bed, wire mattress, swagger wash stand and a long consul looking-glass, oilcloth on the floor and a crimson spring blind, lace curtains, but no place to hang up one's clothes so have them on the floor. Get into bed but it is very uncomfortable, as there is only the mattress and no blankets, so sing out for Margrét and tell her what is wanted. She goes into the shop and brings out one of those quilted bed covers sailors use nowadays. I put that under, and the down quilt over, and so got warm and sleep well, but still for all that it's not so cosy as the Guðmundarstaðir bunk.

In asking Jakob about his whereabouts etc., he had not seen my pieces of paper but had seen the footprints of the horse and, as it happened, I must have been the only traveller that way that day. He judged from that that I was ahead of him and so came on.

July 26th

Was awakened by Halldór coming in at 8am. He had returned during the night. He had on all his best clothes, white collar and dicky and cuff and looking quite a toff, so much so that I felt rather small, seeing I had no collar but a coloured silk handkerchief wound around my neck and homespun clothes and heavy boots, but that didn't matter, he was very glad to see me. After the usual greetings, I got up and dressed and came down to breakfast to find it a miserably wet and cold day, cold wind from the sea. Margrét lighted up the stove in the best room, which is tastefully fitted up with German furniture: inlaid table with unequal legs and it wobbles; settee (very stiff, upright affair); six chairs, all covered with apple-green plush seats; two windows with gold cornices; expensive curtains (lace); spring apple-green blinds; paper costing seven shillings and sixpence a piece, also apple-green and gold; a beautiful, brass oil lamp costing £5 hanging from the centre. The ceiling is very nicely decorated and panelled but, to Halldór's grief, no carpet. He had ordered a Brussels costing £15 but it had not yet arrived. Gilt cornice all around the room and in the corner a long consul looking-glass with marble-topped table beneath.

We had a yarn after breakfast about fish etc., and he had been fortunate in the night getting 2,000 herrings for bait, which is kept in an ice house, fresh. The fishing had only just commenced but his boats had done well to that time and so had the Faroese. A crew of Norwegians had first come so there is every hope of its being a successful season with him. His premises are built on a cliff projecting into the bay (it can hardly be called a fjord, for it's similar to Torbay and Halldór's place would be about on Hope's Nose). There is a little cove on the east side for landing in bad weather and where the boats are charging up, but for fishing purposes the fish is landed on the rocks below Halldór's store and carried up some rugged steps cut into the rocks. Flat rocks at the bottom form a sort of quay where the boats throw out their fish and are then rowed around to the cove and hauled up. All the day it's cold, raw but the wind is from the south-west and off land so the boats can land their catches, and at four o'clock they come in, loaded each one. They get about one to one and a half tons of fish per day if it's fine enough to put off the beach, and there are five men in each boat so it must pay the men very well as it's only a short distance, only about one hour's row to the fishing ground.

I don't say anything to Halldór about his grumpy foreman but come to think it over and why he is so. I think it is because, when I was here last, he went with the *Rose* schooner and got drunk and I did not give him any gratuity, so therefore there was no interest for him to trouble about me, but just treated me off-handed to show his disdain for a man who did not recognise his valuable services on the last deal.

After dinner of three courses (soup, fish and potato and pancakes with jam followed by coffee and cigars), we played Icelandic whist until it became too dark to distinguish hearts from spade, and bed.

July 27th

Very strong wind from south-west. Boats unable to go out so the men spent the day washing their clothes and cleaning up their boats and getting their lines in order and generally lolling about. Cold and miserable outdoors. I had nearly a nasty accident this morning as I was going out of the front door, which is approached by a temporary wooden stepladder like going into a bathing machine. Halldór says he intends putting concrete steps but as the house has been built two years these temporary affairs are likely to be there for another two years, as no-one uses the front door but gets in via the cellar and kitchen. Well, as I was saying, I was going out and a puff of wind took off my attention of where I was planting my foot and it slipped down between the step and wall and if I had not had hold of the handle, I should have fallen out and snapped my leg off like a carrot. As it was I got a lump of skin off my ankle. I consider myself very, very lucky indeed to have escaped a very nasty accident and 25 miles off a doctor. Programme same as yesterday.

July 28th

The wind now seems to have cleared the sky as the clouds are high and the sun peeps out between the drying masses. After breakfast, Jakob fetches the horses and then I discover that Halldór has no horse, or says he has none, and asks if he might ride my red one, which he greatly admires. There is nothing for it but to accede to his wishes, although the Icelander, when he knows a horse, uses it very badly and all my horses have been ruined by lending them. He brings out a very swagger new saddle, which I look cross at, for new saddles always make a sore back, so he brings out an old one after Jakob has told him I did not want the pony hurt and would prefer his using an old saddle.

Off we start, Halldór making the red career about and prance and dance, which is quite unnecessary, as he never does it when I am on his back and is quite a nice well-broken animal and a child could ride it, but these people, because it looks nice when they can get hold of a pony, they jig it about all over the shop. Consequently the red used to be all of a tremble when I got on it, but now since I have had it, it's quite another animal.

We are now bound for Þorvaldsstaðir, about three hours' ride from Höfn, to survey the piece of land and cove I bought four years ago for the company and of which they have made no use. On our road, we pass the vicarage and church of Skeggjastaðir where the old sporting parson lived when I was in Bakkafjörður last, in whose house I spent three weeks. He has got a removal to a better church away farther north and migrated there last year, and left his two wives buried in the churchyard here in the care of the next vicar. As I passed the burying place, I saw clothes hung out to dry on the railings surrounding the graves of the two dead vicaresses and the stones nearly covered with grass, so it will only be a short time before they meet with the same fate as the other graves and the rails are destroyed and graves levelled and the stones thrown in a heap in the corner to help swell the heap already there. I hear his Number Three is very dangerously ill and not likely to live out the year, so it must be quite a give and take with the old chap and hard along another.

We got to the place, which is now known amongst the neighbouring farms as Wardsvík,[11] and found that Halldór had carried out nicely all the instructions I had given him. The piece of ground, through having a trench cut all around it, had become perfectly dry and solid ground and the foundations of the projected fishing station all in order, and the little cove looking so peaceful and nice when it ought to have been the scene of activity and work. After taking photos etc., we adjourned to the farmhouse, had a chat with the young farmers there (they are three brothers living with their widowed mother), and had skyr and milk.

Saddle up and leave for Höfn. Having now reached the end of our northern journey, this is the first step towards the return. As we ride back, the fog rolls over us more and we pass Bakki farm. I notice a cross set up in the tún and find it was the grave of a French sailor, brought onshore when the two vicars were changing living and neither was on the spot, so the farmer of Bakki raked in his 20 krónur for allowing the man to be buried in his tún. A simple, rude, wooden cross set up, the poor fellow's name inscribed in rough letter printing done by the captain with black paint, marks his resting place until a stray pony or sheep knocks it down and he is forgotten forever.

Get back to Höfn, supper, cards, coffee and bed.

Sunday July 29th

Thick, heavy rain and wind. A steamer comes into the anchorage and blows a whistle. A boat puts out from Merchant Halldór to enquire if he wants anything but finds that, instead of wanting to buy, he wants to sell herrings as he is a herring boat and has a good catch last night and put in here to sell bait which pays better than salting down. Of

---

[11] Ward's Bay. Pike had bought the bay and farm for £25 and he planned to build a fish station here. The place name Wardsvík is no longer in use, nor the related names Vordsskurður and Vordsstykki which are documented in past use at the farm here.

course news etc. is exchanged and on our boat coming on shore, I find the captain is the same Norwegian I had when I went to Labrador, Ole Jørgensen, and he gives his compliments on shore to me. After 12 noon it clears off fine, and the young men go over to the church and the girls clean up and put on their best bib and tuckers (Halldór having in his employ about a dozen of each) and at six o'clock, Sunday being finished, they all adjourn to the dry fish store, being now empty, start an accordion and have a regular good romping dance until 10pm. Then off to bed.

Monday July 30th

Fine morning. *Prospero*, Wathne's ship, comes in and Halldór loads off his produce, wool and a little dried large fish which he has got ready, and she leaves again about 8am. It's my intention to leave here again southwards today, so tackle Halldór as soon as his work with the steamer is over. I have tried every day since I came here to corner him but he has always evaded the subject, so at the last hour I get him to say yes or no to my questions. As he appears not to like my arrange-ments, I assume a very independent air and after breakfast (the horses having been brought in and saddled), we leave, Halldór riding my red to accompany us on the road so far as is Icelandic custom with their guests. He borrows another brown horse at Bakki where, by the way, the old black chest of which I have a photo comes from and for which I had frequently offered money. It was sent to Reykjavík and offered there for £15 but got no-one to bid for it higher than £10, but a Danish officer took it to Copenhagen and there got £25 for it and the old fellow at Bakki is very sorry as he now feels quite sure it was worth £50. We ride along together, Jakob, Halldór and I until the foot of the ascent is beginning and there stop on a grass plot to finally say farewell. Then Halldór draws me on one side and after a preamble agrees to my business proposition, so my letter book is taken out of the pack and as I had it already written out, he signs it and I give him a copy, so that matter is settled after the dilatory manner of all business up here. We after take a photo of the group, say our final farewells and Halldór rides off on his old pony. We go off also and wave to each other until a dip in the hills hides us both from sight.

We have a very nice ride back, bright weather but little sunshine, but nice for the ponies and they skim along quite nicely. Having now become accustomed to each other and us, we are enabled to drive the loose ones ahead of us. The red is splendid for this and trots along ahead and the old brown with the pack follows him demurely and we follow and chat along as we go.

We come to that wretched river again and I make Jakob enquire at the farm adjacent for the best fording place, and am told that where we came over was the deepest and most fast. I gave the man a króna to come and show us the ford and we crossed over quite nicely, water only up to the girths, changed horses and finally got to Vopnafjörður about 5.30pm after the most enjoyable ride of the whole journey. Although there was no sunshine, still it was just right for the ponies and my stiffness had all gone and the ponies also had got accustomed to my weight and manner of riding, and the roads were not half bad in places, so it was a case of everyone being pleased.

The first person we met was the doctor Jón Jónsson, who had just returned also from his trip, so we exchanged courtesies and all that, and on arrival at Einar's house, we unsaddled, Jakob went off with the ponies to graze, and Elín, Einar's wife, welcomed us back. She busied about getting supper, during which meal the little boy comes in yelling, with his face all covered with blood. In play, he had fallen and cut his forehead and a rich mess it was in, so he had to be washed and bandaged up. A call came from the doctor for me to come up to him to supper, of course I had finished mine but went up nevertheless for a chat. I find that he has two more children since I was there last, so he will soon get a quiver full if it goes on at the rate of three in two years six months. Found Stefán Guðmundsson there, Jón's wife's brother from Þórshöfn, so we had to play whist until the grey hours of the morning.

On getting to bed, I did not feel at all comfortable: cold, chilly, and sleepless, and violent indigestion. I think I must have got cold somehow, for I was very uneasy all the time and could not sleep, except in patches, and I perhaps worried a little as I am always in dread of typhoid fever, as it's so common up here. When the time came to get up, I was very dull and lazy and heavy, and could not eat anything

much for breakfast. Very fine morning, brought nice weather and sunshine and rather mild. I have an interview with Stefán Guðmundsson
(not satisfactory) and had a look around amongst the fishermen and
find the fishing very poor indeed, in fact quite a failure so far. Einar
Runólfsson, in talking, said he was leaving Zöllner's[12] business in
August and was going to open a shop, in fact was doing so. Then, on
the quiet, he asked if he might buy fish from the peasants on my yea.
As I could get no satisfaction from Ørum and Wulff manager, I gave
him leave to do what he could, so hope to scrape up a little by this
means, although I expect a remonstration from Ø&W.

I see Jakob had got in the horses and, after making Elín and
Jóhannes Pétursson's sister's grace with a gratuity, we make prepara-
tions to leave, when I see heaped up on a pack pony two or three extra
sacks. I ask Jakob if he has bought a shop, and then he informs me a
farmer is going our way and has asked him to oblige by taking some of
his gear with our pony, as it would save him hiring another extra to the
one he had. I quickly bundled it all off our pack, I can tell you. The
cheek of these people is beyond understanding, for just then a carpenter fellow came dressed in his best with a saddle and quite con-
fidently asked if he could ride my spare pony to Hof, about three
hours' journey, and he would undertake to send it along after us to
Guðmundarstaðir later on. Well, of all the blank, blank impudence! I
turned wind and gave him what he didn't expect, and he went off quite
crestfallen.

After saying farewell to the group around, we mounted and went
off, and about half an hour's ride out, who should we see resting but
our first friend, the Jökuldalur farmer, pleading if we would only take
it as far as Guðmundarstaðir, he would be glad to pay and to hire a
horse there to go further along, so I had to give in that much. Up went
the two bags on my pack again and off we went and got to
Guðmundarstaðir at 6pm, thick fog now rolling over all. We have
coffee and trout later on for supper, and after supper Icelandic whist
and off to bed.

---

[12] Louis Zöllner was a Dane who lived in the north of England and traded in
Icelandic goods. He was Danish consul in Newcastle and a well-known chess
player.

August 1st

Up at 7am, drip, drip of rain and fog, breakfast 8am to 9am and ponies brought in and saddled. Much to the disappointment of the dear, homely, old widow, I could not take a photo of the house and family. What is more, I think they expected a concert, as the harmonium had been shifted out into the front room and *The Elf King* stood open on the music rest, but sorry as I was to leave, there was nothing else to do but to don oilskins and southwesters, say farewell and ride off into the thick fog, dripping with wet.

Our troop was now augmented by the farmer, Magnús, and two horses he had borrowed, the one here at Guðmundarstaðir and another had been bought here during the night for Jakob to take with us to Borgarfjörður, our next point of destination. Lucky enough it was, for it was discovered in the morning that the extra weight of the farmer's pack had raised a blister on our pack pony's back as big as your hat, so the borrowed or sent pony came in right handy. I pointed out to Magnús what had happened and of course expressed the greatest surprise, as if such a thing had never happened to a non-Icelandic pony before, but as for expressing regret that was another thing, the blister was in the day's march. He calmly took out his knife and wanged it into the puff, saying, 'Oh that's nothing, now I have opened it, it will be all right in a day or so.' Anyhow, I told Jakob to be careful and not promise any more help along the road.

We climbed up and up the side of the ravine, the fog so thick I could not see Magnús ahead. I was sorry about it all as the scenery must be very fine all along the way, as by the maps and what one can see from Vopnafjörður on a fine day, it is very mountainous, rugged and wild. All that one could know was it was all up and up, sometimes rough bottom, others wet, and this fairly good, but that's how we went, where we went. One may just as well have stayed at home, for it was thick as a hedge and very wet.

Old Magnús proved himself rather a chatty sort of old chap. When I say old, he told me he was 50 years old and had a family of 10 children, and brought them up on a farm of 400 sheep and never had a loan. His farm was five days' ride from Vopnafjörður, right under the great glacier of Vatnajökull, and his road lay up the side of the glacier river almost to its source, and he frequently saw the droves of reindeer, especially in the winter when they came down to his tún. I asked him if ever he shot any of them now they had been preserved for 10 years and he said, 'Of course I know they are preserved by law but sometimes in the snows in autumn, if one is found dead I must bring it home.' In the winter they are not worth shooting, being so lean, but in the autumn they will weigh from 250 to 300 pounds. He promised to send me in a hind which he has at home and if by chance one should fall down dead this autumn, he will send that one in also. He was so sorry that I could not find time to go home with him to see the droves.

After a time, the fog seemed to be lightening and suddenly it rolled away and we were on top of the heiði and fine this was, clear. We were alongside a lake called Smjörfjallavatn, or 'Butter Mountain Water'. All around us was fog, but just a circle was clear and there we could see how the land was, all bare and barren, a boulder-strewn gravel heap marked at regular distances by vards, and on our right hand the telegraph poles. We went on until the 'Bone Vard' was reached and here Magnús was to leave us, as he would take the west road up the Jökuldalur. As the next farm was only four hours from here, he took his bags off the borrowed horse and gave it a kick towards its home and it left, trotting off and it will go straight back to Guðmundarstaðir alone. He then loaded up his old grey, had a pipe of tobacco, said goodbye and departed on his way, and we on ours.

After riding about an hour, we came across the Norwegians putting up the telegraph poles, so they are getting well across the heiði. As we began to descend, so we got into the fog again and so everything was shut out until we arrived at the foot of the mountain and at the farm Fossvellir. We did not stop but pushed on to the bridge over the Jökulsá and here off-saddled and waited for half an hour to let the ponies get a mouthful of grass, of which there was an abundance.

4pm, saddled up and off again across the bridge. Here our road branched off from the one we came by and it led east alongside the river for some distance and then south again over rather good track, scrub and grass and plenty of birds. Came to a little farm called Blöndugerði, good tún and seemingly plenty of grass which was cut and piled up into haycocks. Saw no-one but a dog which barked at us, and on again to another farm called Stóri-Bakki. Passed through the tún, saw a man and boy cutting grass but did not stop to talk to them. We now passed over a most magnificent dry mire, long healthy-looking grass as good as one could see in England. It was about three miles across to the foot of the hills and the fog had risen just enough for one to see under and away, right and left. Could see no end to the plain and not a single animal on it. I am sure there was enough grass turned into hay in this plain for all the cattle and sheep in the whole land; it is the most luxuriant plain I have ever seen any place since I have been in Iceland. We went trotting over this on springy turf, much to the dis-quiet of our ponies, who on every available occasion took a running bite at it, and so before we began to get up the hills we let them have 10 minutes, after which we began to rise again over a neck or foot of a big mountain. How high one could not see for fog, and up into the fog again, over some rough ground and then we descended the south side towards the valley of the Lagarfljót. There faintly saw the white shape of the church growing out of the fog and were quickly over the tún, and with a flourish and spurt of galloping ponies, we drew up in front of the vicarage of Kirkjubær ('Church Farm') at 6pm, having been eight hours in the saddle instead of 12 as in the last crossing of Smjörfjöll.

This is a modern built, wooden, iron-clad house, two storeys, the old turf farm having been burnt down some six or seven years ago. After waiting for 10 to 15 minutes, a young fellow came out dressed in his best, white collar and dicky and putting on his cuffs. Jakob told me he was the son of the priest and was a student of law, home for his holidays from Copenhagen. After the usual greetings etc. he asked me in, while Jakob saw about the horses. I got off my outer skins, we talked of where I had been and where I was going, and after an hour the priest himself came in. He had rigged up when he heard I had come and got into his frock tail etc. I know him, he is called Einar and is addressed as Síra Einar and has been a member of parliament but lost his seat on the last election, so we greeted again and had a general confab.

Then two farmers appeared, one old chap with a bible back, much like one pictures old Kruger,[13] and he was not bad (unlike him) with

---

13   Paul Kruger (1825–1904), President of the South African Republic and leader of Boer resistance to British administration.

long hair falling in straggling locks over his shoulders. As he sat in the middle of the room, he chewed tobacco and spat all over the floor so after a little while he was sitting on an island and a red sea all around him. The other was a younger man, about 35, with pale yellow hair that looked as if it had not been combed for months hanging in fingers over the collar of his coat, a pale-faced chap with yellow moustache and whiskers, rather thin and wiry, and a thin red nose sticking out and two troubling eyes, all rat-like face. He amused himself by every five minutes emptying a big sheep's horn snuff box up his nose like a man drinking out of a bottle and then shooting it all out in a big spray by blowing his nose with his fingers. This went on for all time with the regularity of clockwork.

The picture stands: a square room about 14 feet square; two casement windows; door one end; the other end, at the back, a big wooden cupboard; round table; sofa, on which I sit; two chairs in the centre of the room. The two farmers sit on their islands, Jakob on a chair by the window. The student wanders about the room, a word to me, a word to Jakob and a break off to the two farmers, coasting about from one to the other and going on tiptoes when passing the red sea. We wait and wait. I wonder whenever we shall get some coffee and to while away the time the priest hands around cigars. The old farmer lights his with three or four matches and puffs away like a steam engine and chews the sucking end until there is a race which shall get to the centre first, the burning end or the chewing end, but the old chap soon settles that, for when it gets too hot to his lips he calmly rubs out the lighted end on his trousers. He pops the remainder into his mouth and splash, on the floor an Indian Ocean.

Then a smart, clean looking girl with pale ginger hair nicely and neatly plaited, black dress and clean, frilled white apron and smart crimson tie, comes in takes a good stare at me. She produces a big bunch of keys and proceeds to unlock the old cupboard and take out all the best German electro silver (tray, sugar basin, milk jug and coffee pot) and from a drawer underneath some table cloths, and then vanishes out of the door on my side of the room. Wait quarter of an hour. She appears again and drags the table to the fore, displacing the old man's island and settles it in the middle of the red sea. Out again to return with cloth, spreads that. Out, returns with five plates. Out, returns with five cups and saucers. Out, returns with sugar basin and milk jug. Out, returns with plate of cold pancakes. Out, returns with a little plaited basket containing the spoons. Out, at last coffee pot. How thankful I was to get it, as it was now 8.30.

After drinking coffee, the two farmers left and I went out to have a look around. At 10.30, supper was announced: boiled trout and eggs and coffee. Bed at 11pm. Two beds in same room, Jakob in one and I in the other.

August 2nd

Jakob gets up at 7am to see after ponies. Girl comes with coffee, first time I heard her speak, voice like a man's. She is daughter of the priest. Get up, dress. 8am, come down and wander about. Much grass here and plenty of people to work. Son Vigfús also up, chat with him. Priest appears, chat with him. Still foggy but high enough to see under, but the distant scenery (which the priest says is very fine) all blotted out. Right opposite the farm is the waterfall blocking the fljót and one can hear the roar and see the spray rising over it, but it's half an hour's walk and Jakob says there is not time to go there and back before we leave, so give that up. Another of the priest's sons now comes in with an eight pound salmon which he has got out of the net at the bottom of the falls, so expect it for breakfast but was of course disappointed; we had boiled salt mutton and eggs. Pay for our lodgings, say farewell and then the priest asks Jakob to take a letter for him which takes him half an hour to get ready and we are impatient to start, which we eventually do at 11am.

Good weather for travelling as it's sunless and cold but no good for seeing the country. We ride east along the valley of the fljót amongst kopies and scrub, and pass a rather large farm called Hallfreðarstaðir. Many people, men, women and children, in the tún and surrounding grassland. Count 13 cows and several yearlings. Still eastwards over fairly good track, much grass and scrub, plenty of birds, past Gunnhildargerði farm, Nefbjarnarstaðir and Geirastaðir. At the latter farm, we had to get a man to show us the way over the mire as we leave the kopies and strike across the delta formed by the Jökulsá and the Lagarfljót. One very nasty dyke with rushing, clay-coloured, thick water, not broad but deep, was crossed, and then we wished our guide goodbye and trotted off over what seemed an endless plain, the fog hanging so low that one could see nothing of the hills which we know are high above us on each side of the valley.

On and on, jog, jog, bump, bump, southwards, and at 2pm arrive at the crossing place of the fljót. Sing out and wave for the ferryman who lives in the farm on the other side, which is called Hóll, and he comes in a pram. Whilst he is on the way, we unsaddle our ponies and get them ready for their swim. It is very deep here, and clay-coloured, thick water, but a very little stream, about a quarter of a mile broad. When all is ready, the ponies are got together and urged into the water with whip and ho! ho!, and they first gingerly, and then more rapidly, wade out. The old brown pony takes the lead and they begin to swim and head for the opposite shore. We load up the pram with our gear and the man rows us over. By this time the ponies have got over all right and are having a fine scamper and a roll, so that when caught they have to be rubbed clean from the sand on their backs before re-saddling.

Have a talk with the ferryman, who has lived here always and he says he does not know of any Englishman that has crossed over at this place before but he remembers some gentleman once coming up the fljót in a steam launch as far as the foss (waterfall). After paying ferry money and giving his boy a lump of chocolate, for which he had to kiss me, we made a start again and found this side of the delta very sandy, which made it hard going for the ponies. Heavy, black sand and the road wound about like crossing the Warren at Exmouth, only it took one and a half hours to cross.

We came to another river much nearer to the sea, in fact the tides flow up to the crossing place. Get an old man from the farm to come with us, get out his pram, ho! ho! the ponies over the fjord (which was about the same length as the fljót), now over ourselves, find our ponies busy at the grass, saddle up, pay our score and begin at once our mountain climb.

Up and up we went, bearing rather east, the track about two feet wide, often in places overhanging the hillside and one could look sheer down to the beach below. Zigzag path, each path about 20 yards long. Turn, 20 yards that way, turn, 20 yards, turn, and so on until at 5pm, in dense fog, we get to the top of the mountain pass Geldingaskörð. Jakob, being on ahead and two ponies between him and I, suddenly disappears, then the two ponies, and before I could say 'knife', over went my pony, over the ridge as sharp as the ridge of a house, only steeper. I assure you his forelegs were going downhill whilst his hind legs were coming uphill, so sharp and narrow was the neck. I came over; it was one ghastly look down into a bottomless pit, for the fog obscured all and the zigzag led away to the left and I was looking to the right and ahead. I held my breath for an instant, for I could not see Jakob or the other ponies and nothing but a sheer up and down precipice. Anyhow, Blackie pulled himself together, took in the situation and bore away to the left, downwards, got hold of the path, came to the end of the zag, turned right, end of zig turned left, end of zag, and so down, I holding back in my saddle until I touched the saddlebag at my back and my toes about level to Blackie's eyes. Going up is bad enough, but the going down is a bit off, especially when one comes to the end of the zigzag, for there is nothing but nothing to see right ahead, and one wonders if at that moment the pony should stumble, how far would one have to fall before the bottom was reached. Going up or down quay steps is child's play to this mountain path. We must have come down about a thousand feet when suddenly the fog rolled away and gave us just a fleeting view of the valley below us, and just a glimpse of the high, sharp mountains around us, and then it rolled back again, even before I could get out my camera, and blotted it all out again. I am terribly disappointed as the photos would have been unique.

We crawled down to the valley of Njarðvík, which is a small cove with a sandy beach but an almost impossible landing as it is so open to the Arctic Ocean, and so is not used by fishermen. Only one farm is here, which we pass inside of and have it and the sea on the left-hand, over a small river and then up the side of the mountains again. This time the road, instead of going over, skirts the foot of the mountains and follows the line of the coast. It leads us over a narrow path about two feet or less wide, some 300 to 400 feet above the sea, in and out, up and down, as it were, along the face of the cliff, which is shaped as a series of Vs poking out into the sea. We have to go out to sea to the point of the V, get around the corner and into the cliff, turn that corner and out again to sea. When we get out to sea and begin to turn the corner, the left leg and left side hang over a straight up and down precipice, and underneath are the black rocks and clashing rollers of the Arctic. One instantly inclines to the right and the right leg and shoulder brush the cliff. The turn is so sharp that after going up, the turn down rather makes one hold one's breath and screw oneself up into a button until the turn is taken and the latter half of the pony follows the fore half around the corner. The pony goes step by step, cautious, along, downwards, following in the very footsteps of the forward pony. As we gaze also at those footprints, we notice one half of it over the edge and you know for certain your pony will put his foot in exactly the same place and wonder if that place will hold up, and what would happen if it broke away.

So we crawl along, dot and dot, in and out, up and down, until half of this horrible place is crossed, and there in the inside V stands a wooden cross with a Latin inscription on it of, 'Jesus Christ – save us'. Here, it is said, in old days lived a mountain spirit and he on occasions, especially if single people were crossing the skörð (as this road is called), used to kill them and throw them over the cliff after sucking their blood. One day, a very strong priest was going alone over the road and the spirit sprang out of the corner, but the priest clung to him and got him down on his back and put his silver cross on the spirit's breast so that he was unable to get up again. The priest went off and got assistance from the people in Njarðvík and they chopped off the spirit's head and buried him there. They set up the cross over him, and the legend goes that as long as the cross is maintained with the inscription on it, so long will people be able to pass the skörð in safety. It's very seldom indeed, true, that any accident happens here of course, because it's so dangerous that every caution is taken and when speaking of it since, I find that many a man who has to go over it for the first time turns back and will not face it. The hotelkeeper in Seyðisfjörður tells me he went there once and would not go more than one V.

Anyhow, we had to go on, there was no other road and when once again we began there was no room to get off, or turn round and go back, only hold on, and go on, but I hope I shall never have to do this again, and thankful enough I was when it was all over. It took us half an hour to get over it. I daresay you remember seeing the navvies working at cutting back cliffs and standing on a ledge with a rope around them, well it's something like that, only an awful lot worse and fancy riding a pony along that ridge! I really am not swinging the hatchet now and as I look back on the job, I would not do it again for any money. The only regret I have about it was the impossibility of taking a photo of the dreadful place. Well there, all's well that ends well, so after taking a good long breath, we gallop off over the grass towards Borgarfjörður, being now on the point forming the north side of the fjord, which is more bay than fjord and about the size and formation of Torbay.

We arrive in at the village about 7.30pm, wet fog and everything looking smaller. We pull up at a merchant's house and shop called Þorsteinn Jónsson, being the best place in the village, and find Þorsteinn at home but he will be leaving for Seyðisfjörður in a motor boat that night. As his wife lives at Seyðisfjörður, he has a caretaker and his wife here, so he gives me his room and the caretaker, Eiríkur, gives me food. We have coffee without milk and Jakob goes off with the ponies and, as he is very well known here, he gets his lodgings in another house. At 10.30, we get fried fish and sea biscuits and more milkless coffee, and are waited upon by rather a good-looking girl, but she sniffs horribly and bubbles in her nose, which takes off the charm of her appearance.

At 11pm, Eiríkur says the bed is ready and I return and find an iron bedstead with a modern mattress which looks rather doubtful for a good night's rest, however beggars must not be choosers, so I make the best of it. Þorsteinn comes after I am in bed and wishes me goodbye, and as a nightcap tells me he is selling his fish to a Leith merchant and is getting a much higher price for it than I am offering, so I have to put that in my pipe and smoke it.

Wake up at 5am. Hear it raining heavily but feel a lot of tickling in my back. Have an examination and discover black sheepskin is used for an under-blanket, so have a hunt in my jacket and find! Throw out the skin, turn in tickling legs, turn out, hunt, find! Turn all inside out trousers and jacket, try to sleep again, more tickles, more hunts, more finds! So decide to get up and dress, which I do, but as it's still raining heavily, I do not descend to the lower apartments but sit in the bed and read. At the same time, I imagine I have tickles in my pants but it's only imagination, for I do not make any more finds, although I search diligently amongst the bedclothes. I expect though that the sheepskin was pretty well-populated. I expected the sniffer at 8am but she did not come with the coffee, but Eiríkur came at 10am, August 3rd, and announced breakfast as being ready.

Last year about 150 Norwegians and 30 or 40 boats came here but the Icelandic merchant was too cute for them and swindled them and brought them in debt. Consequently their boats and gear were seized for debt and they did not come this year.

WHEREIN IT IS VALUABLE

'A REPUTATION for truthfulness is a valuable asset.'

'Yes?'

'Yes, indeed. It enables a man to lie so effectively.'

August 3rd

Come down to breakfast, reasonable affair. It was fried fish balls (which is boiled fish pulled to pieces and mixed with potatoes and boiled again, and one can imagine either the sniffing girl or the dirty woman mixing up these fish balls), sea biscuits and butter, and milkless coffee. After breakfast, it clears a little and I go out to have a look around, as I expect to get a good bit of business in this bay from the Faroe fishermen who are in the habit of coming here and fishing during the summer months in small rowing boats, three men in a boat, and selling their catch to the highest bidder in September when they leave. This Þorsteinn does not care for me to dabble in, but rather let him buy and resell to me, and that is why he gave me the parting shot last night.

There is another man here called Helgi, but find he is at sea and expected in tonight as well as all the Faroese.

One boat is just come in with about 72 tons of cod and one cod enormous, weighed 72 pounds and six feet long. I was sorry not to be able to photograph it, as well as a large halibut, seven feet long, 250 pounds weight and five feet broad, for it was thick with fog, calm, and raining heavily again. Go indoors but it is a very uncomfortable place, five or six dirty-nosed children constantly in one door and out the other, crying and unruly, and one little baby that screams all day and night, and Eiríkur wanders in and out. I don't like Eiríkur, he is one of the biggest rogues in Iceland, and that is saying a good deal. Unprincipled, unmitigated thief, a spare, hungry-looking fellow, impudent face, rough, unkempt hair and whiskers and big, thick, round glasses, and he has a self-satisfied smirk on his face all the time. I know him of old so am cautious, but as he is only the manager for Þorsteinn, I do not talk business to him beyond pumping him and getting information.

Dinner: sweet sago soup with raisins and prunes in it and boiled salt mutton. Why on earth they do not give us fried fish, I cannot think. In the corner of the room is the daintiest little cradle that it is possible to see, wickerwork body with a red down quilt decorated with the finest openwork embroidery, little pillow ditto, and a broomstick nailed to the back forming a canopy of white calico, also beautifully embroidered. I am sure if it was put in a shop window as it stands it would be quite worth £10, and yet these dirty-nosed children crowd all around the table whilst we are eating and put their fingers into everything. The father remonstrates but they go on just the same, under the table, over the table, chairs; a perfect racket and mess all the time. One feels induced to smack them all around the room.

Moon about smoking, for it's still raining and after a while supper comes, cold mutton and sea biscuits and milkless tea this time. At 10pm, go off to bed hungry, fall off to sleep but awake again at 1am. Rather dark for hunting but highly necessary. Turn out the skin again onto the floor, put stockings on to keep my friends from crawling up my legs, fasten a neckerchief around my throat, bind up my cuffs and try that, but at 3am wake up again having a feeling of a horse race being held in my hair, or hide and seek games. Clear those jokers out, overlock my safeguards and try to sleep again, and do so all night.

August 4th

Still rain, and heavy overhead. My intention was to have left here today, as I had got, with the help of Jakob, all the information I wanted, but Jakob comes in and says he is dubious of being able to cross a certain mountain torrent after so much rain. As the brook which runs through this village is swollen to flood size it looks as if his surmises were right. The thick, heavy, wet blanket sky, or rather clouds, hang low over all. A most depressing day, especially as we only had cold salt mutton for breakfast and that horrible concoction called fish soup for dinner ('couchon lavez',14 it's simply horrible but it had to go, I was so hungry) and the boiled fish, a disgusting mass of bones and fish which all looked as if scrambled up in the hands and cast onto a plate, and sea biscuits.

This morning it was said a motor boat would leave for Seyðisfjörður, and if I liked I could go with it. As it looked as if I should have to remain here for an indefinite period, I said I would go by it as it would take about five hours to do the journey, but just as it was ready to start, it was discovered that the cylinder wanted cleaning and so daddled about all day taking it to pieces and putting it together again. Meanwhile, a heavy sea began to roll in and break on the shore so it looked as if there was wind outside.

As it had stopped raining, I had a look around and got over to the Faroese settlement. Jakob had been there and got all the information but I thought I would go and have a chat with them. What a horrible, dirty state their place was in. When I got inside, there were some six or seven men sitting on boxes or fishing line buoys and small kegs, grouped around a square wooden trough which contained steaming lumps of black porpoise meat and lumps of blubber with an occasional potato. They were grubbing it with their fingers and sheath knives, all heads together, picking out the best bits. In the corner was the small cooking stove with an iron crock bubbling over with some fatty looking

---

14   A lost term, unrelated to Icelandic names for fish soup.

soup. Outside in the fish store there were two young fellows skinning a seal which they had shot in the morning and stuffing the skin with salt to preserve it, and all over the floor one filthy mess of mud, blood and fish refuse. In fact the whole village is the dirtiest place I have ever seen, even for Iceland. Fish refuse in every direction, houses dirty, people dirty, beaches dirty, maggots by the ton and a frightful smell of decaying filth, everything wearing the air of dank, damp miserableness.

At 10pm, after supper (also cold salt mutton and weak tea) and just as I was thinking about bed, in came the motor boat man to say he should start in one hour. I was a bit sick about going at that time of night, as it had now settled in for one of those dismal, heavy nights with a cold air from the sea, which with us in England in November time means a gale of wind before morning. However, I donned my things, oilskins etc., and got ready to go. On getting to the beach, found too much surf to get off there, so had to get to a cove about half a mile southwards which was more sheltered from the heavy roll. On getting there, found a group of people and, on asking what it all meant, was informed that seven women and eight men were going as well. These, with a crew of four men, meant, with me, 20 people in an open boat so I said no, thank you. It's all right if it goes right, but all wrong if it goes wrong. It seems as if some sort of Providence looks after these people, for of all the foolhardy things to do was to go with all that lot on an open sea voyage as long as Exmouth to Brixham in the face of such threatening weather. One would not mind so much if only the crew were there, but if it should blow up and the boat ship some water, what a disaster. I returned to my insect-infested nest and turned in, but determined that whatever the weather in the morning, I should leave the place on horseback and trust to luck to get over the river all right. I find afterwards that the boat got to Seyðisfjörður all right at 8am, being eight hours instead of the four or five as was talked of, and a fearful mess they were all in.

August 5th

The next morning, it had knocked off raining but still heavy fog resting over all, so sent for Jakob and told him to bring the ponies, expecting him quickly after 10am and breakfast was finished. As luck would have it, it was fried fish, so I got in as much as I could, and I thought of the boy at the school treat when pressed to take more cake, 'I could chew, but could not swallow more.' Dressed up for the bad weather, paid Eiríkur his charge, and waited for the ponies to arrive.

Meanwhile I heard that the priest had come from Seyðisfjörður last night, where he had been to see the parliament men who had returned from their visit to the King of Denmark in Copenhagen in the *Botnia*, and that he had crossed the river about a mile further up than the usual crossing. When Jakob turned up at 12 noon, I named it to him and he then said he knew of that crossing but it would take one hour more, so I had lost a day only because of that hour. Now he comes to say he has lost my bridle, for which I am sorry as it had a silver bit and was a present to me and I have had it a long time, but it's no use grumbling. We have now lost two hours and, not seeing the saddle on the pony, I ask if he had lost that also. 'Oh no, it's in the store here', and on bringing it out, there was the bridle under it. I think Jakob wanted to put difficulties in the way of not going today, as this Borgarfjörður is a very favourite place of his and, it being Sunday, there may be some jollification going on in the evening which he wanted to join in. He is an unmarried man and I suspect he has got some sort of a sweetheart here, but I was determined not to stay here any longer so at 1pm we set off, still fog and heavy overhead.

The road led us straight from the sea into the back of the flat marsh-land to the foot of the mountains and there was the dreaded river. Jakob plunged in and we followed, that is the ponies and I, and we struggled over. It certainly was very strong and furious but only up to the girths, but as Jakob explained, this was the higher crossing. Well that was got over all right, so we began the ascent of the mountain. The way went as usual alongside a deep ravine, up and up, and the higher we went, the rougher it got, until instead of resembling a dried brook bed, the stones got larger and larger until they got up to 20 tons and at least 100 ton boulders, a perfect chaos of fallen rocks scattered about the ravine. We wound our way in amongst them, sometimes over and sometimes around them. Still creeping higher and higher, what a pity it all was that the fog should envelope us on every side, for it must have been awfully grand.

Still a steeper ascent and my Blackie bearing me well, at last we came to what looked in the fog an impossible way, for it was the foot of a stone slide. Up on this Jakob went on his old brown and we followed. I cannot by any means give you any sort of description of this climb, for I don't think it possible for anyone without seeing it to believe anything I can say of it. It was almost perpendicular. I lay on my pony, grasping his mane, my nose almost six inches off his ears, my toes about level with his tail. I likened myself to a monkey on a dog's back in a circus, up and up, straight up, no zigzag but straight up on end, Blackie digging his toes in between the stones and literally hoisting himself up like an acrobat on a horizontal bar, then digging his hind toes in, fairly standing upright until he could get another grip of his fore toes. So we went on until I thought he would never do it, and I sung out to Jakob, 'Should I get off?'

'No! No! Hang on, it's nearly finished', and so it was, for if it had not been, I am sure my Blackie was, and there was Jakob and the other ponies standing on the neck between the two valleys.

This neck was broader than the Geldingaskörð and was just enough to hold us, so we stop for a blow and change saddles, the red bearing me after this to the descent. The way was now first over a glacier sloping away to our right and we went right across it at right angles. I would have given anything for a photo of this for the slightest slip would have sent pony and rider slipping like a shot out of a gun down the icy slope. I am sure it was a lot more slanting than the roof of a house, but previous travellers had made, by ponies' feet, a sort of foot-grip right across and our own ponies followed this and so we got over all right, then zigzag down, still enveloped in this dreadfully thick fog, and down and down until we got under the blanket, and there spread out was the valley of Loðmundarfjörður.

We made a halt at the foot of the hill and let the ponies have a roll on the wet grass and then on again, past a farm and then to the river, over which we ferried and the horses swam, then began another ascent and more of the 'fly on the wall' business but it was not long, for this is a gradual ascent after the first nip. Our ponies now have become very accustomed to each other and the loose ones follow us like dogs. There is no need to lead them first on ahead, they will run, nibble a bit of grass, and as we get out of sight, they come trotting and neighing after us and getting on ahead again and so on. They are no more trouble to keep in sight so we let them go their sweet way.

We are now passing along Hjálmarsdalsheiði, gradually ascending, good road, so we can ride abreast and chat and at last arrive at the top. We bear away to the right along the top of the ridge, or as much as one can see it's a ridge in the mist, and here comes the vard, marking the beginning of the way down. As soon as I saw what was coming I slipped off my pony, preferring to walk down as it was almost perpendicular and these zigzags are alarming, especially when the turn comes at the end of the zig. I shall always do this in future, it's much quicker to go down that way, leading the pony, as he has got rid of the weight and can come along. Tell about driving a cab down to Labrador Strawberry Gardens,[15] it's child's play to getting up and down these mountains. The only grief I have is it was so foggy that photos were impossible, but this last descent into Seyðisfjörður I shall be able to get, for we are now only two hours off and it will not be much one bright day to ride out here and take some views of the road. Down and down, I am bathed in a bath of perspiration although I have taken off all coats and wraps, yet one would wish to go in shirtsleeves, but that's foolish and it's still wetting fog.

At last we come to the priest's house and farm at Dvergasteinn, on the north side of Seyðisfjörður, and we trot along to soon come to Vestdalseyri and in half an hour are at the hotel door in Seyðisfjörður village, where we arrive at half past ten at night, nine and a half hours from Borgarfjörður. We get a hearty welcome from the hotelkeeper who says all his people are in bed and can get me no supper, so I open a tin of brawn, get some bread and butter and a jug of water and munch my hunger off, at least the edge of it, and so to bed, Jakob having gone off with the ponies to the usual grazing ground. So ended that tour of 15 days in the saddle seeing nothing but fog, and it stands in my report to the company:

---

[15] The Labrador Tea Gardens inn was situated half way up a cliff in a cove near Teignmouth, and was famous for its summer strawberries.

'Went land-ways to Bakkafjörður, Vopnafjörður and Borgarfjörður, made arrangements for shipping in September and returned to Seyðisfjörður after a 15 day ride.'

So it's summed up in a few words and seems easy enough to do.

Before going to bed, enquire for *Vesta* and find that she came in this morning and left again to her time, of course. This is always so if one should overstay the time: the mail boat is to date and leaves punctually. But if you are in time, then the thing is two or three days late, so it is. I enquire of my obliging host if there are any letters for me by *Vesta* but he says he was in the post office in the afternoon and saw none, so must wait until morning to see how it goes, so goodnight.

August 6th

Awake several times during the night, terrible thirst, drink and drink the decanter empty. Get up at 8am and dress, but more to get more water. After a good drink, go to the post office and get four or five private letters which had been addressed to Reykjavík and had been brought around here last week by the Danish man-of-war *Hekla*. I am surprised there are no business letters by the *Vesta* nor any home letters. Very fine day, bright sunshine and everything nice and warm. Jakob sick today, obliged to go for a doctor, and I am drinking water like a … I found afterwards that Jakob and I must have been somewhat poisoned with that tin of brawn, which accounted for my terrible thirst and his illness.

Sponge, loll about all day and have an after-dinner nap and a general relaxation, read my letters and snooze. Turn out my wash and get that in a line to be cleaned. After supper was surprised to get another two or three private letters which had come via Reykjavík and Akureyri in a land post here, so I hear from everybody and some extras. No business letters, but on making an examination of the time-tables, I have some suspicion that they are with the *Holar*, which boat leaves Leith about a day before *Vesta*, and all Icelandic mail must have gone by that as I even do not get my newspapers, so must wait for *Holar*'s return here August 9th.

August 7th

Another fine day, get my photos out and get them developed. Some are rather thin, which I thought quite possible, but I hope they will print all right. Jakob still sick so suggest getting the ponies and riding to Vestdalseyri as they want looking to in their shoes, so ride out there and am afraid that my red is pricked, as his hoof is bleeding in the nail holes. Hope it's not so, but he seemed all right coming back. Had that beastly mess 'couchon lavez' for dinner, and the boiled fish that accompanies it, so I jib and leave the table and go and get a tin of fruit and eat that instead. Got good news of the first buying at Vestdalseyri, the man there having got many promises for September as the peasants prefer to sell to me direct and not through the merchants. As the merchants have refused to sell to me and prefer to go to Leith on spec, I am getting to windward of them I hope by treating direct with the peasant. Q.E.D.

This starving process is not very comfortable whilst it goes on but I can feel in myself a distinct advantage, as I can now lace up my boots without puffing too much, but at the same time there is a great void, a sort of 'apartments to let in the middle flat'. I don't think I can have been really well the whole tour, as I had dreadful indigestion and heartburn all the time. I thought at first it was the result of nine hours bumping and jerking, but the stiffness wore off after the third day and I felt nothing more of it, but now Jakob complains of the same. Perhaps it was the fog that caused it, as I had a throat tickling all the time, which is not at all usual for me up here, and it could not have been I smoked too much, for I only used half a tin of tobacco where I am accustomed to use two tins in the same time, and even of that half a tin, Jakob helped himself. All the tour there was a feeling of a romped up, sick monkey sort of feeling. However, the last two days I have felt nothing of it and am very fit indeed. I only wish the *Holar* would come in so I can be off again southwards to see where the *Rose* is, as I expect her at Norðfjörður about now and I want to see my friend the vicar there and see how he is getting the stuff together.

August 8th

Cloudy and cold, thick fog over the tops of the mountains and I should not be surprised to hear there is snow in the passes over the heiði. Had my hair cut today and walked out to Jón Stefánsson's. Find that he is getting a lot of salt fish and sending it to Grimsby, so the man there is evidently making a pay of it as he has not advised Jón to stop buying. Very annoying but cannot be helped. Better dinner today, 'least my boys, beat, glorious beat!'

Spend some time writing up my doings and so to bed as it's the warmest place. Jakob still complains of being unwell. Glad to say he reports the red pony all right and not lame as I anticipated. Fully expect *Holar* today.

August 9th

No *Holar*, very annoying. Bleak, cold day, spend the whole of it writing in my room. Jakob still unwell but I have given him something to do, and that is look after our ferðataska (travelling bag) which has become damaged a bit, straps pulled off and wanting the saddler's attention, which he is supposed to be doing today but I suspect he is in bed. It was a rattling good thought of mine, that oilcloth wrapping for my things. It has saved the situation and now I shall know what to do another time.

August 10th

No *Holar*. Bleak cold day and Jakob still unwell but he got the pack saddle all completed. I am sitting in my room with great coat on, writing, miserably cold.

August 11th

Still bleak and cold. The annual holiday for the shopkeepers commences today and all the young fellows are busy getting horses together for a trip to what they call a forest at the end of the Lagarfljót. They ride to Egilsstaðir and take the motor boat there to the end of the fljót, where this famous forest is situated. I am told there are trees there of the birch species quite ten feet high and six inches through the butt, by far the highest and largest trees in the land. I daresay it's very nice there, it's very nice on a fine day, but with only about four degrees Réaumur of heat (equal to about 40 degrees of Fahrenheit) with a wind blowing off Vatnajökull glacier and heavy wet fog, I don't think it will tempt me to join the jollification, especially as so many young people are going. The only sleeping accommodation for the night out will be on the damp hay in the hay house. I tried that once and it took a week to get the smell of damp hay steam out of my clothes and nostrils.

4pm the *Holar* comes in and brings some home letters and one business letter, from which I judge there is an important business letter still missing. It may be it's on board the *Kong Inge* which left Leith about the same time, so I must wait for her arrival. As she was in the next fjord when *Holar* passed, it may come tonight. With *Holar* came the news that the *Ceres* was stranded in the Faroe Islands and that the telegraph communication between Shetland and Faroes was completed. They were enabled to wire to Copenhagen and the *Laura* was dispatched to take on the passengers and mails, so instead of getting that mail on Monday it's quite indefinite, so shall not wait here after *Kong Inge* arrives but go to Norðfjörður as quickly as possible.

One of my men, Sigurður Haflidason from Ísafjörður, has come with *Holar*, bringing me the latest news from that place and saying the cutter *Gudrun* has been dispatched to Exeter with half a cargo, and that the salt vessels have been successfully unloaded and all in order. He had come via *Esjan* and had been to his home at a place called Garðar and there had made some business for the company which I hope will bear fruit, and as I have also given my other man, Jóhannes Pétursson, orders to go there as soon as the Ísafjörður business was in order, I hope that some will result, Q.E.D. Got home letters and glad to find all well. Jakob a little better, I fancy he must have had stomach catarrh owing to getting wet on our journey. Red pony not lame and all the rest well and we are all ready for a fresh start. I had fried eggs and ham today (what ho!) and boiled trout for dinner, so I am like an alderman, but Siggi, my man, says he is surprised how thin I am.

August 12th

Cold, wet, snowy, bleak day. Yarn with Siggi. Jakob better, gone for a ride with the holidaymakers so suppose he is all right again. Once a year, in the summer, it is the custom amongst the shopkeepers to have a free day off, and that was chosen for tomorrow. So as a matter of fact, today being Sunday, they get two days' holiday and ride up into the country. I cannot see much fun in that this weather but they went all the same.

Whilst we, that is Siggi and I, were sitting talking about the business, in came the Vopnafjörður postman land-ways with some of my letters. The silly fellow here in the post office had sent all the *Vesta*'s letters up to Vopnafjörður, stupid of him. But what was my consternation on opening my business letters to find the company had decided to send the schooner *Rose* out to Newfoundland instead of here and I must get a vessel here. Well, well! Here was a pretty kettle of fish. I expecting the *Rose* to be ready at Vopnafjörður and waiting to commence loading. I have told people along the coast the vessel will come to their places and collect the stuff and now I cannot keep my promise. In consequence of this, my dinner was nil, so went out for a walk and 'smoked'. Did four hours walking and walked it off. This is a proper hole and how am I to wriggle out of it, goodness only knows, but there! Trust to chance, I suppose. As Old Captain Cockle used to say, 'Iceland was found by chance and everything has gone by chance ever since, there is not anything you be sure of here, not even death, you might be drowned.' He, poor chap, died on a steamer in a gale of wind between Faroes and Iceland. There were many Icelandic passengers on board and they begged of the captain, who was Norwegian and on a Norwegian steamer so didn't have any sympathy with this Englishman (or rather, Scotch man) dying on board his boat, so the superstitious Icelanders prevailed upon the captain to throw poor old Captain Cockle overboard, which he did. The gale abated and they got in next day and so the poor old chap after all met with a watery grave.

Went to bed very sick at heart but the four hours' walk had tired me, so soon forgot my troubles in the arms of that sleeping chap (is it Beelzebub?).

Woke up August 13th, cold and bleak still. Found Jakob back. Wrote letters and instructions to my agents along the coast what to do now *Rose* was not coming and so got ready for a start tomorrow to Norðfjörður.

Perhaps, after all, the *Rose* not coming is all for the best, as I should have had to coast about in her and perhaps got stranded or foundered. If lost at sea, neither myself nor anyone else would know where I was, but now if I fall off a horse or off a cliff and kill myself that way, I and my friends <u>will</u> know where I am. It's like poor Sam Hutchings used to say when describing any unlucky speculation or particular misfortune: 'It's like batterings in big waves.' You hold on to a rope (Hope) and see a big roller coming and you think, 'Now surely I shall be finished with.' You hold your breath and hold on to the rope, close your eyes and grunt, then whack comes the wave and nearly tumbles you over, but when you open your eyes and take a breather, lo! Behold, it has passed and you are in a calm, and so this is a big 'wave' just passed.

I get the horses and ride out to Vestdalseyri to see how my chap there is getting on, as he reports the stuff coming in. Found all satisfactory there, came back and bed.

August 14th

A little finer but still showery. To our great surprise, *Laura* in place of *Ceres* came in, correct to time, and brought the mails, which were all satisfactory, but no papers. Posted all the letters I had ready, together with the first volume of this wonderful *Book of Lies*, when a sudden thought came to me to send my man Siggi to Ísafjörður with the *Laura* to see if he could get a Norwegian vessel which I know was coming there with timber. She would be there about the time that Siggi would get to his post, to his great delight as he also was first out now that there was nothing to do now the *Rose* was not coming. If he succeeds in getting the captain of *Elise* to come here, he will be back again sometime about end of September in the vessel, which will be time enough at any rate to get two-fifths of a cargo here and Norðfjörður, but his insurance will not allow him to go to the open places such as Vopnafjörður, Bakkafjörður or Borgarfjörður. As these open and exposed places are the best fishing stations, there is the greater part of the cargo to be shipped there, so I must try and collect it best manner I can into Norðfjörður, which is a good harbour and I have a store there. If I cannot, the stuff must be wrapped in bagging and sent to England by steamer. When, goodness only knows, but that is the only way I can

see to fulfil my promises to the men or at least show them I am trying
to fulfil them. The expense will be frightful. Cold, wet, miserable
evening.

August 15th

Awoke early, that is to say 7am. Found the weather better and the sky
looking clearer so get up and have an inspiration. Send for Jakob but he
also had seen the clear-up and had gone out to look for the ponies, as
he expected I should be wanting to make a start if it cleared sufficiently
by breakfast time. Heard from the pony boy who I employed to water
the ponies that two of them could not be found, and at breakfast time
Jakob came, being unsuccessful in his search. Just then a man came in
from Vestdalseyri and said he thought he had seen them out there, so
off trotted Jakob. I meantime packed up my ferðataska and got that
ready and donned my travelling clothes, and just as I was beginning to
think the journey was off for that day, Jakob came triumphantly in with
the mob so we saddled up and, with the usual delays, got off at 2pm.

Weather still cold but clouds high with a glimpse now and then of a
blue sky. Went up the valley in fine style and began to climb. I was
riding Blackie, as he is the strongest and was saving the red for a
scamper across the heiði, but during the climb I thought Blackie was
not easy in his wind. As he is a sulky beast and has fits of temper, I
thought he was annoyed because he had been brought from a good
feeding ground, but as soon as we got to level ground I found, on
trotting, he had got the limp. Got off, held an inspection of his feet and
found a stone wedged in his off fore foot and had a job to get it out.
Changed saddles and sent him and the piebald off ahead, but still
Blackie limped and he limped all the way across the heath.

Halfway we had to make another stop and don oilskins and southwesters and were soon treated to a heavy snow, a sleety, cold downfall.
We drove on, passed two or three droves of ponies on way to
Seyðisfjörður but did not stop to yarn but drove on and were soon
across the heath, making the descent into Lagarfljót valley. Here the
downfall lightened a bit and one could see the land with glimpses of
sunshine on it here and there, just like when we look up and see the
blue sky through the clouds, so we could look down and see the green

sward (good word this) and sunshine on the water through the falling snow. Getting down to level again and under the clouds, it was fine. We passed a farm, in the enclosure of which the people were tweedling about the hay to dry with their little, small toothcomb sort of rakes, and by the time we got to Egilsstaðir it was seven o'clock.

We off-saddled, hobbled the ponies and messed about waiting the usual invitation to come in, but found from one of the farmhands that the missus was not at home (by the way, the mistress of the farm is called the húsmóðir or 'house mother' and the master is called the húsbóndi, from which we get our word 'husband') and that the húsbóndi also was not at home either, and then Jakob could tell me that he had seen him in Seyðisfjörður the night before. Anyhow, he was expected that evening so we had to kick our heels about until 9 o'clock, when he and another man came bustling in. They had heard we had come on and had tried to catch us and had come in four hours. Coffee was soon underway and then in came another lot, a party of four, and they had coffee and a yarn but they were going farther on. Icelanders like to ride in the dimpse[16] as they say the ponies go better in the evening than in early morning, or what they call early, which is any time before 12 o'clock. After getting rid of that party, we kicked our heels again and waited, wondering what we should get for supper. Seeing as I had had nothing since breakfast, I was beginning to think like the boy at the farm in Ivybridge, Devon: 'What about the Fude?' This boy used to accompany us on rabbiting days and bring along the basket of provisions, and when told to carry dead rabbits as well, he always asked, 'What about the Fude?!' I will say that for him, he may forget half a dozen rabbits but the 'Fude' was always to the fore; he and the basket were inseparable.

Anyhow, at 11pm the maid said 'Gjörið svo vel' which is Icelandic for 'if you please', and that meant the 'fude' was ready. By this time the twilight had got to nearly darkness inside the house, but these people are like cats and can see in the dark. No lamp (although a rather swell one was hanging over the table) was lit, nor candles (there on a corner shelf) offered. I gave out a sort of hint that we should have to light matches to find our mouths; it only called forth a snigger. I could just

---

[16] Devon dialect for dusk.

see something steaming and on closer examination found it was trout, boiled, so get at that. Instead of a nice supper of this delicious fish, after a mouthful or two I found it was one of those things a dentist-filled mouth was not adapted to, for although in daylight time there do not appear to be many bones, in darkness it's all bones and no fish. Rather than create a scene by making a sudden dash in the dark for the outside door (which I always am compelled to do if a fish bone tickles my throat), I reluctantly had to give over and after making a sort of speculative jab with my fork in the dark, I got hold of something flabby which might be anything and turned out to be a junk of 'rengi', which is the name given to whale. As there are no bones in this, I fired into it and got a supper, such as it was, and had to be contented, especially as there was no bread, only what is called 'kringler' which are imported from Denmark and are really only paste baked as hard as iron and dotted here and there with caraway seeds, or at least some of the spots are really caraway seeds and the other spots may be anything. These kringler are about the thickness of one's finger and are coiled up into a sort of true lovers' knot, and as my incisors were not designed by W. Goodman to walk into kringler, I had to go breadless.

After the whale came weak tea without sugar or milk, which is the custom at supper. The people give it a right name: 'tevatn' = 'tea water'. Then after a bit of a jabber, the husband says, 'Verði þér að góðu' and we say, 'takk fyrir það'.[17] We get up, light our pipes and the maid says, opening a door, 'Gjörið svo vel', and Jakob, the other man and I troop into a sort of cupboard in which there are three beds. We say, 'Góða nótt' (goodnight), make a choice of beds, quickly undress and slip in under the eiderdown in our vests and pants and socks. I always up here look out to keep my socks on as it prevents crawling things getting up my legs. I can often feel them trying and an occasional adventurous chap now and then gets to windward of me by getting down my neck, although I safeguard that also by a silk neckerchief and my arms by a string around the wrists, but generally before he makes the discovery of how to get inside it has become daylight again and then it's sudden death to the explorer. These two,

---

[17] Polite exchange of well wishing and thanks.

Jakob and the other man, jabber and jabber and smoke cheap cigars and I gradually fall asleep.

Am awoke in the morning by Jakob stamping his wellington boots on; he is out to see the ponies are all right. The other fellow gets up and performs his toilet (which is done in a teacup of water, corner of the towel wet, wipes out his eyes), lights the stump of cigar, rigs up his collar and dicky, puts the rest of his clothes on, gives a sort of wriggling shake together, a satisfied grunt and goes out. Then I get up and look out and find it a glorious, sunshiny morning so I go out also and find Jakob with the ponies all right. The other fellow gets a cup of coffee, says goodbye to us and rides off so as to get to the next farm at breakfast time instead of waiting here until our breakfast is ready. It's glorious in the sunshine once more but then that has its drawbacks, as being so close to the water of Lagarfljót the flies are worrying, and they are such stupid things, seem almost too lifeless to fly but just suspended in the air and get into one's eyes, nostrils and ears. They don't even buzz but flop lifeless on to anything that happens to bump against them. Stand still and you are all right, but just move and squat they go right into your eye, swarms of them.

This Lagarfljót is glacier water, white almost as milk, being fed from the great glaciers beyond which are slowly advancing, or rather descending, into the valleys and grinding the rocks into powder which moves with the melted ice and forms this 'flowing milk' stream, or rather lake with a little tide sea-wards. The stones by the waterside are thickly covered with the condensed milk and the whole has a Kingsteignton clay works look about it, so that one almost expects to see a lighter sailing down-tide loaded with pipe clay. Here one sees a clay bed being formed with which some fortunate clay merchant in 20,000 years' time will make a fortune.

Whilst waiting about, a caravan of pack ponies come to the landing place, some 80 to 100 of them, and the men unload them one by one, depositing their packs on the ground in a heap. The ponies go off one by one as unloaded, by themselves towards home, up the fljót. The farmers have bought a motor boat which plies from this place up to the end of the waters and the ponies are thus enabled to go back light in one to two days instead of four or five if loaded, thus saving a deal of time to the peasants, which is of great value this season of the year. The drying of hay time is so short, they are obliged to take advantage of every hour to enable them to cut, dry and save enough hay to keep their flocks from starvation during the nine months of no grass.

I noticed great baulks of timber strewn about the vicinity of the farm and enquired what it was and where it came from and how it was possible to bring such enormous pieces of wood up so far in the country. I was told it was drift timber which came from the forests of Siberia, got into the Arctic stream, came all along the north of Europe and eventually drifted on shore at the mouth of the fljót and got embedded in the sands of the delta. In the winter, when it is all frozen over, the farmers go down over the ice and dig up the timber and drag it here on sledges, which they tell me is quite easy to do although some of the trees were 30 to 40 feet long and two to three feet thick and must weigh two or three tons weight, as the wood is much like mahogany in colour but rather closer in grain. By the way of how heavy weights are taken about in winter, I saw here for the first time, or at least it was the first time it came under my notice, a rig-up to bring heavy goods such as a barrel of petroleum oil. It is two pieces of wood like the shafts of a cart, the thin ends fasten to a pony's neck and trail backwards so the ends (which are shod with iron) trail along the ground. It is kept in place with a cross bar and on this rests whatever weight they have to bring and the pony drags it over the frozen ground, a very primitive but useful contrivance. I have seen pictures of North American Indians' horses rigged out with the same sort of contraption. I regret I did not get the farmer to rig up one to take a photo of.

After this look around, and getting waxy with the flies, breakfast was announced. It now being all right with the light, I make a hearty meal of the trout, have another junk of 'rengi' in lieu of bread, two cups of coffee, interview the farmer, pay the scot and then ready to be off, when I hear Jakob making enquiries about the road. I chipped in I did not want any more Columbus work so I got the farmer to let us have his son, a lad of 16 or 17 years old, to go with us so far that he could show us the direction we should go, so at 10am we get off.

The track leads us backwards for about half an hour, over the little wooden bridge to the side of the little river and there, bearing south, we follow on the banks of the stream, past what is called a forest but is really birch scrub. I have seen a better forest on Haldon in a furze brake,[18] which, by the way, these so-called forests in Iceland much resemble, about the same height of growth and about the same bushiness, only no prickles, only leaves. It was a lovely ride, bright sunshine, not a cloud in the sky, high, rough-peaked mountains on each side, not a sound to be heard except the babbling of the running waters on our right hand, not a bird of any description to be seen or heard, only the deep silence of utter loneliness.

We amble along the steep track, come to a farm called Dalhús, pass through the tún, see a man and two women cutting grass, past the front of the bye, cannot be said to clatter past but sploshed past, ankle-deep in mud, a chorus of barking dogs yapping at our heels as it is their duty to drive off stray horses from the tún grass. As they see us going right through the middle of the Forbidden Ground, they come barking and yelping at the ponies' heels. That puts a bit more life into them and we scatter off at a sharp amble and out into the sheep track again.

We go on like this for three hours with only one stop to change horses, which as Blackie is still lame means shifting the pack onto his back and my getting onto the pack pony and a nice old pack pony it is. It's bump! bump! bump! until your boots seem to have changed places with your hat. As we approach the end of this valley, three passes appear up amongst the mountains and I began to see some more 'fly on the wall' work ahead, but we passed what looked to be the worst pass and the lad then pointed out to us the way we had to go. Had a rest and a smoke, gave the boy a new sixpence (or what is equivalent to a sixpence) for himself, paid him the farmer's charge for the loan of the pony and the boy's time, said goodbye and began to climb.

First it was an ascent, slightly rising, then a bit of mire, into a bit of which my pack pony flopped and got stuck up to his girth in black slimy mud and then calmly collapsed on his side as much as to say, 'Here you get off, I am not going to try to get out of this with a great fat lubber on my back, so don't you think it.' I could quite imagine him saying that, but if I look fat I don't feel it and more resemble a boy's

---

[18] Devon dialect term for gorse thicket. Haldon is a ridge of hills between Teignmouth and Exeter.

halfpenny coloured balloon with half the wind out of it, all over wrinkles. Anyhow, I had to get off very gingerly, cocked my leg over the other side and gave a spring and landed on hard ground, or at least a bit harder than where poor Brown was stuck, got hold of the bridle, gave the necessary twick and yell, a great struggle, more floppings and with a grunt of satisfaction got him out, or rather he got himself out, so I decided to walk over this mire and did, towing my worthy steed after me. Jakob, he got stuck twice and then followed my example and at last we got to harder ground and then up the side of the mountain.

The track lead upwards, east, gradually ascending but upwards all the time, skirting the side of a mountain down the sides of which stone, slide after slide, had fallen until it was one mass of fallen rocks. Over this we picked our way, following the barely marked road which in some places was not to be discerned by me, but my old pony seemed to know more about it than me and went on all right. I had to go on ahead as the other ponies which run loose always follow old Brownie's lead. Right ahead of us but slightly on the left, a wild, black-looking chasm ran and far up one could see a high waterfall and hear the noise of the tumbling water, but our road had about half a mile to the right so did not go near enough to see if it was larger than the Seyðisfjörður falls. Before getting right up to the summit of the pass I took a photo but I don't think it can give any idea of what a desolate valley of rocks it is.

On arriving at the summit, we found a bitter blast of wind, primarily cold, which was a great change from the summer-like heat of the valley where we had been riding without our overcoats, so it was quickly into them. Jakob wisely got his oilskins also over all but I foolishly thought we should be down the other side into a valley again, instead of which we had to pass over a long, dreary heiði, slightly descending but all bare glacier-grooved rock, rough and strewn with boulders. It's wonderful to think however these proud boulders came right in the middle of the plain, not a mountain top within half a mile for them to have fallen from. In fact the heiði is a mountain top itself and is about the usual 3,000 feet high, a bare piece of rock as flat as a table and about half an acre in size. Dotted all over the surface are round plum puddings, some as large as a football, others as large as a ball you see acrobats walking on, and others as big as a lump of chalk, and not a bit of sand or gravel near them. The question is always before one, 'However did they get there?'

Flat piece after flat piece is passed, and then suddenly right before us is the fjord of Eskifjörður. This heiði is called Eskifjarðarheiði. As we plod along, the bitter wind slipping into our backs, a great wreath of cloud fog drives past on our right and I watch it curl around a peak and, as it were, encircle it lovingly and make a sort of necklace of cotton wool, with the sharp, black peak just peering out over the soft, fluffy swansdown like a collar. Another wad comes floating past and goes flop into a big, black ravine and there remains like a bit of medicated wadding on a cut chin.

The wind got more and more fierce, but just as I was shivering, the road led downwards suddenly into a ravine and we got shelter and also sun again. We followed this ravine down and down towards the plain and at last got to grassland once more and the ponies bucked up and I got bumped up. Right ahead, about half an hour's ride, was our destination, so I changed over to my red pony so as to cut a decent appearance in riding into the town. Well there! It's called a town; a collection of stores, cottages and merchants' houses. Here is also the residence of the sýslumaður and a doctor and a newspaper, two piers, and the whole is about 20 buildings and about 3,000 inhabitants, but it's considered a very important place on the east coast. It is the birthplace of the managing director of the Thore line of mail boats and he is called Þór Tulinius but lives now in Copenhagen. He is a half breed, his father a Dane and his mother an Icelander. He has got on well but his father was a successful merchant of the good old money-making days and so he had a good education and capital to begin with. His brother is sýslumaður here and is called Axel who is married to the Bishop of Iceland's daughter.

Þór Tulinius has, to his own expense, made a connection from Eskifjörður to Egilsstaðir with telegraph and sent up his own poles and wires. He tried hard to get the head station there but the engineer sent up to pick out the best fjord recommended Seyðisfjörður as having a sandy bottom, whereas Eskifjörður is rocky and guarded at the entrance by several bad reefs just showing above the water. Very little business is being done here now except its being a coal depot for Þór's boats, only some three or four motor boats fishing out of the place, but it lay in the way to Norðfjörður so I had to pass through it.

We ride into town at 5pm, seven hours from starting, and ask the first decent man we meet where the house is that lets out lodgings, but was informed there was no house. That's the worst of these 'trading stations': no place to get a bed, no inn, no nothing. If there is an inn it's called 'hotel', but if there is a small place it's only a drinking den and if, as in this case, no-one has a licence to sell drink, no-one will keep a tramp house. Oh yes, by the way, the sýslumaður Axel Tulinius, when-ever I met him on board the mail boats, he is very gushing and is always saying, 'You never come to see me, always glad to see you', and all that sort of thing, but here am I just outside his house (and in a few minutes everyone in the place knew I was there), and he did not come out. I heard afterwards he had his father-in-law the bishop and his wife with him. I knew them also but they, of course, had the guest room so he would not show himself until I was housed.

Well it was no good sucking our thumbs and as usual several small boys were around us. We asked them for a blacksmith as I was anxious to see if Blackie had been badly shod, so as the boys are much sharper and readier than the men, they volunteered to show us. We found the man, who examined the shoes and tapped the nails but said it was not that. He thought it might be a strain with the hobbles so had to let it go at that, but I was not satisfied, for I believe it was a nail. Anyhow, the smith offered to take us in for the night so went to his house and was introduced to his wife and a small cottage it was and she was afraid we could not get much to eat but she would do her best.

The house was four-roomed, two down and two upstairs, wooden affair, about a two shillings and sixpence a week cottage and smelling badly, as if it was a washing day and a big wash on. The lady was very tall, very fat, very little hair which was brushed right back from the forehead and tied in a knot at the back, so tightly that it seemed to pull most of her gutta-percha-looking[19] flesh back with it, so that her eyes stuck out and the skin stretched tightly over her nose. It only wanted a prick to fly asunder and the bone would come out like the breast of a boiled chicken, and her mouth, oh my! No lips, with protruding teeth

---

[19] A type of latex extensively used in Victorian Britain.

which waggled as she spoke, and over all a sickly, 'Don't care a shoe-maker's lump of wax if you come or not, either way is the same to me, take it or leave it', so we had to take it.

There was an old-fashioned sofa one side and a very stout table, between which and the sofa I squeezed myself. I wondered why the thing was so firm, as most Icelandic tables are so joggly that if you only breathe on them they shake most of the things on it onto the floor, but on examination of it I found it was from a shipwrecked steamer and had carved dolphins for legs and was really a very nice affair.

After about an hour coffee turned up, and then we were asked to get out for a walk, so we did. Had a chat or two with some people, all workmen etc., but all the merchants kept close as they did not want to be saddled with me for the night. Went back, found supper spread: cold chips of salt meat, some horrible cheese, sea biscuits, some motor car butter (this butter I call motor car is mixed with tallow and the combination gets rancid and the smell, poof!, it's strong enough to drive a motor car, hence its name), salt anchovies, and a round or two of cheap German sausage and five boiled eggs. At the same time the lodgers were there, three Danish carpenters employed by Tulinius, where do they all sleep in a four-roomed house and where will Jakob and I sleep? Anyhow, sit down to make the best of it and growl with Jakob why he had not got out a tin of our stuff, but he said the old woman would not warm it up and serve it up as it might annoy her lodgers to see us eating hot stuff for supper and they not getting any of it. Of course, if I had known this before they might have got a hot supper, for I would have given them enough to go round. So supped on one egg and biscuit and cup of 'tevatn' and then told to clear out again. Luckily it was not wet but it was chilly, and just as one got warm with five people breathing in an eight by eight feet room for half an hour, had to turn outdoor in the cold again and hang around, Jakob and I still wondering where we were to sleep and what time we should go to bed.

At 11.30, just as we had made up our minds to have a shot at having a trial trip around the house just to show we were there, a girl comes round the corner and says 'Gjörið svo vel' and we slink in and find I have got the sofa and Jakob got the floor. It is curious amidst all this squalor, the sheets and pillowcase were, as usual, beautifully embroidered, and one of the smartest monograms worked in Hedebo embroidery that I have ever seen. So we stripped and got in, but where those other chaps (the permanent lodgers) hung out, Jakob and I never found out, but we found out the lady had two servant girls besides and where did they sleep? It's beyond me where they stow the people in these rabbit hutches. I took the usual precaution against explorers but at daylight had to turn out and hunt and find and kill.

Jakob kindly snugged down in his corner and I heard nothing from him until almost 6am, August 17th, when there was stumping about overhead, rattling of pans and kettles and buckets in the next room (which is the kitchen I suppose, for I did not get a look there), and a stumping downstairs and banging of doors. Then Jakob, he got up and dressed and went out to see how the weather was, and came in and said it would be a fine day, and would I get up as the lady wanted to tidy up the room. At the same moment one of the girls appeared with a tin of water, about a pint, and a towel, so that was another hint. As there was only one pint, Jakob generously gave me first bath and after having a good swill, which by the way finished up the water, I got out of the house and had a breath of fresh air.

I wandered about whilst Jakob fetched the horses in from the hillside and found Blackie still lame as ever, very sorry and disappointed about that. It cannot be helped but it means taking a longer time doing our journey, besides the risk of ruining the pony forever and breaking down the red one, but we got to do our work so had to put it out of our minds and think about breakfast. The old girl would <u>not</u> heat up a tin, and as it was a sort of Irish stew called 'Army Rations' and cannot be eaten without heating (well I say cannot, I mean cold, fat gravy is not pleasant), we gave up the idea of it and trusted to luck and luck we had! Substantial breakfast: one boiled egg and sea biscuit and a cup of coffee, this time without milk. The old girl said if she gave her lodgers hot breakfast or supper once, even if they knew I had provided it, they would want it always so would not run the risk of a grumble, and if they grumbled after this she would be able to say, 'Not good enough? When Mr Vard was so pleased!' and so would have a good saw to saw with.

Whilst we were waiting for our sumptuous repast to be prepared (which by the way was of course in our sleeping room, which had not been aired, only the beds removed), the sýslumaður comes along, smiling, full of 'bonhomie'. He is really a very fine, handsome man with a winning smile and shakes hands very heartily and says he heard <u>this morning</u> (!) that I was in the town and hoped I had had a comfortable time and a good bed and sleep, and I assured him with the same winning manner and the same bonhomie that I had never been so comfortable in my life and was sorry to go and hoped soon to come back again and enjoy the húsmóðir's generous hospitality (this is what the old girl will hang her hat on). So he expressed himself delighted to hear it. I knew he was telling lies and I expect he knew I was also, but we were both mutually pleased and so, again shaking hands and wishing me a good journey, we waved each other a most enthusiastic farewell.

I then squared up with the old girl and she charged me a most reasonable four krónur each, eight krónur, which is nearly nine shillings and in England would be equal in value to being charged at a workman's cottage 30 shillings each or £3 for the two. I paid and thanked her very much for her extreme kindness in taking us in for the night and hoped she did not mind our calling there on our way back, to which she did not raise any objection. So after bidding her goodbye with a most blank smile (the sort of smile one puts on when the vicar of the parish calls on you once a year and you want him to see you with your best points sticking up, as it's so respectable for the vicar to think well of you, and such an honour for him to condescend to call on you, even if he does ask you for a subscription for his blanket club or soup kitchen or curate's fund), we were all pleased. It seemed for Jakob sleeping on the floor has its advantages, for as he chews tobacco in bed he hadn't so far to get rid of the juice, and the old lady was pleased to find she got eight krónur and got a whip for her lodgers. The sýslumaður was pleased because he had got rid of me for the night, Jakob was pleased because he hadn't to spit so far, and I was pleased because I thought I had pulled all their legs and at the same time expect I was the biggest muggins of the lot. Anyhow, I know I have added a few more wrinkles to my diaphragm since yesterday morning.

We began our ascent of the mountain at the back of Eskifjörður right at the back of the house. We got on a zigzag path and were quickly high over the town. It was a bright sunshiny day with the fleecy clouds high over us just gently sailing along, quite a summer's day sky and the sea right beneath us, just a gentle ripple on the surface and clear so that one could see the patches of weeds and sand on the bottom. One could nearly imagine oneself to be in Italy, say Naples as one sees it in the second-coloured pictures. We zigzag up and up until about halfway up the mountain a sort of shoulder is reached, and then the path leads towards the sea. East along this path we jigged, quietly along as there was no hurry, and the weather was grand, no overcoat, warm and clearing and away out at the mouth of the fjord the Arctic Ocean was sparkling, and in the fjord the mirror-like water reflected the grand old hills until it was almost impossible to see where land joined water.

As we rode along, the breeze gradually worked into the fjord and one expected to get a whiff of the ozone, when whaugh! Whatever is it? It seemed to strike against one's nostrils like a heavy blow.

'Whatever is it Jakob?'

'Don't know, expect it's something dead!'

'Dead! Something! A pretty big something!'

Then I remembered there were two whaling stations just beneath us, they are about six miles out of the town and we had just caught their 'Odour of Bouquet of Roses' wafted up by the breeze. Caught suddenly by us in the clear mount air, it seemed like running against a brick wall and we must have been at least 2,000 feet above their level. However, we hurried a bit after that so got to windward of it. Now the road wound around a neck and led us more northward and, after getting a bit higher, made towards a sort of pass which was nicely grassed and in which a man and woman and a boy and girl were engaged in cutting grass and twiddling it. We stopped and had a yarn and to ask if we were going right, and right we were, so onwards, upwards, onwards etc. Still nice riding but could not go fast, neither did we care to as Jakob had never been that way before and until we knew what diffi-culties we had to encounter, we thought it best to keep a reserve of activity in case it should be wanted.

At last, right over our heads as it were, we saw a vard, which meant that was the mark of the pass, so then we knew what was to be expected. To prepare for this, we off-saddled and let the ponies nibble a little and we laid on the grass, I to get a smoke. Jakob remarked, 'Oh I am hungry!' and then thought I was also, so we got out an 'Army Ration', opened it and dug out a lump of cold, fat meat and a carrot or two. It looks like beef tea does in the morning after having been left overnight in the saucepan. Began to eat and then discovered we were real hungry. Thought I would try the gravy: good. I had the first drink, Jakob finished it up with his trial drink, so we demolished the tin between us and both nearly at the same time said what fools we had been the night before not to have got one of our tins out after the old woman had put us to bed. Anyhow, it will not catch us going hungry again whilst we got a tin of 'Rations' in our locker. Had a good drink out of the brook, smoke and saddle up and begin the 'fly' business.

On arriving at the top, we gave the ponies a breather and took a view, then across the neck and took another view. The neck was about ten minutes to cross over and there was spread out before us a very nice valley sloping gently to the grasslands at the bottom, and away on the right a glimpse of the sea outside Norðfjörður. We zagged down to the grass and then a fair road down, down, until we came to a ravine with a very nice fall, and still down until we came to the plain, which is intersected with a river, or rather a large brook. Over this we cross and get into the marshland, plenty of grass, few farms, and now the ponies race towards the sea and right before us on the north side, nestling under the great hills, is the village of Norðfjörður looking eight times its size in the bright sunlight.

We see several French fishing schooners in the anchorage. They come here to wash their clothes, fill their water casks, get fresh meat and clean up provisions to make their departure for their homes in France as now their season's work is done, and good or bad they all timed to be back to Brittany in September. Most of them come from Paimpol and St Malo but there are also some from Normandy and Dunkirk. They have had a bad season, only filled about two thirds of the average catch. We get over the marsh, through one or two byes where the people are busy about their haying and some peasants recognised me and sung out their greetings.

Now alongside the fjord, skirting the hills, and then the houses began to come and we clattered past them, and the people washing and cleaning fish. We heard 'Það er Ward'[20] at every group and so on. We finally brought up at the priest's house, Síra Jón Guðmundsson, our final destination. Priests are the only people who have a prefix to their name and are always addressed as Síra Jón or Síra Einar or whatever their name might be. We off-saddle and presently he made his appearance and great shaking of hands and greetings. Then his wife Guðný and his sister Ólafía came out and bade us come in, so taking off leggings, oil trousers and other outside wraps and coats, we go in and Jakob drives the horses out to the hagi (Icelandic for grazing or feeding place). By the time he had returned, the coffee and cakes were ready and we fall to and enjoy ourselves.

Yarn and smoke, go out with Síra Jón to see how much fish he has already in stock and generally mess about until 8pm, when we return to the house and find Guðný busy getting the table laid. She remarks she fully expected me today as she dreamt she was making up a bed on the sofa last night, but thinking it was far too short, and so on waking she said a tall man will be here today and I am sure it will be Mr Ward. She got us a lovely supper (tinned Norwegian meats, boiled eggs, white bread, lemonade to drink), so that after it was all over and finished with coffee, I felt at peace with the world. After a little chat, she said bed was ready and I had my usual snug room to myself, clean bed of iron frame (English), and so fell asleep and slept like a top until 7am.

August 18th

Find it all clouded over and looking dismal out of doors, dress and go out. Jakob went to see about the ponies and says Blackie still lame. Breakfast lovely, fried fresh cod, delicious, well cooked and looking a picture on the plate. All sorts of nice things on little plates and the room nicely warmed by a lighted stove as it had turned in bitterly cold outdoors.

---

[20] It's Ward.

I forgot to say that whilst in Eskifjörður, I heard that the Danish exploring vessel to the east coast of Greenland had been there to get whale meat for the sledge dogs. She is called *Denmark* now, but is the *Belgica* which went to the South Pole Belgian expedition[21] in 1900 and on her return was lent to the Duc d'Orléans for a shooting trip in the Arctic. I saw her in Reykjavík together with the Duc two years ago on his return when he bagged seven polar bears and had two living cubs on board. The *Denmark* had so many provisions and all sorts of stuff on board as to be loaded to the water's edge, and people expressed their astonishment that such a loaded vessel should venture into the polar ice, it was simply courting disaster, so we shall see how it turns out later on.

We go down to the stores again and have a look at the fish. I am not at all pleased with the quality but, as Síra Jón explains, we have got a competition in the fjord and if we do not take it the other does, and so it comes with any competition: dearer goods and worse quality, for the peasants are quick to take advantage when possible. It is raw and cold. We yarn with the people up and down the village and return to the house for dinner, another fine spread, three courses and coffee.

It is fairly good fishing in this fjord and they have from 25 to 30 motor boats of a better class than the Ísafjörður boats, larger and more powerful, but strangely they do not get any more fish than the small rowing boats with three men in them. It's so incomprehensible to me how the men cannot see it. The small boats row out with three men about 2am with 20 lines which have about 1,500 hooks. They are laid out, baited and moored with an anchor and buoy, and after waiting about an hour, are hauled up and the catch is generally about five to six hundred fish. They then row ashore and get in about 10am. The motor boats go out about midnight and go a long way out to sea with 60 lines, 4,500 to 5,000 hooks, and return about 3pm with about the same quantity of fish. I ask why this is and why they don't fish where the row boats fish and then they would get three times as much, but they scorn the idea of a big motor boat fishing amongst the small boats and they go far out in order to try and get larger fish, which they do not get.

---

[21] The first expedition to winter in Antarctica, after the *Belgica* became trapped in pack ice, 1898–1899.

It's so ridiculous an argument but they will not see it and grumble that motor boats do not pay. Seeing a motor boat with lines and equipment represents £300 and a rowing boat with all its gear is only worth about £20, one cannot wonder at its not paying when they go so stupidly to work. At Ísafjörður, they still keep to the accustomed ground and consequently fish well all the time and the boats only cost £50.

Lovely and warm in the house, and if only there was any chair except a Windsor wooden chair to sit on, it's a bit tiring to sit bolt upright for five to six hours. Anyhow, after supper I got off to bed until the morning of August 19th.

Awake and cold, bleak, heavy rain and a strong wind out of the fjord, of which the Frenchmen take advantage and sail home. Another fine day's feeding, everything of the best that can be got here, well cooked, and what is more no nasty smells coming out of the kitchen. We sit and yarn, stand up and 'wild beast' walk up and down the room, complaining of the weather, yarn, smoke, and twiddle our thumbs. One of the peasants on the opposite of the fjord, it appears, in the spring found what he thought was a vein of coal in a ravine. They are always finding mares' nests now since gold was supposed to have been found in Vatnsmýri, and he sent off for the government geologist Helgi Pjeturss[22] to come here and report. Last week he came and was shown the deposit but made nothing of it. I could not find out what he called the stuff but it was not coal, so that excitement fizzled out.

After a long day, it seemed almost a week, the evening came so off to bed, and awoke August 20th to find the hills all round white with snow, for it had fallen heavily all night. Gale of wind and heavy snow squalls, so Jakob went off to one of the stores and got a pack of cards and we played all day, which made it seem better than yesterday. Very nice indoors but bleak and uncomfortable outside and I was continually patting myself on the back that this had not happened at Eskifjörður.

---

[22] The first Icelander to receive a PhD in geology, Helgi Pjeturss (1872–1949) discovered that Iceland had been formed through repeated periods of glaciation and warming. He also published ideas about the nature of dreams and the unity of all life in the universe.

August 21st

Ditto day: eat, smoke, play cards, drink coffee and to bed. Impossible to go out as there was nothing to do there and it was bitter weather.

August 22nd

A little finer, clouds higher and a gleam of sunshine now and then, but clouds all heavy and it might come on bad at any moment. Jakob goes out to look after the ponies but comes back at 12 noon, says he cannot find the red. After dinner has another search and finally gets hold of him amongst another flock of ponies towards the sea so that's all right, but reports that Blackie still lame.

All today I felt uncomfortable pain under my right ribs and it caused me much anxiety. I was not quite certain if it was indigestion or what it was. A shorting, stabbing pain and the slightest movement caused it to give me 'gee up', so I knocked off supper that night and on going to bed could not lie down. I grunted and squirmed all night, sometimes it was under my shoulder blade and other times in front under my ribs, for certain it's appendicitis or else pleurisy. I rubbed in embrocation three or four times during the night but no better. Took two or three doses of ammoniated quinine but it got no better, so I huddled in the only position in which I could get ease and wrapped the eiderdown around me for heat, but I was uncomfortable and miserable as a sick monkey. On finally giving over trying to sleep, I dressed amidst various ejaculations and went out to find it was a finer morning.

August 23rd

Jakob had got the ponies in. Heavy fog hung about the hills but it was much warmer. After breakfast, of which I only took a boiled egg and a cup of coffee, the priest announced that he would go with us to Eskifjörður to visit the bishop, who was there with his son-in-law the sýslumaður, and so his pony was brought in and then it had to be shod and that took two hours so it was 1pm before they were ready for a start. The pain I was suffering from was acute and I tried to get on the pony and at last decided I would not try it but remain here, especially as there was a steamer expected in the next morning on the route north, one of the Wathne's boats, the *Prospero*. I sent Jakob on as he was particularly anxious to get back to Seyðisfjörður to see the opening of the telegraph by the Icelandic minister Hannes Hafstein on the 25th, when there was to be a great feast and message to the king of Denmark and all that sort of thing, speeches (of which the Icelanders are very proud), and in fact a regular drunken spree. So he and the priest left at 1pm. Blackie still lame but it looked as if not so lame as before, so perhaps it will pass off.

On the 18th, the London Cable Constructing Company's[23] steamer the *Cambria* of London came and put the end of the cable onshore at Seyðisfjörður and sailed again for the Faroes to make the junction there, as the cable is already laid to Tórshavn. I was sorry I was not at Seyðisfjörður to see this but my friend the chemist there took several photos of the landing and has kindly given me a few prints. It is expected it will all be in order on the 25th of August but the land work between here and Reykjavík is far from ready, so it was decided that the minister of Iceland should come here from Reykjavík in the Danish man-of-war the *Islands Falk* (Icelandic Falcon) and have an opening ceremony, hence the drinking spree which Jakob was so anxious to join in.

After they left, I went for a walk to try and walk my pain off and it came out nice and warm. I soon got into a bath of perspiration but the pain was there all the time and gave me sundry jabs and I gave sundry grunts and on returning to the house I decided to get to bed. The priest's wife and sister were very kind and wanted me to eat something but I would not, thinking a starving cure would be good, so they gave me a teaspoonful of opium. I tried to stretch myself out but could not, so wound up in a ball in the corner of the bed and at last fell asleep. Anyhow, it was dark the next thing I remember and I was awakened by a fearful stab, so I get up, take more quinine and rub more embrocation in but all no good. At 8am, August 24th, Síra Jón comes in to enquire so I give a ghastly smile and a squirm. He then said he had

---

[23] Properly called the Telegraph Construction and Maintenance Company Ltd. The laying of this cable enabled the Marconi Company's rival, the Great Northern Telegraph Company, to connect their stations at Tórshavn and Seyðisfjörður, allowing mainland Europe and Britain to communicate with Iceland via the Faroe and Shetland Islands.

asked the doctor at Eskifjörður what he thought it was and he said 'flatulemery' and had sent me a bottle of peppermint water. I take some of this but will not eat but starved all day. As the pain had now become unbearable, I asked Síra Jón to send off a man to fetch the doctor from Eskifjörður as I was really now beginning to think it was pleurisy. Sundry visits from the family, all day in and out, and so whilst waiting for the doctor, I 'ejaculated'. It takes about five hours there and five hours back, and an hour to get doctor ready, so at 10pm began to expect him or the boy with the message but nothing came, and so I get another teaspoonful of opium and fell off to sleep only to awake at 3am, August 25th, by a steam whistling which proved to be the *Kong Inge* outward bound, but as I had written and posted all my letters, I had nothing to do with her. She sailed again at 8am.

I fancied I was a little easier when the priest came in but would not eat anything. At 10am, the man came back from Eskifjörður without the doctor, who he said was ill himself and could not undertake the journey. 'Lazy' I expect was the name of his attack. So what was to be done now? I pictured all sorts of things and told Síra Jón that if I died I was to be pickled in a barrel and sent to England which he solemnly promised to do. But I was decidedly much better, which I attributed to not eating anything and from that I thought, as I had no fever, that it must be 'liver', the good things that Guðný had made for me and the two days indoors. Stuffing three times a day with sundry coffees in between was more than 'Little Mary' could stand, especially as I had been accustomed to two meagre meals per day and much exercise, but it was no joke, the stabbing pain and the grind and twist it gave on every moment.

The *Prospero* should have been in ere this but to our surprise the *Mjolnir* arrived from Copenhagen at 4pm, and on board her was a doctor called Jónas Jónsson, a young fellow who has a district up in the country and he had been out doing a round of Danish hospitals. As soon as Síra Jón heard, he sent off on board and got him onshore and he came and had a look at me, made the usual examination, tapped etc., then said it was a congested liver. I asked him if it was dangerous to go aboard *Mjolnir* and go to Seyðisfjörður, as I would prefer to be in hospital there than in a private house, and he said, 'No not at all, only keep yourself warm.' So I dressed whilst he had coffee, packed up my few traps and went off with him after thanking the household for their kindness. I am coming back here again in September so did not make any final farewell.

Left in *Mjolnir* 6pm and got to Mjóifjörður 7pm. Left again 8pm and arrived at Seyðisfjörður at 10.30pm. Found the *Vesta* at the quay so we had to let go anchor away from the pier. After waiting a long time a boat came off enquiring if we were the *Islands Falk*, as she had not yet arrived. This man gave us all the latest information and said that owing to the minister not arriving, the sýslumaður had sent the congratulatory message to the King of Denmark but no answer had been received, and they had at 5pm sent another but that the reply was that the king was dining, so they sent back to say they were dining also. Anyhow, they were having a fine spree onshore according to this man's account. As it was raining heavily, I decided to remain on board and so did the doctor. He gave me some medicine and I turned in and, for a wonder, slept until seven o'clock.

August 26th

The boat came to the quay. I dressed and went ashore but it might have been a town of the dead, not a soul to be seen, and up at the Hotel Seyðisfjörður only a very sleepy-eyed girl and she told me they had all just gone to bed. I asked for some bread and butter, got that, and as my room was occupied, I laid down on the sofa and had a snooze but I was feeling very, very miserable, feeling like a washed out egg, seeing I had had no food for so many days. The medicine the doctor gave me did some good and although the pain was still acute it was much better than yesterday.

When the people began to stir, I went to the post office and got a whole budget of letters, some two months old which had been following me around and I finally got them here. At 1pm I got some breakfast, boiled fish and boiled eggs, and felt much better, especially as the weather was fining off. At 4pm the *Islands Falk* was seen entering the fjord and anchored, hoisting all her flags and of course too late, but the minister went on shore and sent off his telegram and several he had brought from Reykjavík. The man-of-war had been delayed by bad weather, 24 hours in the Westman Islands. She is only a small boat and is more like a tramp steamer of 300 tons than a smart gun boat. She is employed here on coastguard duty watching the foreign trawlers do not fish inside the home waters and is around with one quick firing gun in order to intimidate the poachers. With her came more delayed letters from Reykjavík so had a nice lot today, together with my delayed newspapers from Vopnafjörður.

Fine evening and the farmers with their wives and sweethearts get ready to start for home and a very fine set of men some of these peasants are, over six feet high, about 30 to 35 years old, long hair, big-boned, straight-limbed, fine, manly specimens. I can see now that the men we see in the trading stations are the weeds who are too lazy and not strong enough to work in the country. Very fine men indeed, but clumsy. The women were small as a rule and rather plain. Some two or three hundred of them made their departure during the evening, whilst the town boys and girls adjourned to the Good Templar house and town hall and had a dance. I could hear them up to midnight, stump, stump, to the squeak of an accordion, dancing away, as the hall is just outside my hotel windows.

At 7am, August 27th, I woke up by the sun streaming in on my head. It makes its appearance at that time over the tops of the mountains right opposite our windows. As there was a white hoar frost all over the ground and our iron roof, it was wonderful how in five minutes it melted and drip, drip, made one think it was raining, instead of which it was the most lovely morning anyone could wish to see, quite calm, not a cloud in the sky, a lovely May morning. Got up and went out to bask in the sun and the course of medicine had made a decided improvement. I felt really all right but still there was a stab now and then when I took liberties and wanted to be a frisky lamb. Went to the telegraph office, sent off a couple of telegrams,[24] had a good breakfast of boiled trout, of which there was a plentiful supply as the town authorities had, in order to get a supply for their spree, fished the stream by a net drawn by two ponies on each bank upstream and so

---

[24] Pike sent a message to his mother in Teignmouth. It read, 'All's well, Pike.' It was the first telegram sent from Iceland to England.

got over two hundred fine fish. Walked about and then, feeling tired, wrote letters for the rest of the day.

August 28th

Very fine still, nice morning the same as yesterday. Awoke by the *Islands Falk* firing a salute, making the hills rattle and echo. One could hear it for quite a time after, answering from side to side. The Icelanders call it 'bergmál' or mountain language. Now feeling nearly all right so sent Jakob off for the horses to go out to Vestdalseyri to see about my man there, hoping the shaking up will quite make me all right again. After breakfast, he comes with them and I was delighted to see Blackie was all right again, or at least did not seem lame, so I saddled him for a trial run, two couples together, and we clatter off at a good rate.

On arriving at Vestdalseyri found my man was doing all right and, as Blackie and I were all right, decided I would go further on as it was such a lovely day and do the climb up from the shore at Dvergasteinn to the top of the mountain on the road to Borgarfjörður and see if I could not take a few photos of the road. Although this is not so bad a track as from Borgarfjörður, still it's rough enough to give some sort of idea what it's like and what a worse one would be like.

Síra Jón Guðmundsson came in here today from Norðfjörður. He has to attend a county council meeting and reports all fishing well at Norðfjörður. There came also a crew of the Norwegian steamer *Rapid* of Haugesund by a Faroese fishing cutter, having been rescued from the steamer which was stranded on the north side of Langanes four days since in a thick fog. She was loaded with salt herrings in barrels for Norway from Øfjord[25] and on hearing this Wathne dispatched his steamer *Prospero* at once up there to see if he could salve any of the cargo. Much better this evening, pain nearly gone.

August 29th

Another very fine day, Seyðisfjörður fishing motors coming in full of fish. This is the best night's fishing they have had here since end of

---

[25] The Danish name for Eyjafjörður.

June, one boat having got a thousand fish, which would weigh about five tons. Great excitement and boat owners going about with smiling faces stretched out a foot each side. Towards evening a fog began to grow and at nightfall was so thick that it was impossible to see the houses opposite, but nice and calm and not at all cold, just pleasant. We are still being fed with scraps from the Great Feast and have a sort of brown Irish stew for breakfast and dinner and cold for supper, a gruesome mess, and as one finds ends of German sausages here and there, it makes a sort of impression the stew is composed of plate scrapings, which destroys the appetite.

August 30th

Fog risen but hangs a heavy, wet blanket half up the mountain and dripping with rain but calm. A beautiful three-masted auxiliary steam yacht came in this morning. She had been bought from Southampton this spring by Norwegians to be used for herring fishing. She is called *Fulmar* and is quite as large and sightly a craft as Lord Brassey's *Sunbeam*,[26] but the Norwegians have taken off the yards from the foremast and she looks dilapidated and dirty. They gave £900; she must have cost in building at least £10,000. It's like putting the Derby winner in a scavenger cart. Spend the day writing and getting the stock which is accumulated here in the store and at Norðfjörður insured against fire. In the evening went to the river to try for trout. I got nothing but my friend the chemist (apótekari) got three very nice fish.

August 31st

Over clouded and a breeze from the north so suppose it will soon be bad weather again. Towards middle of the day it cleared off a little and I have a try again at trout fishing. Got seven little ones which we have fried for supper. Very cold towards night and a film of ice on the ponds.

---

[26] The luxury schooner *Sunbeam* was famous for long distance ocean cruising, taking Lord and Lady Brassey around the world.

September 1ˢᵗ

A most beautiful day. Went walking out to Vestdalseyri and after dinner the *Prospero* came in from her salvage expedition to the wreck of the *Rapid*, she got 800 barrels of herrings. In the evening a motor boat came to fetch Síra Jón but it's bitterly cold and the man in the boat says there is a north gale outside.

September 2ⁿᵈ

A most horrible day, gale of wind, heavy driving rain, sit all day shivering with great overcoat on and fur hat indoors. I was in hopes the hotelkeeper would light a stove but he does not offer to do so, but gave us beef for dinner, for which I was grateful and had a good gorge as we only had a cold breakfast. Go to bed directly after supper which is also cold. Pain in the side still there, I don't seem to get rid of it in a hurry. It wakes me up in the night so suppose the congestion is still there.

September 3ʳᵈ

Rather brighter morning but as the day went on it clouded over and rain came on so it's as cold and miserable as ever. My friend the chemist got hauled up before the sýslumaður today for slander. A man here who runs the tannery is often pressed for money and comes to the apótekari for a short loan. In consequence, the apótekari thought he had a right to hint to the tanner that his daughter was out often late at night with one of the sons of the shopkeeper here. The tanner retold this at his home and the young fellow came to challenge the apótekari, and so both got angry and the apótekari said before witnesses that which was best unsaid. So, Iceland for the Icelanders, the apótekari (who is a Dane) got fined one hundred krónur and the boy promptly got drunk on the strength of it. As I point out to the apótekari, Icelanders are one large family and they will slander and backbite each other to any extent, but only let a foreigner chip in and then he gets the whole family on him. Although there is no doubt the apótekari said what was true, he in any case, when it came to law, would have to (and did have to) pay the piper. I hope it will be a lesson to him not to interfere in the doings and the morality of the Icelanders.

The chief of the Norwegian engineers who are setting up the tele-graph posts and wire came in today and says that last night he was in the tent on Smjörfjöll heiði and snow fell six feet deep. The tent got full of drift snow, but he was in a sleeping bag. The snow was so dry that it could easily be brushed off his bag but outside it was all a dreary waste. I asked him if he did not think of Nansen[27] when he awoke to find his bed all over snow. He laughed and said, 'Oh no, I thought of myself only.' He reports the line all connected up to Vopnafjörður and hopes it will all be finished by the 15th of September so he can get back to Norway, out of such a bleak, bare, blizzardly barren country. In coming over the heiði, the wind was so great as to split his oilskin up the back and so he was dripping wet through and glad to come in and get a change.

This morning, I tried to take a couple of photos of the fog and clouds on the mountains but, owing to the pneumatic arrangement of my camera having become deranged in March last on *Vesta*, I had to use the trigger and the results are bad, all shaken so I shall not be able to use plates. The films are fairly good and do not show signs of shake out, only under exposed, but all the plates show the shake of the trigger as you will see in all of them which I have taken on plates. These today I took on a stand and was very careful but the results are all the same, 'all shake'.

My man at Vestdalseyri reports the stuff coming in slowly and he has got five tons whereas by this time fifty tons should have been stored ready for shipment, but it's all going to my competitor, which is only to be expected seeing he is giving a higher price than I authorised to do. 'Couchon lavez' today for dinner, consequently I am a bit hungry and it's bitterly cold, great coat on indoors.

September 4th

Rather finer day, just a glimpse now and then of the sun but towards evening rains sets in again. It has not been so cold today. This morning a man came in from Borgarfjörður, a little merchant there called Helgi

---

27 Norwegian explorer Fridtjof Nansen had undertaken his famous North Pole expedition ten years previously.

Björnsson. He is buying in opposition to Þorsteinn Jónsson and has a fair quantity of fish. As the Faroese fishermen are leaving this week, he thought to steal a march on Þorsteinn and came to me for an advance of money so he could buy up as much as he could lay hands on, especially as he would be able to show the money to the Faroese, so I bundled Jakob off with a supply of needful and he and Helgi left at 12 noon. I hope this will lead to some business being done there. If any is obtained Jakob will weigh it up and pack in hundred pound bundles and ship it in the first steamer that will call there but that is uncertain as both of Wathne boats, the *Prospero* and *Egil*, are off their advertised route. Instead of just coming in from Europe, they are just going out, and both of them are here now taking in coal and both loaded with herrings from Siglufjörður and Øfjord in the north where there has been an enormous catch of herrings. One captain told me there were 180 Norwegian small steamers in Siglufjörður three weeks ago and they had taken big catches, so Wathne's boats have snatched the opportunity to load out with full cargoes. Herring pay a good freight so they have let the regular traffic slide.

September 5th

Rain. Rain. Nothing but rain all day but it's quite calm and not so cold so can dispense with the overcoat. Spend the day writing outward letters as the mail boat *Laura* will be here soon now, bound out.

September 6th

Rain and calm. Hear today that the *Laura* will not come but the *Thyra* has been put in her stead. She is a very old and slow boat and one cannot ever know when she will arrive, consequence is that some fifty Faroese fishermen have agreed with a Norwegian herring fisher to take them home to Faroe at twelve krónur a head and left that morning. I am anxious to get letters from Ísafjörður to know if the vessel *Elise* I have sent for is on the way.

September 7th

Rain but calm, consequently not so cold. *Thyra* came towards the evening and I thought to have received letters from Ísafjörður about *Elise* but no, there was not a word about it, only one letter from Vopnafjörður, so now I am quite in the dark. It's very annoying and disappointing especially as my two men, Sigurður Haflíðason and Jóhannes Pétursson, both are what may be called dependable men but there it is. This place is full of disappointments and very few agreeable surprises to make up the balance.

On board *Thyra*, I had a very long talk with a man from Glasgow, a Mr John S. Boyle, a herring curer and fish salesman there. He has been at Øfjord with four steam drifters and a cargo steamer and a large barque used as a store ship. He has been fishing there for herrings since July and has done as well as he could expect for the first trial, but he had a lot of trouble with his crews just as I had when at Hafnarfjörður. He might have done better could he have controlled them but he, like myself, found that the men considered it a picnic spree instead of hard work and he was up night and day superintending even the smallest detail. He says he began life as a trawler boy and has worked all his life until he is now 57 years old, but never in all his career has he had such a stiff time of it as now and was glad when the season was over that he could get back to civilisation. He said he had heard about me and was glad of the opportunity to compare notes with me. He has got together, he thinks, enough herrings to pay expenses, that is if they sell at average price, but this he will not know until about middle of November.

There was also on board a gentleman and his servant who had been to survey a river near Húsavík which has a big reputation as a salmon river. He had been fishing this summer in the accustomed salmon rivers near Reykjavík and had heard of this lovely river here in the north so made an expedition to see if it was as represented. Of course, as usual, everything was exaggerated. He found that it had been netted and trapped to such an extent for a number of years that it was almost useless, and there was such a number of wild ducks on it that he was sure they downed all the new spawn and that, as usual, the Icelander was asking such a fabulous price for the fishing that it could not be entertained.

Whilst at a farm on the river, he was opening a tin of jam with a clasped fishing knife when the blade closed on his fingers and nearly severed the forefinger and deeply cut the other two, so that before the bleeding could be stopped he fainted. As his guide and interpreter of course was not on the spot, he could not give the people any instructions what to do to stop the bleeding, although he is an army officer and has gone through the usual course of ambulance training. As it was his right hand, he could not do it himself in time before he fainted, but after he was senseless the women bound it tightly and sent off for the doctor. He came after 36 hours and dressed it but there was danger of blood poisoning so he had to remain there for two weeks and keep the doctor with him, as there was every evidence that the wound might mortify and he would have been compelled to have his hand amputated. Fortunately, the worst fears were not realised and he recovered sufficiently to be able to get back to England with the *Thyra*, but it was a very narrow squeak.

Strangely enough, his man-servant heard me say I came from Devonshire and enquired of me what town, so I told him and it appears that his mother comes from Teignmouth, although he had never been there. She was called 'Pound' and I think I remember in my very young days there was a family by that name there of working people, and they had a son who was a telegraph message boy, but they must have all emigrated a long time since. Anyhow, there is a street there called Pound Street or Pound Lane.

September 8th

Still cloudy and occasional rain but not cold. *Thyra* left after midday with mails so hope all will soon have my letters.

September 9th

Cloudy morning but towards the middle of the day the fog and clouds rolled away and it made a most lovely evening. The moon rising over the entrance to the fjord lighted up the black, forbidding-looking mountains and a track of fire on the still, mirror-like water with not a ripple on the surface, and all looking so peaceful and calm, like a trans-formation scene in a pantomime. It had every appearance of a frosty night, but towards morning it clouded over again and September 10th came out dull as ever but still calm, but towards the middle of the day blew up to a gale from the south-west. One could hardly imagine the peaceful scene of last night when looking out on the fjord to see the wicked gusts of wind whipping up the water into spouts and howling as it whistled around the corner of the house, shaking it to its very foundations.

The Norwegian engineer left this morning for his final journey here to Reykjavík, making an inspection of the poles and wires as he goes. He will take about twenty days to do the journey and has made in all six trips this summer here and back, so he will have had enough pony riding for one year when it is all finished. He tells me that they are nearly all linked up and hopes to be able to telegraph to Reykjavík next week.

September 11th

Last night in the gale, a strange thing happened. Suddenly it became calm, the clouds rolled away, the moon came up and a warm air came from the south-west over the land and it became really sultry, so much so that the thermometer rose from nearly freezing point to 60 degrees of heat. So it continued all the night and when the sun rose at 7am over the hills, one might have imagined it to be a spring morning in England. A most lovely day it proved to be, not a cloud in the sky, quite calm and the heat was very oppressive and relaxing. The thermometer rose to 70 degrees of heat in the sun. I have never seen it so high here before.

I had rather a busy day and bought 80 tons of fish from one and the other, quite a field day. It all came so unexpected but the reason of it was the small merchants had become tightened for money and I was the quickest and safest outlet, so one came to try and as soon as he succeeded I was soon overwhelmed with clients. Jakob also returned from Borgarfjörður with requests for money. I am rather pleased as I think I have secured the principal man who has been giving me a lot of trouble in competing with me and will be the means of getting rid of the competition and lowering the price from this date. Anyhow, he sent off a messenger to Norðfjörður to stop his agent there from buying any more, so there is one good result from today's work.

September 12th

Alas! The clouds have gathered over us again and the wind is from the sea, cold and chilly after yesterday's glimpse of summer weather. I get today my first cablegram from Exeter. You will see by the number the enormous business this cable brings to the island. It is now 18 days since it was opened and the number is 76 up to date! Olsen lives at Patreksfjörður and it will take six weeks for me to send to him, so I do not see what good the news is to me here.[28] It may have been sent by letter from England direct to Patreksfjörður and got there sooner than via here.

A violent storm all day and in the evening much rain and, for the first time I have ever been in the island, I saw lightning and heard thunder. I have often asked about it, as I thought perhaps in these high latitudes it might be unknown, but it's very seldom as you might guess, seeing this is my first experience. The echoes were tremendous and reverberated back and forwards echo after echo. The chemist had a birthday party and gave a lovely supper, to which I was invited. The eating was prolonged for three hours and then the steady drinking until 2am, at which time I left. The party was mostly Danes, the telegraph operators and three Icelanders.

September 13th

Still stormy but as the wind is south-westerly, it's not cold but furious gusts with heavy rain and squalls. The chemist goes this afternoon on a shooting trip with a Dane called Hørring[29] who is here as government naturalist and is making a tour of the Islands shooting and classifying birds. He came up last year and I met him on board the *Vesta*, very nice fellow but he does not talk English. He is engaged for three years, this

---

28 The telegram, dated 11th September 1906, reads, 'Have paid Olsen's balance, sixty five.'

29 Believed to be Richard Hørring (1875–1943) whose collections of Icelandic birds are now held at the Natural History Museum of Denmark.

is his second. He came now from Reykjavík via Øfjord and will return via the south coast. He has eight ponies with him and one man to look after them. The chemist will accompany him for two days out and return here again but Hørring will get, with luck, to Reykjavík in about 3 weeks' time. I am thinking he has put it off too long for the back trip southwards as there are many glacier rivers to cross there and no bridges, but it's in his programme and he is a good, lusty, strong fellow, about 30 years old, so suppose he will struggle through all right. His journal must be very interesting, seeing he will be about four months in the saddle.

Anyhow, he and the chemist have got a nice start this afternoon, blowing a hurricane and rain, so much so the whole staff of telegraph engineers are busy repairing the wires between here and Egilsstaðir which have blown down during the night and today. One of the tele-graph people tells me the copper used in the wires is too hard and too much alloyed so they will not bear the strain and even now, although not all connected up, there are constant breaks and repairs. This is owing to using a cheaper material than should be used and will cause no end of expense and will necessitate the renewing with best copper wires before next year, a question of penny wise and pound foolish, as is the usual Icelandic policy, everything on the cheap, but in this case cheap is dear.

September 14th

Fine morning but came on to rain after midday. Last night something went wrong with the fellows staying here in the hotel, for they all got firmly intoxicated. One man who has just passed his examinations as a priest and is here looking out for a vacancy got very uproarious, began singing and shouting and finally kicked up a fine shindy and was, with great difficulty, got to bed with the help of the others, who also were drunk, a case of the blind leading the blind. After they had got him in bed, he got up again and went out in the rain strip stark naked and had to be chivvied in again. It was a case of the greasy pig at a regatta, nothing to hold onto except his hair, and I saw one chap tugging away at that as they dragged and pushed him up the stairs. It was one o'clock before the house got quiet again. This morning he was very subdued and sheepish. It seemed hardly possible that this intellectual fellow with a clear face and head, and quite gentlemanly-looking, should have been the drunken beast of last night.

We have also here a Danish captain of the Navy who is retired on half pay and is the superintendent of the Danish Fishermen's Society. He is here to enquire about fishing places so that the Danes can come here now they have motor boats for two or three months in the summer to fish cod. He and I have become great pals, talking about future prospects etc. This morning, he had his first go at a whale but it didn't go well. After the first two or three mouthfuls, he had to give it up but, as I tell him, a week here will put that all right and he will be able to go at his lump as well as I can. Spent the best part of the day in the Co-operative Society's stores looking after the repacking and salting of fish which I have bought through the Society, and which will be stored here in a salted state until the spring of 1907.

September 15th

Rain but calm. Went in motor boat to Brimnes to look at some fish. This is about two hours' journey to the mouth of the fjord and only get-at-able by boat. Got back to supper, after which, just as we were going to bed, there came a motor boat from Borgarfjörður with six girls and eight men all like drowned rats. They wanted a place in the hotel but only four girls could get a bed. Where the other poor things held out, I don't know. However it is these people do not die with exposure, I don't know. Six hours in a boat, dripping wet, cold and seasick and they come here on a pleasure trip for Sunday!

September 16th

Rather fine day but heavy fog. Go out again in motor boat to Seljanes at the northern end of the fjord, opposite to Brimnes, also to look at some more stuff but got back by 4pm to dinner. I hurried up as I saw a sheep being killed yesterday and so, as this Danish captain is here, we shall have new mutton for the first time this year. These last few days it has not been cold, that is for here, as the thermometer stands at about 45 degrees, about the same as a mild winter's day with us in England. Very nice dinner, I should have made some folks stare at the quantity of fresh mutton I put away, and we had blancmange with strawberry jam and dessert after of some wind-blown apples and coffee. A regular red letter day, especially as close after dinner the *Kong Inge* came in and brought the English mails so I had the pleasure of reading all home news, which were satisfactory and I was glad to hear all were well and enjoying their summer. I see the papers complain of the heat; we could do with a little of it here. Towards evening a fresh breeze sprung up and made it bitterly cold again.

On board *Kong Inge* was my old friend Mrs Anna Stephensen, sister-in-law to the old governor, Magnús Stephensen (of Hall Caine's *Prodigal Son*). She was returning from Copenhagen where she had been since June, having gone there with her foster daughter, Marie, who had been very ill all winter in Reykjavík, first with typhoid and after with pleurisy, so the doctors recommended her going to a warmer climate. She is now in a convalescent home in Denmark but Mrs Stephensen wishes to come to the south of England next winter so I recommended Torquay, and I expect they will write to me when I get back in November.

With *Kong Inge* came a huge bale of hessian stuff for packing fish in, so I got the captain to call into Vopnafjörður with it where it can be sent over the mountains on pack ponies to Bakkafjörður. There the fish will be packed in hundred pound bales in readiness for the *Kong Inge* to call there on her return voyage, so I am getting out of the mess caused by the non-arrival of the schooner *Rose*, but it will cost a heap of money which might have been well saved if only my instructions had been carried out.

September 17th

Fine, bright day but fresh wind so everyone is delighted and fish is spread out in all directions to dry. *Kong Inge* left last night and took our Danish captain, or admiral or whatever he is, with her and so that this morning we sank back into our old routine and had boiled cod heads with the mouths stuffed with cod liver, the usual plate of whale, and all the other unsavoury dishes which are the accustomed Icelandic spread.

A motor boat comes from Norðfjörður from the vicar asking for money, so he must be getting a good lot of stuff together, and it looks like as if the vessel which I expect from Ísafjörður (if she comes, which I doubt) will have a full cargo. I cannot understand why my men at Ísafjörður have not sent me a letter about that vessel, but I suppose it's like the man who lived in America and had a brother in Iceland and never wrote to each other and the reason given was, 'He knows he's all right and I know I am all right, so what's the use of writing and spending money on postage stamps?' So I suppose my fellows know where they are and they know where I am, and I know also where I am, and so they just let it rest at that, but it's very annoying to be kept in the dark as to the whereabouts of the vessel and if she is coming or not.

My friend the chemist returned from his shooting expedition. He got one duck for his trouble and that he ate in the farm of Egilsstaðir for his supper. Had a shot at a falcon but too far off, and so ends <u>his</u> summer's holidays.

Just as I thought! For now the Danish captain is gone, we get regaled with the horrible messes the natives delight in at this time of the year. Now begins the slaughter time for the sheep and everyone revels in blood. We had for dinner today blood pudding, and the water it was boiled in was served up as soup. I fished out half a boiled heart and with potatoes managed to squeeze through, but it was a most revolting mess, that is to us English, but the way the ladies and gentlemen who grace our festive board stowed the disgusting stuff away was enough to make a pig stand aghast. They simply gorged themselves and wallowed in the soup. Thank goodness there were pancakes for the after part of the meal. I wonder what we shall have dished up for tomorrow.

We have a relative of the hotelkeeper staying with us from Akureyri. She is a lively young party, about eighteen or nineteen years of age but a thin, consumptive, anaemic girl, but she keeps the place alive, being a sort of actress in an immature way, and has a string of young fellows always at her beck and call. She leaves next week for home by the *Ceres*. We have part singing every evening and our future priest makes the lamp glasses ring with his bellowing, and in between songs Hilda gives recitations and parts of Icelandic plays. She is far from shy but I think she will die in the winter as she had pleurisy last winter and complications. The doctors have told her in as many words she ought to go to a warmer climate for the coming winter, but she is a self-willed girl and will, like all Icelandic young people, have her own way were though she dies for it. She says she would rather die in her motherland than in a foreign country, and meanwhile she is determined to get as much out of her existence as is possible up here. She has never been in church since she was confirmed, except of course to a wedding, so has no religious thoughts which is, as I have said before, very common with the people here.

We hear the *Vesta* has arrived at Eskifjörður this evening and she will be here tomorrow with the latest news from England.

September 18th

Foggy with occasional showers. SS *Vesta* came in at noon and had letters on board but as she followed so quickly the *Kong Inge*, I did not get any papers, only one home letter but of course I could not expect more. Only one English tourist on board, a Regent Street, London, shopkeeper travelling for his health. He has tuberculosis in his throat and thought the cold dry air here would do him good, but from his appearance I should say he will soon have a wooden overcoat. From him I heard the result of the Cambridge Holland boat race and was very pleased to hear England won. Had supper on board and she left again at midnight for Reykjavík.

September 19th

Very fine day, bright sunshine, warm air, one of the best days for the whole year. Got the ponies and went out to Dvergasteinn to look at some fish. Had negotiations with a small merchant but think the business will fall through as he has got a letter by *Vesta* telling him the price our company had given for a parcel in Leith, consequently he would rather ship on his own speculation than sell here. Had boiled blood pudding for dinner with the water they were boiled in for soup and I jibbed and had bread and cheese.

September 20th

Another extra fine day. Rode out to Hánefsstaðaeyri to look at some more fish which was ready for shipment. I really do not know what is best to do with this stuff I am collecting together, as I can get no news of the vessel to take it to Exeter and I am afraid to pack it up in bagging as that will make it more costly if the vessel does arrive, and if I do not pack it up it deteriorates. I shall not be able to ship it until end of October as all the steamers are upward-bound now and will not return south for some weeks. It's very puzzling.

The farmers are now driving their fat sheep into the town for slaughtering, hundreds of them coming in every day now. They are killed in the open, hung up on nails to dry and, when cold, cut up and salted in barrels for either export to Norway or home consumption.

At 9pm a motor boat came in from Norðfjörður, bringing the welcome news of the arrival there of the little Norwegian vessel *Elise* with my man Sigurður Haflðason on board. He was nine days from Ísafjörður and had commenced loading that morning, so I sent instructions for him to continue loadings so as to take advantage of this fine weather. I must remain here until the *Prospero* arrives, so as to arrange the shipping and unshipping of any parcels he has on board and get the whole into Norðfjörður and put on board the *Elise* there to save the expense of unloading and reloading here.

The Northern Lights were brilliant tonight, lighting up the heavens as if a bright moonlight night. The weather was gloriously fine and the fjord like glass reflecting the Lights, but at the same time cold (about five degrees of frost) and on September 21st, early in the morning, the fjord was sheeted with thin ice. I made arrangements for Jakob to go at once to Bakkafjörður to hurry up my man there and to see he shipped all the fish he had in stock on board the *Kong Inge* so as to get it to Norðfjörður for the *Elise*. I tried to hire a small steamer but of course he had something else to do that day, but would do it next week. I would not wait for that, so dispatched Jakob with three horses so he can hurry up. I expect he will get there in three days and I hope will succeed in getting the lot shipped. Jakob telegraphed the arrival of the vessel to Exeter.

September 22nd

Also a very nice, fine day, quite summer-like, but the fjord is covered with thin ice which makes it bad for the motor boats as they crash through the glass-like sheets, for it cuts like a knife and soon eats through the soft wood planks, so all are busy nailing iron plates over their bows. At 11am, we get a telephone message from Eskifjörður to say the *Ceres* had arrived there and left again so that at 4pm she came in here and brought mails, which were of course very meagre now, seeing all the boats have come a day or so after each other, and there will be nothing more to come for a whole month.

Went on board *Ceres*, had a yarn with the captain about his stranding in the summer at Faroes. The vessel went full speed against a wall of rock and smashed her forefoot in, but as it was in the ballast tank no water came into her holds. In less than ten minutes all the boats were out and the passengers in them, 89 people in all, and had to remain for one and a half hours until it was found the vessel had not received dangerous damage. Reshipped passengers and boats, returned to Tórshavn and sent them on shore there until the *Laura* came up. A salvage boat was sent from Denmark to accompany *Ceres* back. They got to Copenhagen under their own steam all right but the repairs took a long time. Captain says all were exonerated from blame in the enquiry and all passed off all right. He attributed the disaster to the strong tide setting the vessel broadside land-ways. As the channel here is only about two miles broad, he was steering a course right in the middle but hit one side instead. It was calm sea, no wind but dense fog. The vessel looks quite smart, all fresh painted and scraped up after her repairs. Had some dessert on board (pears, plums and bananas) and supper in the evening. Only one first class passenger, an Icelander for Øfjord. Our lively lass Hilda returns to Øfjord with this boat.

September 23rd

Weather still holding fine but a fresh wind and the sun is getting a sort of misty veil over it in lieu of the clear blue sky, so suppose we shall soon be having our old friend bad weather with us again. No news of *Prospero* although it was some days since she left Øfjord on return voyage. I am getting anxious now to get into Norðfjörður as I expect the *Elise* will have got most of her cargo on board. Very alarming news from Exeter about the Labrador fishing, quite a failure and vessels returning empty, so their policy of hold back here is also a mistake and instead of 'Bearing' I should have bought all I could lay hands on, but now it's 'Too Late'. This is the third year of 'Mistakes'.

September 24th

As I thought! Today, and in fact all night, was a violent gale of wind. Terrific gusts strike the house and seem to try to tear it up by the roots, but these houses are different from the Reykjavík houses. There they use frameworks with loads of paper nailed over them but here they are built with three-inch planks set on edge and morticed at the ends and firmly screwed together so that they are as solid as a ship. In fact, the church at Vestdalseyri, being so built but empty and consequently light in weight, a gust of wind tore it up from its foundations, completely capsized it and it fell some hundred yards away and pitched upright again. There they have let it remain on the flat. The spire of course was destroyed and the whole structure shaken up a great deal, but it retained its shape. That was some ten years since, so that when a gust extra to the others shakes the house, one imagines it being capsized, bottom up, and all the people inside (oneself amongst them) crawling out over the bottom like bees out of a capsized beehive.

The gusts seem to come straight down and when they strike the water of the fjord, it's just like a big rock had been cast into it. It does not travel fast but seems to come straight down, whop! One of the most curious things about it is that for one half hour now and then a quite warm blast comes along, making the thermometer fly up to 45 or 50 degrees, and then quite as suddenly all the rest of the day an icy cold wind with eight to ten degrees of frost. They say here that it often happens in January and February, the warm blast, but it's always in a gale.

Yesterday I was at the chemist's. He can only supply spirits on a doctor's recipe, and a man came in with one pasted on a piece of card, quite dirty and almost obliterated, but he got his bottle of fire water and the paper handed back to him again. In about five minutes another countryman appeared with a ditto paper and he got his bottle, and then another came. My curiosity was aroused, so I examined the paper and saw it was given out in July 1905, more than twelve months since. On enquiring, the chemist laughed and said, 'Oh yes, it makes no difference to me, it's a doctor's recipe and they have the right to keep it, just as you do in England.' You get the recipe from the doctor, go to the chemist to get your medicine and keep the paper for future use. They do the same here and hand it around to each other until it's worn out. It cost two krónur (two shillings and sixpence) to get a recipe from the doctor. It put me in mind of Mark Twain's story of how he was once in a whiskey-forbidden state and came in the evening to the hotel where he was stopping and asked, as he was tired, for a whisky and soda. He was told that it was not to be had in the hotel but that the chemist sold it. He went to the chemist and was told that whiskey was only supplied to a man who had been bitten by a snake. Mark asked where the snake was and was informed it was down the street. He enquired the number, knocked at the door and enquired of the man if he had a snake and was told yes he was the owner of one. 'Well' says Mark, 'I want to get bitten.' The owner gave a sickly smile and said very sorry he could not oblige Mark, and it was turning money away, but the fact was the snake was so tired of biting people all day he could not open his jaws anymore! So Mark had to do without his whiskey that night and so in all lands where a law is made, there is always a way to get around it and get what you want.

Bad day for the sheep today, everyone busy cutting throats and today is 'Gangnadagur' or 'Walking Day', in which all the farmers in each parish meet together and climb over the mountains and drive all their sheep and lambs into a particular valley where the sheep are penned and sorted and marked. They begin today and take nearly all the week to do it. Towards evening it fined off a bit and at 8pm, to my great surprise, Jakob Jónsson came riding in. He reports having been north and on arrival at Vopnafjörður found my man there had not forwarded the bale of packing to Bakkafjörður. He therefore at once hired a motor boat and went to that place and found Halldór Runólfsson taking things very easy. Although I had arranged and sent messages, he had done nothing and was waiting for the *Holar* in the middle of October to send on our fish, and here was I waiting with the sailing vessel for it. However, Jakob put some energy into him and he has promised to send about 16 tons by the *Kong Inge*. I am very annoyed as I quite expected 35 tons by the same boat, and even now I have doubts I shall get even the 15 tons. A very good man Halldór is, if one is with him all the time driving him on, but he does not stick to his promises and I find he put 35 tons of his own fish on board *Prospero* and let ours remain. Of course one cannot blame a man to look after himself, but at the same time he should fulfil his promises. It's all the same with these Icelanders, they cannot go straight. However good the man is, he requires constant watching, therefore I am always asking for a motor cutter so I can get around to all these agents unexpectedly and prick them up. I am very annoyed with him but what can I do? At midnight *Prospero* comes in here.

September 25th

Fine day but strong wind off the land, not cold. Get an unexpected letter from Vopnafjörður from a man there saying he is sending by *Kong Inge* about eight tons of fish, also one from Norðfjörður saying the *Elise* will be finishing taking in the stock from there but not stating the quantity and asking for instructions. I had already made arrangements to go in *Prospero* and she leaves tomorrow after breakfast so I shall go with her and I expect shall return here in the *Elise*. Later on in the day I altered my plans, thinking it best to remain here to meet the *Kong Inge* so as to stop the fish here. Sent a telephone message to Eskifjörður, and thence over the wires to Norðfjörður, to tell *Elise* to come in here immediately. I think by doing this I shall save time and be able to get the vessel off earlier from here than if I delayed her in Norðfjörður for my coming there.

September 26th

Very fine weather as regards warmth etc. It might be in the middle of summer, really quite sultry in the eye of the sun, but a most violent gale of wind is blowing and tearing everything up by the roots. Dust and small stones are hurled against one walking and when the gust strikes, it's hold on to anything or crouch down, so that walking out is impossible. It seems to tear the very coat off your back but it's warm, marvellously warm, and if we had had this in July what a blessing it would have been. The sun now gets over the tops of the hills about 9.30am and sets again at 4pm.

September 27th

Bitterly cold, fog over all, greatcoat on all day. The village is full of countrymen and sheep and mostly dogs. They howl all night, hundreds of them, I think there must be more dogs than sheep. The hotel is full of men who walk about all night, up and down the stairs, talk and sing and carry on finely.

September 28th

Still cold and raw and heavy fog all over. Clear up with Jakob and send him off to Borgarfjörður with all the ponies for their winter quarters. They will be fed and cared for there and given hay and corn so as to be fit to use in the spring if necessary, but the rule is to let the ponies feed as much as possible now until the snow comes and let them pick up moss by scraping the snow away with their hoof and eat seaweed on the shore all the winter. Consequently, when spring comes, they are all so thin and miserable and utterly unusable until July, so to be sure the ponies are ready when wanted, I get them fed with hay and corn in the winter and keep them fat.

Very miserably cold all day. I am cramped up like a bear with a sore head and have what my mother calls a 'Heavy Cold', sneezing and shivering. My friend the chemist prescribes a German innovation which is cotton wool saturated with a preparation and stuffed up the nostrils, which is certainly a great relief. All the people in the hotel are the same but no stove lit yet as it's not the date to light up, so at 6pm crawl to bed and try to get a little warmth.

September 29th

Still raw and cold. 'Heavy Cold' still on in its greatest force. Altogether a miserable day.

September 30th

Broke out fine this morning. Clear blue sky and summer weather again, and at noon Sigurður Haflíðason came in reporting the *Elise* in the fjord. He had been put on shore and had walked up here to let me know. He reports 60 on board, which is about half the vessel's cargo, and I expected at least 80 tons. In the afternoon the vessel gets into harbour and is moored alongside the town quay.

October 1st

At 6am, am awakened by a steamer hooting and dress quickly as I expect it is the *Kong Inge*, and sure enough it was. Hastening on board, I find that Halldór at Bakkafjörður and the man at Vopnafjörður had put the fish on board but had consigned it to Leith instead of here. Of course the captain of the steamer would not deliver to me here, but after negotiating (which meant paying full freight to Leith and a gratuity to Captain), I got the fish on the pier here. Find it's 22 tons from Halldór and five tons from Vopnafjörður, and as the steamer left again at 9am it was sharp work, as the negotiating took up most of the time. I had just time enough to close my letters and get them off. Away went the boat, being of course in a great hurry, being so late on its time-table. Got the *Elise* alongside the quay and loaded that lot into her and then got her back to another quay where I got 10 tons more in store. By getting the fish from *Kong Inge*, I saved the rail carriage from Leith to Exeter, which is great, but lost half in freight here to Leith. Very fine day and my 'Heavy Cold' is going.

Today I made a perfect 'ass' of myself. I bought a motor boat. I have been looking at it all the time I have been here, and as it was a petrol engine and started by electric batteries, of course it was always going wrong. The merchant who owns it had at last given it up in despair and offered it to me at a third of its cost. I in a weak moment offered him half of that, and today he came and said I could have it. It was new in July, boat and engine, but I suspect the engine has been damaged so shall unship it and send it to England by *Elise* and have it overhauled. At the same time I know quite now I have, as I said before, made myself a perfect ass and bought trouble.

I suppose I cannot help this madness at times, it is the result of my early education and the atmosphere I was schooled in at the 'academy' I finished in.[30] I passed six or seven years there from '65 to '72 and was officered by three brothers named Silvanus, Josiah and Caleb. Fancy being taught by men with such names? The chaplain of the school was their father, the Very Reverend Theophilus Allen, called by we boys 'Old Billy Goat' because of his white whiskers. All four were shining lights in the Congregational Chapel and I remember well the building of the new chapel. We boys were coached for three months beforehand to save our weekly monies for the great opening day 'bazaar'. To the last we were all <u>permitted</u> as a great treat to attend, for which purpose we were granted as a special favour a whole half holiday in order that we may be able (also with special permission and a great favour) to spend our savings, together with the result of our special monthly letter to our dear parents in which an intimation that the bazaar was to be held and asking for funds to assist.[31]

The whole school was really managed and generalled by the mother and wife of the three men and Old Billy Goat. She was called by us boys 'Old Curly', out of respect to two corkscrew curls that hung each side of her frowsy old cap. She was really the 'Boss' of the whole show and ruled all hands with a rod of iron. She it was who superintended the cutting up of the bread and butter and poured out of the big tin urn the mixture she called 'tea'. She it was who cut our slices of meat which came with great regularity: boiled beef on Mondays; cold boiled on Tuesdays; roast leg of mutton on Wednesdays; cold leg of mutton on Thursdays; hot hash on Fridays and cold cottage pie Saturdays. On Sundays was cold roast beef, but this was an extravagant joint and only indulged in on Sundays. I can see her commanding figure even now, with white apron and white sleeves around, with a three-foot long, sword-like blade, shaving off slices of meat as thin as wafers (looking on the plate about two pounds of meat but in reality two ounces), and her two curls shaking and dancing up and down and her commanding searching eye, all the time watching. The boys did not begin before all was served and then, at a rap by the handle of the knife on the table, all

---

30   Plantation House School, Dawlish, Devon.
31   The new chapel opened in 1871, when Pike was 15.

stood up and the chaplain said a long-winded grace, and at the word Amen we all sat down again and fell to. Woe to the boy who said yes when asked the question if he wanted more! It was the strict etiquette of Old Curly to ask the question of each boy, 'Will you have some more?' but he was expected by an unspoken law to say, 'No thank you Mrs Allen.' If, mind you a big IF, any unthinking or new boy said by chance, 'Yes please', the look of horror and disgust on the old girl's face was grand. The poor victim had to stand a running fire of ejaculations and set phrases from the old girl, remarks of how she was surprised at some boys' enormous appetites, and hoped he would not make himself ill, and the effects of overeating. Then the eyes of a hundred boys fixed on him all the time he was getting through his second half, and in the afternoon, if he should be behind in his lessons, one of the three brothers would sneer and say, 'Oh it can only be expected, such dullness from a boy who gorges', and many such remarks. That it was a lesson for life, or at least whilst at school.

At the age of sixteen, I left that school fully educated and with visions of being a 'Merchant Prince' or 'Lord Mayor of London' and all sorts of wonderful things. After a lapse of ten years, I revisited the scene of my scholastic days and on approaching the entrance gate, expecting to hear the joyous laugh and voices of the hundred boys who used to play in the back yard (which was called in the prospectus a 'spacious recreation ground'), I saw a big board on which was printed in black letters on a white ground, 'Lunatic Asylum'!

On making enquiries, I found that Silvanus had married a very beautiful wife, a confectioner's daughter from Clifton, and she used to serve in the shop there Bath buns etc. She was such a beautiful exterior but a regular fiend interior that when she entered the fold of lambs at the Academy, she wanted of course to take charge and oust Old Curly out. That occasioned rows and the consequence was the school gradually went down from a hundred boarders to three. The old people died from chagrin, the two unmarried brothers packed up and went off as missionaries, but what became of poor Silvanus I never knew. The whole affair was sold up and the property purchased by the

Wonford Asylum people as a seaside residence for their better class of inmates.[32]

It is curious looking back that over the 35 years since I left, out of the hundreds of boys who I must have met there, very few have come under my notice. One fellow called 'Lily' I came across a few years ago had married to a rich wife years older than himself. He had jibbed after a while and had joined the Roman Catholics, and was walking about with a shaved head, long, monk-brown, sack dressing gown, sandals on his feet and no stockings. Another I met wandering about the seafront looking as if he had lost a shilling and found a farthing, unmarried, and dealt in rags and bones and old scrap iron, and spent his leisure in picking up bits of paper on the point of his umbrella and pocketing the result. Another called me last year. He had been in America 'speculating' he said, and he looked it: a thin, cadaverous-looking chap and had come over to speculate on his friends. Another wanders about Exeter, I often see him dressed up like a monkey on a barrel organ. Another, a farmer's son, hanged himself. In all, I think I have come across some six or eight, and all are inoculated with the taint. I myself, instead of the Merchant Prince, I am up here 'Fish Buying', living in a tramp house at three shillings a night, feeding off dogs' meat (and not the best of that), and just by the skin of my teeth keeping out of Newton Abbot Workhouse, which I suppose I shall do until I bust like a ripe gooseberry, but as I said before, I cannot help making an ass of myself owing to my early training.

October 2nd

A most charming day, bright, calm, not too warm but with just enough sharpness in the air to make crisp. Got all my packages of fish on board the vessel and only want the little parcel at Vestdalseyri, but of course the man there is busy slaughtering and cannot attend to it today. These Icelanders are the perfection of 'Put Offs', everyone must wait their time but woe be to anyone who keeps them waiting! He says he will try to do it tomorrow and when tomorrow comes it's a gale of wind or

---

[32] Plantation House was taken over by the Wonford House Hospital for the Insane, based in Exeter.

something else turns up. They are! Well there! They are! Late in the evening, he turns up with a motor boat full of fish and we got on board and then had news that a couple of tons more would come from another man in the morning.

October 3rd

Another fine day and at last we got all the stuff on board the vessel. The crew then fastened up the hatches and prepared for sea. On reckoning up the total, found we had got 100 tons on board and as she only carries 110 tons, I was quite pleased with myself for having got together so much. I made out the bills of landing and cleared the vessel from sýslumaður or sherriff's office, Sigurður packed up his traps and came onshore, and all ready for a start in the morning. Wished Captain goodbye and so another stage of the year's work is reached. Right glad I am that I wriggled out of the hole I was in at August month, and so it's no good to meet troubles halfway but just take things as they come.

Late in the evening, a man from Borgarfjörður came in and said he had 20 to 25 tons already put up in bundles and packed for shipping. It was this parcel I have been after, for which I sent Jakob to Borgarfjörður to tweedle with. I had a sort of a hint yesterday that this man had to meet a bank draft for £250 tomorrow and so was prepared to meet his overtures. At the beginning of the negotiations, he opened with a very insinuating manner that Þorsteinn Jónsson had been trying to buy this parcel but he would much prefer to let me have it, as he did not like Þorsteinn. Now, Þorsteinn I knew was in a worse predicament for want of money than this Helgi was, so that cock did not fight. I was very off-handed and we had a confidential talk, and many compliments from each other to each other, he pressing forward, I drawing back, and so it see-sawed. Then he scribbled over a lot of paper with figures and I offered a low price, and came up inch by inch until a full stop, and then broke off negotiations until the morning of October 4th.

Another fine morning with just a little breeze out of the fjord, so *Elise* sailed away to Exeter and I wired to Exeter her sailing. After breakfast, Helgi turned up again, and with him Jón Stefánsson, and we began our see-saw again. All went as merry as wedding bells and before the bank opened at 11am we closed the bargain at £1. 10. 0, less (far less) than the company had been giving in Leith. We trotted off to the bank to make the payment in advance of about two thirds of the parcel, the remainder to be paid on shipment in the coast boat *Holar*. It will arrive in Leith November 9th.

It is very cold night and morning and the fjord has a thin sheet of ice over it, but there is no wind and bright sunshine when she comes up. That is not until 10am when she comes over the hilltops and goes again at 3pm. Soon she will not rise over the mountains at all, and for 23 weeks the sun is not seen. We hear from the telegraph people that a storm is raging in the Shetland Islands but we have lovely weather here, much to the chemist's disgust as he has been predicting every day, 'Look out, tomorrow we shall have bad weather', but it does not come. *Ceres* should have been on her way here and we should be leaving here tomorrow for Reykjavík, but she has not arrived yet so it looks as if a week's wait is before us.

This fearful slaughtering is going on in every direction. Hundreds, I may say thousands, of sheep are being killed and pickled in barrels for shipment; everything reeks in blood. It's frightfully cruel: the sheep are penned and taken out one by one, laid on the ground, one man grasping its legs, the other man seizes it by the nose and cuts the jugular vein and the blood gushes out into a wooden tray. A woman stirs the blood to prevent it clotting. When the blood ceases to run, another jab is made and the windpipe and arteries are cut and a fresh stream flows. Finally the head is hacked off and the man sits on the carcass to squeeze out the remainder of the blood. All this time, the poor thing is groaning and gasping, and one can hear some 10 or 12 poor things at the same time. This goes on from early dawn until late at night, day after day, until everyone you meet is bloody and greasy and the smell of dead mutton fills the nostrils until one thinks one will never touch fresh meat again. It's a gruesome sight: heads, carcasses, skins and entrails all over the place wherever one looks, and the dogs can hardly move they are so filled out with titbits. Hundreds of them sit and lie around and gasp and blow and are too lazy to get up and bark at a fresh flock.

Telegraph wires all gone wrong between here and Reykjavík, only coming in jerks and the latest news is no news of *Ceres*.

October 5th

Mjolnir came in from Leith, brought two bundles of papers but no letters. I post some for Vopnafjörður and Norðfjörður and *Mjolnir* sailed again after a few hours' wait.

Very fine weather still. We hear that *Ceres* arrived at Reykjavík during the night and there the communication stopped again. It's all going wrong, this Icelandic telegraph. The cable of course is all right but the land wires are dreadful and what it will be in the winter with storms and snow and ice; I expect it will be more often in bits than in working order.

I am now all paid up and all cleared up, and on reviewing the results of the year's work so far, it seems it will not be so very bad after all. It will be about 500 tons I have got down, including the salt fish stored here, and I hope to get a bit more down and a bit more bought at Reykjavík, if I can only get over there. I am beginning to feel more easy in my mind, a sort of relief that the year's work is nearly finished.

October 6th

Fine day but cold, as the sun is in a sort of mist, and has all the appearance of finishing up the fine weather. It only wants wind now to make it very uncomfortable. As it is, a great coat is necessary to sit indoors in, but of course outside one can keep warm by walking about.

October 7th

Rain all night, overcast and heavy fog on hills and a bleak, cold, southeasterly wind blowing. Very raw and miserable. Spend most of the day in bed as it's the only warm place. I really do not know how it is that I do not get pneumonia or pleurisy or some lung trouble, I am sure I should if I were in England with the same cold temperature. I am cold into the very bone and shall be glad to get to Reykjavík where I can light up my stove and get a little comfort.

October 8th

Rather fine but fresh wind. Waiting for news of *Ceres* and hear by wire that she left Reykjavík last night.

October 9th

Very fine day but a strong wind south-westerly which brought another wave of heat so that all day it has been really warm. On walking out to the telegraph station it was almost overpowering, so suddenly has the heat come on the top of such cold weather we have been having. It is very remarkable indeed, these heat waves, and I have never come across it up here before, although the people say it often occurs even in the depth of winter. As an example, last year at Christmas day a heat wave came along. The thermometer had been standing for a month at 16 to 18 degrees of cold and suddenly, pop, up it went to 50 degrees, which is 18 degrees of warmth. That was late in the evening and lasted for two days so that the stoves had to be discontinued, and then just as suddenly, whop! Down went the quicksilver again and the cold continued. This island is full of surprises and uncertainties.

At six o'clock we get a telephone message from Hof at Vopnafjörður saying a large steamer has just come in the fjord which is of course the *Ceres*. Afterwards a fishing boat came in and said they had seen her going north at midday so at last she was in reach.

October 10th

Heavy rain and cold. *Ceres* came in hooting at 6am. Got up and went to enquire when she will sail again and find she has to take in a hundred tons of bunker coal and fill up tanks with fresh water, as this is one of the few places where there is a quay. That was built by an English fishing company some years ago and abandoned. It is constructed of wooden piles and the largest steamer can lay afloat at all times alongside. A water pipe has been carried to one of the waterfalls right behind the quay so all it has to do is to fall on board the ship. Here the engineer takes the opportunity to blow out his boilers and refill with fresh water, so that the vessel will not be cleared for sea today.

Return to the hotel, have breakfast, finally pack up and get my gear sent on board, pay my bill, say goodbye and takk fyrir þetta skiptið (thanks for this time). Go on board and have a jolly good warm in the smoking saloon, which is steam heated, a jolly good dinner and a yarn afterwards with the captain. Then we made up a party for supper and invited the telegraph clerks and some other friends, wives and daughters. We had the saloon piano going until twelve o'clock, by which time the weather had cleared away and our friends also did the same. They gave us three cheers and we responded, and goodbye, good voyage, happy homecoming, and we parted and went to bed.

Five

Return to Reykjavík

We were awakened at 6am, October 11th, by the steamer getting underway and leaving for Norðfjörður, where we arrived at 8am. It's a very
short way by sea, out of one fjord and into another, but two days' ride
around by the land road. Went onshore, cold raw morning, and as the
postmaster is the pastor and the pastor is my agent, I went in the post
boat. As we only had two hours to wait, we got through a lot of
business, cleared all accounts for the year, gave instructions for the
future, said goodbye to him and his wife, kissed his sister (nice girl but
spits at meal times which takes off a bit of the glamour), and get on
board just as the last whistle is blowing, just in time for breakfast.

Took in here a lot of fishermen and fisher girls, so that we have by
now nearly 300 of them pigging it in the empty hold. Each one makes a
sort of cubby house with their chest and a bag of straw or shavings to
lie upon for the voyage to Faxa Bay, Keflavík and Reykjavík where they
live and will pass the winter. All are returning after their summer work
on the east coast with their earnings in their pockets, so all are glad and
drink a great deal. They have an accordion and they play and sing all
the time after they have wriggled down into their places.

We come to Eskifjörður and here we take in more passengers for the
hold. We are only three men and three ladies in the first cabins: my
man Sigurður Hafliðason; a Norwegian engineer on the telegraph staff;
myself; two young girls, daughters of the priest at Vallanes on the
Lagarfljót, going to Reykjavík to learn things; and a widow woman
from Norðfjörður to Reykjavík. These were all we had for the voyage.

We came out of Eskifjörður and into Fáskrúðsfjörður by 5pm, by
which time it was quite dark and inclined to be foggy, so the captain
decided to remain the night at anchor. In this fjord is a rather good
hospital built two or three years ago by the French government for the

use of the French fishermen. Consequently in the fishing season there are many schooners here and there is also a French priest and two Sisters of Mercy stationed here, all overlooked by an Icelandic doctor called Georg whom I know very well. He is about thirty years of age and was married this spring to the daughter of the Norwegian merchant Wathne of Seyðisfjörður, owner of the Wathne line of steamers plying between Norway and Iceland. A very handsome girl she is, one of the most beautiful amongst the beautiful Icelandic girls, but she is half bred, father Norwegian and mother Icelandic. The captain proposed we should go onshore to pay the wedding visit, as this was the first time he and I have seen them since we called at their father's house in March on the occasion of the nuptials, but it came on to rain and blow up a bit so we abandoned the idea and played patience until 10pm.

On the morning of the 12th October, 4am, we sailed again. Now we are on our way to sea to Reykjavík, all along the inhospitable south coast where there are no harbours for hundreds of miles, only one long stretch of bare, barren mountains backed with glaciers which press down into the sea, causing a moraine to be formed and pushed out into the sea. The debris is washed out miles into the Atlantic Ocean and forms a dangerous sandbank of shoal water which has been the cause of vast numbers of shipwrecks and loss of life ever since the island has been known, the shore from the eastern horn to Portland[1] on the south-west side being strewn with wrecks of steamers, steam trawlers and sailing vessels.

On coming on deck at 8am, found a bright sunshine morning with a fresh breeze off the land and alongside the island of Papey, or 'Pope's island', a name given to it by the Irish settlers of many centuries ago. They came here from Ireland on the conversion of the Icelanders from heathenism to Catholicism and were driven out again when it was re-converted into Lutherism, which, by the way, was a bad thing. Owing to the lax energy of the priests of this latter faith, it has allowed the people to drift into atheism, whereas if it had remained Catholic the priests would have kept them in order and saved their souls. Now they

---

[1] An old English sailors' name for Dyrhólaey, probably because of its likeness to Portland in Dorset. Dyrhólaey means a hilly island with a door in it.

are only animals, and as they come more and more in touch with the outer world by the increased communication of steamers and telegraphs, they become more and more distant from Christianity. Their sole aim is to get money and get it quickly, honestly if possible but it's too slow, consequently they are up to every move to swindle and cheat on all sides. I really believe if it were possible for a man to cheat his own self, they would do it, for fathers, brothers, grandfathers count as nothing. It's all self, nothing but self, no-one gives the other a helping hand, everyone helps himself if he gets the chance and he is always thinking and trying out ways and means to get that chance. Not one is above a bribe and any man can be bought, but at the same time it's wonderful: I can trust a man with £1,000 in hard cash and not see him for two or three months and he will turn up with the right quantity of fish and correct accounts. It is altogether incomprehensible, altogether indescribable and the whole place is a bunch of contradictions.

After breakfast, come on deck again and remain all the morning, telescope in hand, watching the passing scenery. We are opposite the eastern horn, which is a bunch of black, forbidding mountains rising into sharp peaks, sharp as needles, rising straight up from the sea and cutting into bright Arctic sky as if cut out of black paper and stuck on a blue sheet; bunches of peaks in bunches. The distance is too great from us for photos, but to see it all through a powerful telescope (and the captain has a rare good one of English Dollond manufacture, the one used by him when in the navy) is grand and requires the pen of a really good writer to be able to give anyone not seeing it any idea of the wild grandeur of the views.

On rounding the horn, the great expanse of the tremendous Vatnajökull, or Water Glacier, comes into view. During the many years I have passed and repassed this coast, never have I seen the unmeasurable vastness of this glacier brought so plainly, so vividly, to my eyes. It is a sight that one can remember to the end of one's days. Right away in front of one stretches peak upon peak of black mountains, and where the valleys should be is the great mass of glistening ice, white and yet green, green and yet white. It fills the valleys and passes out between the black peaks in an overwhelming pressure, spreading out and downwards towards the sea with the power and weight of 8,000 square miles[2] of glacier ice which every year is being added to by the fall of snow and which never melts, only adding and adding to the weight and thickness. The height of this glacier is over 6,000 feet and is the highest point in the island. When you consider that it takes us 24 hours to pass in front of this panorama, you can form some idea of its vastness. Owing to our distance from the shore (which would be about 20 miles, as it's dangerous to approach nearer owing to the shallowness of the water, and yet we only seem to be a couple of miles away), here and there one can see storms of snow and wind hurling against great masses of clouds down the glacier. Here and there bright open sunshine gleaming like diamonds on the whitened surface; here and there the black, helpless-looking, sharp needle-like peak of an overwhelmed mountain protruding like the hand of a drowning man endeavouring, as it were, to keep back the onward pressure but in vain. Press and press it goes, pushing its moraine out into the sea. We are far enough out to sea to look over and into the fathomless interior of the island and see nothing but ice.

Look on the map of Iceland and you will see that a third of the land is covered by this glacier, the great Vatnajökull, the top of which in clear weather can be seen 130 to 150 miles away. It can be seen as a white-peaked cloud up in the sky, hours and hours before any land can be made out. This is what Ingólfur the Norwegian[3] saw first when he discovered the island in 875 and it was at the foot of this glacier he first landed. The spot is called Ingólfshöfði and this we pass about 3pm. It juts out into the sea in the form of a wedge of cheese with the thick edge landwards. It appears as if detached from the mainland but it is not. It is about two hundred feet high on the thick end, flat on the top and sloping seawards to a sharp point. We round this, the most southern point of the island, and then dinner is announced.

---

[2]   It seems that Pike is confusing metric and imperial measurements. Today, Vatnajökull covers 8,538 square km (3,150 square miles). Its name more correctly means Lakes Glacier.

[3]   Ingólfur Arnarson is believed to be the first permanent settler who came to Iceland. Surviving versions of the *Book of Settlements* (*Landnámabók*) from the 13th century claim that he stayed in Iceland from 874, although archaeologists now believe settlement could have begun a few years earlier.

Reluctantly, I leave the deck and leave bright sunshine, smooth sea with dancing ripples, and seawards a great shoal of porpoises leaping out and splashing down into the green blue water, only to come on deck again at 4pm and find the sun set and a great heavy, angry mass of clouds growing out of the south-west and the feel of the heavy rolling sea gradually increasing, foretelling a big blow at the back of it all from the south-west, which is the whole North Atlantic Ocean. Here we pass five or six German trawlers who only fish these banks and have only been two or three years at the game. As they prefer cod and haddock, they stick to the cod banks, whereas the English trawlers only want plaice and halibut and consequently fish closer in shore and poach on the small bays and fjords within the prescribed limit. They get pounced upon by the Danish cruiser and lose their catch and gear and a big fine in money when captured in illegal places.

After passing Ingólfshöfði, we come to the most desolate, most uninhabited and most dangerous part of the coastline of Iceland. Here in the bay between Ingólfshöfði and Portland, or as it is sometimes called Dyrhólaey, is a vast stretch of quicksand where the great weight of Vatnajökull presses downwards as well as seawards and forces up the sand, sea-washed moraine. It stretches miles and miles out to sea, covered only at high water with a foot or so of water and on the ebb tide is dry and seemingly firm but it's all one death trap. Woe betide any vessel that touches the bottom of this bay, she is lost and no power on earth can ever save her. I have never seen it but people who know say there are numerous hulls of steamers, steam trawlers and iron vessels still standing intact and as good as the day they were built, all strewn along this shore, the sand being soft enough not to damage them and the waves only large enough to beat them farther and farther inshore but not sufficiently heavy enough to destroy them, owing to the long distance they have to roll on the shallow water, the sands acting as a breakwater, diminishing the height and weight of the mighty Atlantic rollers which beat and roar on the outside edge of the shallows miles away.

I know that in 1900 a party of English salvage men tried to get off an English trawler called the *Richard Simpson* which had stranded there. Although she had been there two years, exposed to all weathers, she was as good as when she was built, which was three months before she stranded, and being worth £7,000, the insurers tried to save their money. They were seven weeks with 200 men with every modern appliance for salving vessels, but they had to abandon the vessel and she is still there, as good as ever, only all moveable gear (especially copper and brass parts of the machinery) has been ripped out by the natives. They tell me that when they want an amusing day or a holiday, or a knock off work day and carry bricks holiday, they make up a party and go to these stranded hulls and probe and rip out bits of copper, just like our people do at home when they go blackberrying. Wooden hulls are what they like but the days of sailing wooden vessels are almost days of the past. Except an occasional unfortunate French fishing schooner, they got very few good windfalls there now. A good wooden vessel with all its masts, sails, cordage and hull will fetch at auction about £25 to £30 and her original cost might be about £1,500 to £2,000, but a steam trawler costs about £7,000 will make only £2. 10. 0. to £5. As there are only two or three farmers with a priest amongst them in the immediate vicinity, they make a pool and do not bid too much at the auction, which is held by the sýslumaður as a matter of form. He gets his fees and a bit and gets the job over quickly and the farmers get the lump.

It had now become dark and stormy and the vessel began to sling about, being empty, and at 10pm we passed Portland, or Dyrhólaey, the place mentioned in Maurice Drake's prize story in the *Daily Mail*. Here the captain stopped the ship and took soundings and bearings and went slowly along so that he should arrive at the Westman Islands in daylight. We got there about 5am on October 13th and he blew his hooter but it was not really daylight until about 6.30, when some boats came off. The Westman Islands are a group of islets, only one of which is inhabited and has a population of about 500 people. Here we landed several of our hold passengers and took on board several for Reykjavík. The morning was one of those black, forbidding, early mornings; black, heavy clouds with a clear space in the east which was tinged red with the rising sun. Away on the mainland was the chain of mountains standing out like sharks' teeth and in the centre was the summit of Hekla, the celebrated volcano, but not now in activity.

At 8am, we left again and made a beeline for the cape of Reykjanes and the island of Eldey, or 'Fire Island', which stands out plainly. Owing to its formation, the Danish and English sailors call it the 'Meal Sack', as it looks just like a sack of flour standing up against the sky. It is about 300 feet high and looks like a fully-rigged ship when seen on the horizon. It is about three miles from the mainland and the point of Reykjavík, on which is a lighthouse, and between the island and the cape is our course. By this time, 2pm, it became very bad weather but fair wind and it gradually blew up into a gale with heavy snowstorms. It thickened all around us so that on leaving Reykjanes at 4pm it was as dark as a bag. As we had altered our course to come into Faxa Bay, the wind was on our starboard side and she lay over at a good angle and soughed and wallowed along into the dark and stormy night.

We should have seen another light on the point of Skaginn but saw nothing, so after running his distance, the captain drew into the small bay in which the village of Keflavík is situated. As we had about 200 passengers for that place, he had promised them if possible to set them on shore there instead of taking them on to Reykjavík, where they would have been compelled to walk home a distance of 14 or 15 hours' walking. We now got into a fleet of steam trawlers, as this is one of their favourite fishing grounds, and hooting and hooting is to be heard on every side, ahead and astern, a regular howdy-do. We got through them and gradually got into the smoother water of the bay, but as it was impossible to see hardly the length of the vessel for the snow and baggy darkness, the captain let go the anchor to wait for daylight and we got our supper in peace.

It was a very bad night, wind howling, snow falling, black, angry sea surging against our sides and slopping back, lit up with gleams of light from our portholes, and all around as black a night as if in a coal hole.

Next morning at 6am, October 14th, we upped anchor and crept towards the vík of Keflavík. As daylight gradually dawned, we came to anchor and blew our whistle, and at 8am had got our people on shore. The wind, although still strong, was off the land. The landing was smooth and the dispatch was quick, seeing it was all a living cargo we had. About 200 went on there so we had only 100 left for Reykjavík.

Some 10 or 12 English steam trawlers were at anchor around us taking shelter, and as many more were coming in from the fishing grounds and steaming towards the anchorage.

We left again with the wind right after us and gradually the city of Reykjavík began to be seen. At 10am, we pass between the islands of Akurey and Engey and into our final anchorage. Find three or four cargo steamers at anchor and half a dozen trawlers. When all was clear, Captain and I took breakfast and after that was over, about noon, my man Jóhannes Pétursson came off with a boat to take me onshore, as there is no pier or landing here except for boats. Everything, cargo and passengers, has to be landed in open boats and lighters. At 1pm, landed on the town slip and go up to my diggings which had been made ready and the stove lighted. I squat down in my armchair with a sign of thankfulness and a feeling of, 'Now I have come Home.' The town slip; 'pier' they call it here, but it's only a stone slip.

At 3pm, go to my boarding house to get dinner but feel all out of sorts, a kind tired feeling, as if the year's work was finished and I had come home to rest. As it is dark at 4.30pm, I light my pipe lamp and, having been at the post office to get my letters (of which I found a miscellaneous collection and some pretty old ones and also a bundle of papers), I sit in my armchair and go through them over and over again. Outside the wind is getting up from the north and I can hear it moaning and gusting around the house, but I am as snug and cosy as it is possible to be.

October 15th

Awake after a good night's sleep and feel very refreshed and fit, but outside it's blowing a gale and very cold, freezing hard. I go to breakfast and return to my rooms and find the fire lighted and all cosy. Soon after 12 noon, Jóhannes and my man Sigurður come in and we talk over the plan of campaign for the winter, and Jóhannes makes his report of his journey to the south coast fishing places and where he has made arrangements for taking the stuff in the spring and had many promises of supplies. Clear up the year's accounts and get all in order, as the *Ceres* is intended to leave for the west coast tonight and these men will return to their homes for the winter.

In the evening, hear an English voice calling into my door, 'Is this Mr Ward's?' I find it is the Marconi telegraph man, a Mr Sergeant, who has come to take the place of Mr Newman who left in May after having got married to the Icelandic girl he had engaged himself to last winter. Had a chat and a laugh. He is a young fellow, about 25 years of age, and has been for four years on the Atlantic liners. He is doubtful of the Marconi company keeping on the station for the winter and is waiting every moment for instructions to return to England. He also complains of the want of interest in the newspaper people and is rather disgusted when he gives out sheets and sheets of press matter to see nothing of it in the papers when they come out. The editors say they have no room in their papers for foreign news; such is the use of telegraphs for press purposes.

Bitterly cold outdoors, gale, north wind, so no communication can be had with the vessels in the harbour. Consequently, *Ceres* will not leave tonight. I get in a barrel of coal and stoke and stoke but cannot get much warmth in the rooms, so I shut up the ventilators (which are holes bored in the window frames and stopped with a cork) and close up my doors, and by evening get it decently warm.

October 16th

Gale still on, and to go out one has to wrap up in fur-lined coat and fur hat and mittens, for it's bitterly cold and the wind pierces to the very marrow. Go to the bank and put our accounts square. There Jóhannes and Sigurður pay me a visit; *Ceres* will not sail today as it's even worse than yesterday. I see in the shops that the postcards are getting of a more magnificent appearance than formerly and that they are getting coloured.

I hear a fine story from the government that is now in about the telegraph wires. They say the wire is quite strong enough and is similar, in fact the same, wire as used in Norway, but the members of the opposition who are farmers scattered along the route come out at night and break the wires. It is curious that the worst breaks are near these farmers so it looks as if there was some truth in it, but they will soon get tired of this. Ísafjörður, which is the largest and most important fishing centre, is left entirely out of the line of telegraph because the whole fjord is in opposition to the present government. Their member of parliament is the leader of the opposition and the government says, 'All right, you don't want the wire and so we have left you out, what do you want?', and so has the laugh of the discontents.

October 17th

The gale gave up in the night and this morning's dawn at 8am was a regular bright winter's morning, clear, still weather, bright sky and sun shining, but cold, about five degrees of frost, but very nice to get out and about and one can go without overcoat in the middle of the day. Consequently the coaling of *Ceres* goes on well and she is posted up as leaving for the west at midnight. Call around to see my acquaintances and meet many in the streets, which are crowded with countrymen and flocks of sheep. 30,000 are slaughtered here for winter's use for the town, or city, alone and none is exported, so it makes it up about four sheep per head. Every house reeks with dead mutton and cooking and all my female friends look as if they have been dragged through a pond of fat, in fact greasy up to the eyes and a bit over that.

Get a visit from the captain and mate of the *Ceres*, the latter very proud and jubilant having had news of promotion as captain and it's very likely will come up next year as master of the *Skalholt*. He is a Swede in Danish service and is a regular Captain Kettle. A great deal of building goes on as usual and the houses are increasing in size and value. For instance, the bank manager has just set up a house costing £1,000. The Young Men's Christian Association are also building a hall and out of the city they are erecting a lunatic asylum, but unfortunately in the last gale, about three weeks since, the greater part of it blew down. I called on Ásgeir Sigurðsson, Messrs Copland and Berrie's factor here, but found he was gone to Ísafjörður on business in the *Laura*.

At 7pm, all my Ísafjörður men with wives, sisters and relations came to wish me goodbye as they were going on board *Ceres*, which leaves at midnight. On going to the door, found it commencing to snow so that there was a foot of it on the ground and the sky overhead deemed heavy and full of it, so expect in the morning it will be over all and the land will have got its coat of whitewash for the next six months, covering up all the dirt and filth. It is still calm so the people will have no difficulty in getting on board, except that it's pitch dark. Why they could not go in daylight, I am at a loss to understand.

I find that the telegraph head office is at the post office although the two departments are distinct one from the other. On sending a message on Monday morning, it took five minutes for the clerk to receive it although it was only three words. He had to take a piece of paper to reckon out three times seventy equalling two krónur, ten aurar (about two shillings and sixpence) and then to write all particulars of time received and amount paid. It seemed a great work and he gave a sigh of satisfaction when he had finished the difficult operation. Then it took ten minutes for him to change a five krónur note, for he had to go downstairs to the post department, and when I gave him a ten aurar piece and asked for three krónur change he was quite nonplussed and confused and he had to count it all over again. I came later and sent off two more wires and was there half an hour. What they would do in a busy office.

A young Icelander has had for some time since a government grant to learn to be a sculptor after the style of the great Thorvaldsen, whose museum sculpture is in Copenhagen. Last year he sent up a plaster model of group which he had conceived out of his own head and he called it 'Outlawed Man',[4] a very fine figure of a man standing 10 feet high on its pedestal. It represents an outlaw in all his rags and sheep-skin clothing, bearing the dead body of his wife strapped to his shoulders and his child clasped in his arms, accompanied by a dog. He is supposed to be on his way to the churchyard to bury the corpse. The wild, hungry, anxious and haunted look of his eyes are very finely done but the figure is not in proportion, the feet being enormous and length of leg also. Child very well done and so is the dog. The hands are larger than the face, but all this could have been rectified if he could have got his grant he asked for to produce it in marble but it was objected to, not because of its faults of proportion but because it

[4] *Outlaws* by Einar Jónsson, 1901. The plaster statue was bought in 1904 by Ditlev Thomsen for the nation. It now stands in the Einar Jónsson Museum in Reykjavík. It is now considered one of the most significant Icelandic works of the 20th century and is seen by many as embodying the Icelandic spirit of tenacity and independence.

represented an Icelander hungry and forlorn. The subject was right against the ideas of the noble native and if he had designed a figure of a Viking slaying hundreds of southern people, he would have got as much money as he wanted.

One fellow today had the audacity to tell me with a puffed out chest that, 'Our nation is the most noble-blooded people in the world', and that, 'We are the foundation of the future Great Northern Race that is to come!' Instead of which, they are the tail end of it all and will die out very fast now the means of communication is improving, especially if the herring fishing which is now only just born should turn out what I think it will and thousands of foreigners will come to prosecute that industry and swamp out the lazy native. So long as they are isolated, they could keep up their own customs and make their ridiculous laws but only let 100 to 200,000 foreigners come in and it will all be changed. I am sure in the next 25 years it will come. Germany is looking for a fishing place to compete with Scotch herrings in Russia and their own lands, and they have only just got a smell of it. Norway having slipped from the Kaiser's fingers, he will look to Iceland and in will come a whole host. Even now the German trawlers are owned by German naval officers who got government grants to try the industry. The captains of these trawlers are all naval men and the discipline is very strict, as on a man-of-war, so Captain Gad tells me. He, having been on the Danish cruiser, used to board these trawlers and was struck with the difference between them and the undisciplined and ignorant English trawler skippers and men. As soon as they make a success of the herring fishing, two boats having been sent up this year to try, look out for squalls. Seeing as Germany takes a whole lot of salted herrings, which up to now they were obliged to buy from Scotland, they will surely try and produce their own supplies by German capital and German boats and men. They will of course succeed, as they can get government grants, which is practically unknown in England.

I came across a postcard of a wire ferry over the Jökulsá or Glacier River which is in use some three or four miles above where I crossed it and took my photos of the bridge and chasm. This wire ferry was in existence before the bridge was built but is still used by the immediate farmers when there is only a small quantity of packs to be ferried over.

In the foreground, you will see two pack saddle horses ready for crossing and the cradle in position for taking over the passenger and his luggage. The cradle you will see is only a square box with four poles in the corners in which four sheaves or pulleys have been placed. This is suspended from the ropes and dragged over by the loose rope in the centre by the passenger, a very primitive and dangerous passage.

Since my 'Heavy Cold' at Seyðisfjörður, I have had my nasty tickling throat cough and I am afraid I shall bring it to England with me now, as it will not go away with any of my many appliances. It's cough, cough every minute, tickling and tickling, and the more I cough the more I may, and I get no 'forardar'. It's exceedingly annoying to get this at the very beginning of the winter and know I have to put with it until next spring.

October 18th

Wind shifted to the south, raw and cold with rain instead of snow, which makes it all sloppy and uncomfortable. Had interesting communication with Mr Schau, the bank director, which lasted two hours about bank business. A funeral today of the captain of one of the vessels lost last April, whose body was found about a week since and recognised by his watch. This has been the only one found out of the crew of that vessel. Also went to call on Mrs Sigurðsson, wife of Copland and Berrie's manager, and found her busy with the cooking of meat for the winter and house reeking with the smell of dead mutton. She has had another addition to the family in the summer, another boy, that makes three now. I did not get much of a gossip as she was on pins and needles to look after the boiling of sheeps' heads, although she has five servants in the house. Although a Scotch lady, she has fallen into all the slovenly ways of the Icelandic húsmóðir.

Some two miles out of the city is the leprosy hospital which was presented to the country by the Odd Fellows of Denmark. Previous to the collecting together of these unfortunate people, they were scattered all over the land, marrying and carrying on the horrible disease, but now the doctors tell me it's very much on the decrease and they hope finally to stamp it out in the course of the next generation. It is not the Asiatic leprosy but the Scandinavian, and is caused by the eating of bad fish and want of antiscorbutic vegetables. It is really a sort of scurvy, only scurvy does not carry on to the next generation, but this does and it is horrible to see.

I had a chat with my old friend Dr Guðmundur Björnsson about the waterworks. He tells me that when he was in England, the town council had an election and he was not elected and so has no voice in the matter, but they had bought the river from Mr Payne (the English-man who had bought it a long time ago) and they had given £8,000 for it, but if it had been bought two years ago, when I negotiated the business, it could have been had for £6,000. Now they have given over the survey of the land and the plans to be made by their own native-born engineer, a young lad of 25 years of age who had succeeded in getting elected on the town council, and in his greatly experienced hands is an expenditure of £25,000 or thereabouts to be entrusted. When they will get the money to carry it out is a mystery to me, but their confidence in a lad who perhaps in the whole course of his exist-ence has never seen a waterworks is marvellous. So I suppose they will wallow through it and blunder and blunder and construct and con-struct but eventually get some sort of a water supply. They are a wonderful people. Iceland for Icelanders!

Dr Björnsson has had a very high appointment given him and he now is government physician, commanding all the doctors in the land and the salary is large, considering the pay of government officials. Besides, he is entitled to wear a uniform, cocked hat and feathers and next summer, when the king of Denmark makes his visit, he will be sure to give him a decoration.

October 19th

Wretchedly wet and raw day, rainy and wind from east. Bad breakfast. Eat meal without milk and as there was fried blood pudding I jibbed and had to fill up with bread and butter. Not a soul visited me today. I suppose weather too bad to get out and about.

October 20th

Rain and cold, bad day. Only went out to meals. Sergeant, the Marconi man, came in and had a chat. He tells me there is a derelict Englishman up here called Rogers who says he is a Cambridge University man but has had many ups and downs in life, mostly downs. He has drifted up here and is trying to get a living teaching English, but how he is to do this not knowing the native language, I am at a loss to see.

October 21st

Another wet day, very raw. Did not have a single visitor today, so spent best part of it in stowing away my Icelandic clothes and packing up that which I am taking to England. Cough still bad but I luckily found an apparatus I got last winter to put over my mouth. It certainly has been better since but it's troublesome, so much so I cannot smoke (and I can hear someone singing, 'And a good job too').

October 22nd

A better day. Still raw and cold but no rain. Go for a stroll around the town's west quarter this time. It's surprising to see all the buildings going on and the cost of them. The county are building a large concrete library to hold the old manuscripts, of which they have a valuable lot and which are at present housed in the parliament house, but as the library is growing with the town there is no longer room there for their books. I expect it will be a big place, judging from the foundations. I have not seen the plans but it is of Danish architecture I am given to understand, and a Danish architect is here superintending the work. Get Sergeant in after dinner and a whole lot of people so had a busy time of it until supper time opening sodas and lemonades!

October 23rd

A similar day to yesterday for weather. Stroll about the city and meet a lot of old acquaintances: Magnús Stephensen, the old governor; Júlíus Havsteen, the old amtmaður;[5] Rector Olsen,[6] the principal of the Latin college, and a lot more, so the morning passed well.

---

5 The post of amtmaður, a senior regional official, was abolished in 1904 when Iceland achieved Home Rule. Júlíus Havsteen (1839–1915) had become a prominent member of parliament and banker.

By the way, I had from the telegraphist in Seyðisfjörður a specimen of both cable and land telegraphy in use up here. The blue, crooked lines are the cable and it reads: Pike Ward, Teignmouth, Devon, Seyðisfjörður, October 5th 1906. The perforated slip is the land telegraph and reads the same.

In the walk around today, I saw everywhere women making what is called sviðasulta. I don't think I mentioned it before about other places, but it is the burning of the wool from off sheep's heads. A sharpened broomstick is thrust into the hole in the back of the sheep's head and it is then held over a portable smith's forge and the wool burnt off it. The women become black as crows. After that the head is boiled and the flesh picked off the bones and put into a tin and pressed together. It is eaten cold as brawn but there is the accompaniment of burnt wool, burnt flesh and ashes. The inside of the mouth and the coating of the tongue is not removed, nor the eyes; it all goes in and when eaten all goes down. It is a very popular and luxurious dish and is only used on very rare occasions as a tit-bit during the winter.

October 24th

Muggy sort of day with occasional showers which make the roads all of a slop. Was asked out to supper and had a roast swan, very good indeed but would have been better if seasoned with goose seasoning instead of prunes, which made the flesh rather dry.

The students, who in all the lands seem to be the first movers of revolutions, held a meeting to discuss the advisability of having their own flag, now they have a change of mode of government and Denmark has granted all their demands to try and keep peace. As is usual with these tin pot communities, one can hardly imagine and call it a nation, although the natives proudly do. It was decided as a beginning that it should be a blue ground with a white cross, on the pattern of the Danish flag which is red ground and white cross. I have been looking for this movement ever since they succeeded in getting the minister here instead of in Copenhagen. Fired by the example of

---

[6] Björn M. Ólsen (1850–1919), former Rector of the Latin School, was at this point a member of parliament and a scholar of Icelandic literature. He went on to become the first Rector of the University of Iceland in 1911.

Norway, they will aim to get a complete separation from Denmark in the end. I questioned one of the malcontents about it and enquired if they were going to get a king.

'Oh no, we shall have as in the Viking times, a republic.'

I then asked a government man and he said, 'Oh, it's only a lot of young students talking and for my part I would like it to remain just as it is, but I tell the students, first get your vessels to fly the flag.' For they have no vessels trading with other countries, only fishing smacks. But nevertheless, I myself think that the students will stir until they get their rag and perhaps at the same time get the rag of Denmark out, as perhaps their new king will not be so complacent as the old King Christian.

The time is now getting close for the final pack-up, although the *Laura* has not yet come back from the west coast. She was due back yesterday but the *Kong Trygve* mail boat has returned and reports very bad weather there.

October 25th

Bad weather. *Kong Trygve* sailed for Leith and I sent letters by her. In the evening, about 6pm, we had a smart shake of earthquake; made the stoves and lamps rattle and gave a rumbling sound. It only lasted a second or two but just enough to let one know shakes were about.

October 26th

Wild day. *Laura* came in from the west coast and also reports bad weather there, but we have news by wire from north and east they are getting fine weather in those districts so the bad weather is following me wherever I go. I get around and say goodbye to most of my acquaintances and finally pack up and have all ready. The *Laura* is advertised to sail in the morning but I doubt if she will as it's such bad weather for shipment of the fish and other goods, for out does not go well and if it were not for motor boats engaged to tow the lighters out, it would be impossible.

October 27th

Wind and rain, very bad day. Nothing done on *Laura* today until about noon when it fined off a little and the ponies were got on board but it's hard work. Some 76 are shipped and a notice is put up at the office notifying the vessel will sail at nine o'clock tomorrow morning, so I send off cables and say so to England. At 4pm, I hire a motor boat and get my gear and myself shipped on board in a snowstorm, for the weather, instead of bettering towards evening, got worse. I am glad to be on board during the night as perhaps in the early morning (and seeing it is not light until 9am) it may be difficult to get boat and men to put me off.

On getting on board, find two passengers from Ísafjörður: a Mr Riis and his wife, both of whom I know, Mr Riis being bookkeeper for the big merchant Ásgeir Ásgeirsson of Ísafjörður. Captain Aasberg, as usual, very kindly gives me his cabin amidships, as the passenger accommodation on the *Laura* is aft and it does jerk at sea; she seems to me to wriggle her stern like a fish whenever there is the least bit of sea on. We chat and smoke in the saloon until bedtime, 10pm. On the morning of the 27th October at 9am, the passengers come on board in motor boats in a bad snowstorm. Being so early, no-one came with them. It is usual when people are leaving for about a dozen to come to see one off. The boats pitch about and make the embarking bad work but at last the luggage is got up and the last whistle blown. The anchor is weighed, we steam out between the two islands of Akurey and Engey which form the harbour, and say, 'Goodbye Reykjavík'.

Outside it is blowing a gale from the south-east but off the land so we can get our breakfast which is served at 10am, after which we go on deck and find it still bad and raining hard. The boat is just entering the little harbour of Hafnarfjörður which is nearly filled up with fishing cutters laying at their anchors, dismantled for the winter. We blow our whistle and the lighters come off with dried fish in packages and barrels of cod liver oil. It takes all day to ship this and the weather was so bad that I did not go on shore to pay a visit to my old friends Mr and Mrs Egilsson. The place has grown immensely since I lived here six years ago, but my old cottage still stands and so does the pier I built which was sold by auction when the station was abandoned. In the evening the place was lit up well with electric light, which was installed here last winter by a man who used the brook to drive his machinery for a joinery works and has put a small dynamo plant in and so supplies his neighbours with light as well. This is the only place in Iceland so lit.

At 9pm, we leave the harbour and begin our voyage southwards. All that night, as soon as we got out into the open, we rolled and tumbled about fine and made very little headway. The *Laura* is a low-powered boat and at her best she can only go about nine miles the hour, and a little wind and sea stops her considerably. I can feel her round the cape of Reykjanes and get into what I call the 'Devil's Frying Pan', that is the stretch of sea between Reykjanes and the Westman Islands, and the sea is all of a boil, the tide being against the wind, and the old crock jumps and nips about in it like an apple in a mill race. I cling on to my bunk and have up the rolling chock which is a sort of garden gate rigged up to the side of the bed to prevent one rolling out of bed, but even then she heaves me half out over it. What those poor chaps are doing in the after cabin I can imagine, being hove about like a pea in a thimble. We should have taken in ordinary weather 12 hours to the Westman Islands but only get there at 2pm, five hours late. I don't think any of us passengers got much sleep since leaving Hafnarfjörður, I know I didn't, for it kept me busy holding on hands and feet, and to my supper, which showed a great tendency to exhibit itself several times during the night but I succeeded in holding onto it. We got into the harbour, as it's called. It is very exposed and the wind was blowing right on shore but by help of motor boats the goods were got out and sent on shore, but nothing came on board. I had my usual pick-me-up of fried bacon and eggs and the other passengers had 'smørrebrød', as the little sandwiches are called.

Of course, as usual, I know all the passengers. First, Mr Hørring, the young Danish naturalist of whom I have spoken before. He is returning to Denmark and taking his 'kærasta' (or fiancée), Miss Þórunn Solveig Kristjánsdóttir, with him, also her young sister Sóla. Þórunn is a plain little thing, about 20 years old. Sóla is 16 years old and better looking and very lively. Both are old acquaintances of mine and used to be at Hafnarfjörður when I was there, running in and out of the cottage and searching in the cupboard for sweets. Two fishing captains going to Copenhagen for a winter's visit; these men earn a great deal of money during the summer and are now on the spree to spend some of their earnings. A young Danish girl of about 18 or 19 years old, the sister of the chemist at Stykkishólmur, she has been there for the summer. A lively young party, she speaks English, French, German and Russian. She has travelled a great deal and has got a smattering of Icelandic as well. She informs me she also sings, so I am teaching (!) her *Goodbye My Bluebell* and *Her Golden Hair Was Hanging Down Her Back*. She says there is not much music in it as I render it. She daresays if she had the music later on she might be able to manage the tune of it, but as it stands now it's worse than a dog howling. A young Icelander, Jón Sveinbjörnsson (a lawyer and son of the lord chief justice of Iceland), makes up the total. So we are not a great number, but as we all know each other, we joke about our sea sickness. Even the two fishing captains have paid their tribute to the sea and the *Laura* frolics.

We all pull ourselves together by supper time, 8pm, and get in a good cargo ready for the start at 9pm. As soon as the anchor was up, we all disappeared like rabbits to our respective holes and the old tank begins her tantrums. Swish, swash the sea goes against her ironsides, and an occasional big one goes whop! against her bows, causing her to tremble and shake like an old tin tray hung on a line to frighten birds away. Portmanteau, slippers, boots and cabin chair play bee-bow with each other and I have continually to hop in and out of the bunk making this and that fast. I finally fall to sleep, only to wake after a bad dream in which I thought myself a flying wonder, for I was jumping on all the door tops and brackets in our old house in my boy days. I had just jumped on to the top shelf of the glass cupboard, when whack! went the top with a big smash. This awoke me and I found the decanter of drinking water had got pitched out of its rest, and it was lying amongst other debris on the floor, all in piles. The steward had closed my cabin door and shut up the deck ventilator, so I was nearly asphyxiated and the temperature was up to about 100 degrees of heat. I had to get out again and put it all square and open the deck light, when squash! came a sea on deck and all over me, but I let it stop; the wet was better than being smothered.

And so the night goes on until daylight begins to simmer in the two portholes. On looking out, there is nothing to be seen but the cold, parrot-grey sea and sky, and the big, heavy Atlantic rollers which are coming in from the north-west, big fellows one can see coming for a long time. Then the boat sinks and sinks down in the hollow and, with a rush, on comes the big one. You expect surely now this one will go right over her but she just turns up a side to it, like a young lady turning up her nose to an undesirable acquaintance, and the sea rolls in under and the vessel soughs down into the valley again, only to go through the same manoeuvre time after time, hour after hour.

October 29th

The steward comes and announces breakfast but I am not in that flock and Captain comes afterwards and says there was only Mr and Mrs Riis up, all the rest were not hungry. At 3pm, I fancy the sea must be getting less, or at any rate was coming more after us. I began to get peckish and on dinner bell ringing, I enquired what was for dinner and had a plate of boiled chicken and some pineapple sponge, so I am evidently getting on. At supper, 8pm, I get some smørrebrød. The literal translation is 'buttered bread', and it is little squares of buttered bread on which is placed all sorts of appetizers. The plateful contains about a dozen pieces and on each one a separate delicacy such as smoked salmon, sardines, pickles, smoked cod roe, olives, raw salt herring, meat of two or three different sorts, two sorts of cheese, pâté de foie gras, etc., etc. Very charming it all is, and I cannot understand why it has not been introduced into England instead of the everlasting and disgusting ham sandwich, very nice in its way, perhaps, but monotonous and tiring, whereas the smørrebrød is one round of surprises and a sort of wonder what is in the next piece, so that is incentive to eat and eat; very delightful and satisfying.

Being in the captain's cabin, I am in the midst of all the nautical and navigating instruments and watch with interest all the manoeuvres of the captain and the two mates, who consult chronometer, barometer and thermometer, and a funny concern in a box for the altitudes and positions of stars. They always seem to be doing something night and day, and entering a mass of figures in a big book, but what interests me the most is the rising of the indicator on the barometer, and that is steadily going up all day so we must be running into a belt of fine weather. In the middle of the night I hear whop! squash! and down streams the water through the ventilator. A big sea has come on board. I remembered once being in a gale of wind on the coast of Labrador in a little sailing vessel and the same thing happened then, and the skipper said, 'Oh! that's all right, now I know we are going to have better weather.' So I turn over and give a grunt of satisfaction, for I know now the worst is over.

Nor was I deceived. On awakening at 8am, October 30th, I could feel the old coffee mill just gently rising and falling, bowing and curtseying like a young shy girl at her first ball, and the glint of the daybreak shining through the ports on to the polished sides of the state room. I creep out of bed and survey and see the rollers are greatly diminished, so much so I can open a port with safety and get a breath of fresh air and find it not at all cold. In fact, the mate told me in the course of the day that it was 50 degrees of warmth, which is marvellous for the end of October in the middle of the North Atlantic Ocean, when often in the summer months it does not stand so high. I leisurely proceed to dress and shave, get on a clean collar (this latter, and perhaps the shave, was for the benefit of the Danish girl) and get up on deck where I find all our passengers except Þórunn and Sóla. A very nice morning and all feeling of sea sickness gone and so I was enabled to have a good breakfast, although the warm part of it was not to my liking as it was 'mock turtle', but I call it 'bits of meat boiled in beer'. By the way, the Danes adore it. I cannot stand it at the best of times, so I just troll along the table and pick up bits of all sorts and make smørrebrød and altogether have a right royal time of it. I skirt the coffee but my Danish sweetheart gets a cup, and is obliged to retire in a great hurry after drinking it against my valued advice. A wilful woman will have her way and she had to stand the consequences, but it interfered with the singing lesson, besides putting on a green complexion and made her nose red, which altogether reminded me of a tomato on a spring cabbage.

After breakfast, Captain and all of us put our time in exercising the dogs, of which there are three puppies on board. Captain is taking them home as a present to his wife. I expect she will put them in the water butt but that's neither here nor there. They amused us by <u>not</u> jumping through a lifebuoy, which Captain was very desirous that they should do, and although he hopla-ed and allez-ed, they just cringed down and refused to even wag their tail. It was wonderful what patience the chap had. I should have pitched them overboard after half an hour's trial, but he kept on all the morning and appeared as pleased with himself as if all his dogs had tin tails. He said, 'Oh, they will do better tomorrow.'

As we get along, we are followed by a flock of fulmar gulls all the way from the Westman Islands and although we are 400 miles from land, we have two or three starlings and a stray snow bunting pitching on the ship. Alongside now and then, up blows a fin whale and although there is still the long, big underswell, it comes with the vessel.

One of the cabin boys had a nasty accident, fell down the lower deck steps and cut his head badly, so Captain had to be doctor and sew up a nasty and deep cut, which took him an hour or so to do, and the poor boy was fainting all the time.

The sun set in brilliant colours and the full moon arose, and as it got later in the evening it was right ahead so that we seemed to be sailing towards England on a golden path. We could not have had a better day even in the summer and it was warm enough for us to be on the deck without greatcoats, so it is going well, very well indeed. The passage I dreaded so much is getting nearly over, as we expect to make our first land fall off the north of Scotland, tomorrow morning about 6am. The Danish girl plays and sings at the piano after supper and Jón Sveinbjörnsson, who is a very good musician, also sings and plays many Icelandic songs, so altogether we are a very happy and contented party and go off to bed at 11pm in good spirits.

October 31st

I am awakened by a blowing of whistles and a steamer answering so thought it was fog, but on getting up and looking out I see a large Danish steamer passing quite close loaded with timber, as her decks were piled high with boards. The Scotch coast in full sight and John O'Groats House standing out clearly in the morning air, for we were passing through the Pentland Firth and quite close to land, the passage being only about two miles across. The sky was heavily overcast and all looking grey and threatening. I get into bed again, it only being eight o'clock and two hours to wait for breakfast. I have the port open and the deck ventilator unscrewed and was building castles in the air, when whop, squash, skat, in comes a big sea through the port. I spring out to close it and whack comes another in my face and, whilst fastening up the screws, a drip, drip, comes on my head from the deck opening. I have a busy time mopping the water which seemed to have splashed over everything, sofa, desk, bed and floor, and filled my boots and slippers. After that was done as well as I could with the towel and a pair of stockings, I had to get out of my pyjamas and begin to dress but the old box pitched and jumped so much that I had to get into the bunk again and be prostrate. Captain came in to wind up his chronometer and said we were passing over the tide race, and as the stream was against the wind, it made it jumpy, and that it would take two or three hours to get through but he hoped that it would be better as we went on and got more in the open sea again. His prediction did not come true, for we met a strong east wind and heavy roll, and as we got more and more south into the Moray Firth she kicked up a fine old dido, so I lost my breakfast (if one may say one had lost that which one never got). I remained in a horizontal position until two o'clock, when I thought I was beginning to get hungry and I dressed. At three o'clock, the dinner bell rang and I was glad to be able to get through with that without mishap, but quickly after had to dive down again to my bunk to save it. At supper it was just the same, and it had now become wet and miserable on deck. There was nothing to see now except the flashing of the lights of the many lighthouses as we passed south along the Scotch coast. The last I saw was Peterhead's lights winking and blinking, so finally retired to rest.

November 1st

Awoken at 8am by the steamer stopping. On looking out of the port, saw Leith Docks' entrance close to us and at the same time felt the shock of the anchor being let go. Dressed and went on deck and there met the pilot who had just come on board and got some letters by him. On asking when the boat will be able to get in, I am told that it will be about 1pm, so go to breakfast and find everybody up, all of us. Have a good and last breakfast and then pack up and get ready for a flit on shore. At 12.30, they hoist up the anchor and get in to the docks, and at about 2pm we are safely moored at the quay. I go onshore to the telegraph office and wire to all my people of my safe arrival, return on board, pay my bill, pass my boxes by the customs house and hire a cab to cart all my gear up to Edinburgh. On the way up, pass all my fellow passengers who stand on the pavement and give me a farewell chorus shout of 'Farvel Mr Vard', 'Gleðilega heimkomu'.[7] And so ends the voyage on November 2nd which, by the way, is my Jubilee Birthday, for I am 50 years old today. I leave by the South Express from the Princes Street railway station and arrive at Teignmouth at 11.30pm. I am glad to be At Home once more, and nestle down in my old bed with a feeling of restfulness after so many months of wandering.

---

7   'Goodbye' in Danish and 'happy homecoming' in Icelandic.

Epilogue

Pike worked in Iceland for a further seven years and had many more adventures, often travelling with Siggi. In 1909, an auction of his belongings was held in Reykjavík. Sale items included a desk, a velvet sofa, two coffee tables, water and wine glasses, a teapot and bedding. After this, it seems that he spent more time in the east of the country, suggesting that he gave up his lodgings in Reykjavík while Seyðisfjörður increased in importance for him.

At some point between 1912 and 1914, Pike's mother Eliza, now well into her seventies, retired from running the shipbroking business at home. With Eliza stepping down, and war in Europe on the horizon, Pike had little choice but to return to Teignmouth full time and take over. Pike ran the business for another 20 years, although by the late 1920s he was leaving the day-to-day work to employees at the Teignmouth offices. Pike Ward Ltd is still going strong and is still based in the town, although it no longer has any connection to the Ward family.

Pike bought a large, elegant house in the English Edwardian style, and made it as Icelandic as it could be. He named it *Valhalla*, after the Norse god Óðinn's great hall. He had been taken with the carvings of sea-dragons and Viking longships on the roofs of some of the new buildings in Reykjavík, and decorated *Valhalla* in similar style. Inside, he panelled the walls with traditional Icelandic bed boards and surrounded himself with Icelandic objects. He gave some whalebones to the town which were erected to form two huge arches on the seafront, where they remained until the Second World War.

Back in Iceland, Jakob fell off a horse in 1908 and injured his right hand so badly that blood poisoning set in and the hand was amputated to save his life. After the fire at his shop that Pike described, Jóhannes concentrated on the fishing side of his business which prospered. Sadly, he fell ill and died in 1917.

The scheme that Pike had advocated with Guðmundur Björnsson, for a pipeline to bring fresh water from the river Elliðaár into Reykjavík, was finally completed in 1909. Guðmundur continued a life of prominent public service until 1932. He became a professor in the medical faculty at the new University of Iceland when it was founded in 1911. He served on a number of national committees as an MP and was the president of parliament's upper house from 1916 to 1922.

Halldór Runólfsson, who used Pike's cash to buy timber for a fish store, built a very successful business. He recovered from his broken heart, married and had a son in 1912. Copeland and Berrie's manager Ásgeir Sigurðsson became British Consul-General in Iceland and received honours from the British, Icelandic and Danish governments. Walter, one of Ásgeir's sons with his Scottish wife Milly, became Vice-Consul but was tragically killed in a gun accident in Reykjavík in 1932.

Despite the fundraising attempts that followed the April 1906 storm, it took another 23 years to get a lifeboat in Iceland. The lifesaving organisation Slysavarnafélagið Íslands was formed in 1928, with Guðmundur as chairman, and a lifeboat was eventually bought from the RNLI in 1929 and kept at Sandgerði.

The fish station at Wardsvík was never built beyond the foundations. Pike's business partners at the company in Exeter wouldn't support the plans, and Pike felt they had lost 'one of the best fishing centres in Iceland'.

Just a few weeks after Pike arrived back in Britain for the winter in 1906, the SS *Kong Inge* ran aground and was wrecked en route to Leith. The *Laura* was wrecked at Skagaströnd in 1910. The *Ceres* was lost during the First World War, torpedoed by a German U-boat in July 1917 on her way to Iceland with a cargo of salt. Three days later, the same U-boat sank the *Vesta* while she was taking herring and wool to Britain.

The Icelandic fishing industry continued to develop rapidly. In 1914, Matthías Ólafsson complained in an article for *Lögrétta* that with Pike gone, corners were being cut and inferior salt-fish were being exported to Spain and Italy. Whether this was true or not, the industry went from strength to strength. The Icelandic deep sea fleet expanded rapidly and trawling was soon by far the nation's most important industry. The new telegraph system gave Icelanders the means to order the supplies and equipment, monitor prices and carry out international bank transactions. A proper harbour was built at Reykjavik with loans from Danish banks and made an enormous difference when it opened in 1917.

The economy took off despite a challenging period between 1914 and 1918, during the First World War. The British government agreed to buy Icelandic fish and keep the country supplied with imports for the duration of the war, but at the price of hindering Icelandic exports to Germany and the occupied states on mainland Europe. Although Denmark and Iceland remained neutral, the difficulties of war meant that Iceland had to manage its own affairs, proving that it could function independently of Danish oversight. In 1918 it became a sovereign state in a union with Denmark, essentially two countries with the same monarch. The link was finally severed in 1940 with the German invasion of Denmark and the British occupation of Iceland during the Second World War. The presence of British and then American troops in Iceland was an economic boon and helped to complete Iceland's transformation into a wealthy nation. Iceland became a fully independent republic in 1944.

After the Second World War, the British market for Icelandic salt-fish declined. The war had brought fishing and import constraints that changed eating habits, and in the 1950s advances in freezer technology and the fashion for convenience food made frozen fish the popular choice. In some parts of Pike's home county of Devon, it remained a traditional dish for Good Friday late into the 20th century, but on the whole the British had lost their taste for salt-fish.

However, the increased demand for fresh fish meant that access to Icelandic waters remained valuable to British trawler owners. The emergence of Icelandic trawling meant that further conflict with the British was inevitable. Four major disputes over fishing limits between 1952 and 1976 became known in English as the Cod Wars. Iceland argued that its action was justified by the country's unusual level of reliance on fishing, as over 90% of Icelandic exports were fish. A letter sent on 11th December 1975 from the Icelandic government to the UN Security Council illustrates how fundamentally important the deep sea fishing industry had become to Iceland in the space of just 70 years: '...no other independent state is so dependent upon ocean fishing as Iceland. Conservation of the fish stocks around Iceland is a matter of life and death for the Icelandic nation.' Iceland was victorious in all four conflicts, eventually extending jurisdiction over its waters from three miles to 200 miles.

For his role in developing commercial fishing in Iceland, Pike was awarded the Cross of the Order of the Icelandic Falcon in 1924. In 1936, apparently at the suggestion of Pike's old friend, the MP Jón Auðunn Jónsson, it was upgraded by King Christian X of Denmark to the Grand Cross; only heads of state can receive a higher honour from the nation. He wrote in acceptance, 'It makes me a proud man to accept this token of esteem from the Icelandic people.'

Pike Ward died in 1937 at the age of 80. He was cremated and his ashes were scattered at sea. This was a very unusual funeral arrangement for the time; in death as in life, Pike followed his own path. Shortly before he died, he wrote to his friend, the photographer Daníel Daníelsson, and hinted that he wished for his remains to be sent to Iceland. In the event, they were ceremonially cast from a boat in Teignmouth harbour.

He left his collection of around 400 Icelandic objects to the Royal Albert Memorial Museum in Exeter. In 1948, Jón Auðunn Jónsson travelled to Exeter and helped to negotiate its transfer to the National Museum of Iceland, where it is held today. The collection includes decorated drinking horns, silver cups, carved boxes, religious figures and altar pieces, traditional bowls and much besides.

In his will, Pike left £100 each to two nephews and two housekeepers, and he stipulated that whatever was left after the administration of his estate was to be given to Teignmouth Hospital for a bed or a ward to be named after his mother, 'one of the best, most unselfish and wonderful mothers a man could have.' Surprisingly, however, he left nothing to Edward, his only surviving son, who is not mentioned. Edward and his wife attended Pike's funeral, but in later life he rarely spoke of his father. The rift was not complete enough for Edward to destroy the photographs and papers, but his grandchildren recall a bitterness towards Pike that was never explained. To add to the mystery, the person most generously provided for was a Teignmouth woman of a similar age to Edward. To 'my friend' Margaret Anne Sarah Vening, Pike left an annuity of £50 a year for the rest of her life. She was 41, her date of birth being two days after Pike's wedding to Agnes. Her mother had been married to a wealthy older man but was now a widow and, two years after Pike's death, Margaret and her mother were both living at *Valhalla*. Perhaps Margaret had been kind to Pike later in his life; perhaps Pike had made an assurance to her father years before; or perhaps Pike knew or suspected that she was his daughter. She never married and had no children, so the question remains unanswered.

Pike's death was announced in the Icelandic newspapers. *Ægir* magazine recalled that he had taught Icelanders new ways to prepare fish, helping them to increase the value of their produce and bringing huge benefits to the country. His obituary told how he fell in love with Iceland, and how everyone who bought and sold fish still knew about Wardsfiskur. The headline in *Morgunblaðið* described him simply as 'Íslandsvinur', friend of Iceland, and he was remembered there for many years more by those who knew him. Ólafur Þorvaldsson was a boy when Pike lived in Hafnarfjörður, and he would sometimes travel with him in his horse-drawn cart. In the 1950s, he wrote fondly:

> 'Ward had been like the best father to me, and I missed him very much
> —and after fifty years I still remember him with respect and thanks.'

Following Pike's funeral, in an article for *The Teignmouth Gazette*, the artist May Morris recounted an afternoon spent in the study at *Valhalla*, 'all hung round with Icelandic treasures'. Like her father, William Morris, she was enormously interested in Icelandic culture and delighted in Pike's reminiscences. She wrote:

> 'Our love of Iceland was a bond of sympathy; we talked of the people, of the rivers and ice-mountains, of the things of artistic and historic value that he has collected... and the time passed unnoticed as we yarned on matters of the North. But beyond all this eager interest in and almost yearning love of the country of the Vikings, Pike Ward will always live in my mind as a man of wide sympathies and hearty friend-

ships, and it will be long before his cheerful personality and boundless generosity to all will be forgotten wherever his travels took him.'

Acknowledgements

It took two years to create this book from the original diaries, and many people have helped me along the way. I am thankful for the support of the Ward family, in particular Pike Ward's grandson Simon, great-grandson Steven, and great-granddaughter Andrea. It has also been a pleasure to meet his great-granddaughters Kathryn and Sally. I am indebted to two volunteers, Dr Sue Skinner at Devon Heritage Centre, who carried out the first transcription of the text with enormous dedication, and Lou Bagnald at Teign Heritage Centre, whose enthusiasm for the project has never wavered. Icelandic history specialist Dr Chris Callow at the University of Birmingham has given unstinting support, sharing his expertise and encouraging me throughout. Icelandic place-name scholar Hallgrímur J. Ámundason has answered my endless questions in detail and made many corrections, always with great generosity and positivity. I am grateful to historian of the fishing industry Dr Jón Þ Þór and food historian Dr Paul Cleave for their kindness and insights into their subjects. Rev Dr Andrew Jones helped me to learn about Congregationalism, and John Pike kindly allowed me access to the Devon Ball Clay Heritage Society archives. Inga L. Baldvinsdóttir at the National Museum of Iceland has helped me to understand the significance of the photographs and showed me the Ward collection of objects in storage. My friend Tyrfingur Tyrfingsson helped with detective work on Pike's unusual spellings, while Scott Pettitt and Linda Banks read early drafts and made helpful suggestions. I am grateful to Fleur Boyle and the team at Amphora Press for believing in the book and steering it to publication, and to Joe Chisholm and Frankie Sutherland for the artwork. For the care of the photographs and access to the collection, my thanks go to the staff and volunteers at Devon Heritage Centre. My thanks also to the following people who have all kindly contributed gems of information: Toni

Booth at the National Science and Media Museum; Professor Jon Fjeldså, Danish Museum of Natural History; Dr Phil Wickham, Bill Douglas Cinema Museum; Jón Sigurpálsson, Westfjords Heritage Museum; Sigurður Atlason, Museum of Icelandic Sorcery and Witch-craft; Dr Conchubhar Ó Crualaoich, Irish Department of Arts, Heritage, Regional, Rural & Gaeltacht Affairs; Þráinn Hallgrímsson, Efling Union, Andrew Findlay and Dr Ros Leveridge. Finally, thank you to my son, Rowan, who has lived with Pike Ward for all this time.

A note on the text

I was fortunate to discover eight volumes of Pike Ward's photographic scrapbooks in storage at the Devon Heritage Centre in Exeter while I was working there in 2016. I was immediately captivated by the story of a fellow Devonian who had fallen in love with Iceland over a century before me. My quest to find out more about him led me to the Ward family and I have been privileged to have access to their private collection of Pike's papers, which includes the notebooks that he entitled *The Book of Lies Volumes 1–3*.

Pike Ward wrote by hand and used very little punctuation. Within each diary entry, his ideas flow into each other as in speech. In this version of the text, therefore, the punctuation is almost entirely mine, with the exception of exclamation marks which Pike used enthusiastically. I have not altered his choice of words, nor changed their order, but I have removed a very large number of conjunctions to create manageable sentences. The choice of where sentences begin and end was often a matter of judgement, taking into account the context, fidelity to Pike's style and ease of reading.

Occasionally, where a word or a clause is illegible or apparently nonsensical in the original text, and has little impact on the meaning of the sentence, it has been removed. References to postcards or other material which the reader cannot see have also been removed. In one case, the second, repeated telling of an anecdote was removed entirely.

Although Pike spoke Icelandic, he used idiosyncratic, phonetic spelling that would be baffling to native speakers and learners alike. Therefore, all Icelandic words have been corrected to standard, modern Icelandic, including personal and place names. Since this approach was taken with Icelandic words, unusual or archaic spellings in English have been similarly adjusted. Any mistakes in the punctuation, editing and standardisation of words are mine alone.

Icelandic letters

Below are the letters used in this book that may be unfamiliar to non-Icelandic readers, along with similar sounds in English words:

Á á	'ou' in 'house'
Ð ð	'th' in 'feather'
É é	'ye' in 'yet'
Í í / Ý ý	'ee' in 'seek'
Ó ó	'oa' in 'goat'
Ú ú	'oo' in 'zoo'
Þ þ	'th' in 'thunder'
Æ æ	'i' in 'icy'
Ö ö	'u' in 'urgent'

Sources

Allen, V. 1998. *Hall Caine*. Sheffield: Sheffield Academic Press.

Alþingi. 2015. *Björn M. Ólsen*. [ONLINE] Available at: http://www. althingi.is/altext/cv/is/?nfaerslunr=89. [Accessed 25 October 2017].

Alþingi. 2015. *Guðmundur Björnsson*. [ONLINE] Available at: http://www.althingi.is/altext/cv/?nfaerslunr=182. [Accessed 29 July 2017].

Alþingi. 2015. *Guðjón Guðlaugsson*. [ONLINE] Available at: http://www.althingi.is/altext/cv/is/?nfaerslunr=173. [Accessed 29 July 2017].

Alþingi. 2015. *Júlíus Havsteen*. [ONLINE] Available at: http://www. althingi.is/altext/cv/is/?nfaerslunr=361. [Accessed 25 October 2017].

Anon. *Eyrbyggja Saga*. Translated with an introduction and notes by Hermann Pálsson and Paul Edwards, 1989. London: Penguin.

Anon, 1847. Tuition: Long-Ashton Academy. *The Bristol Mercury and Western Counties Advertiser*, 9 January 1847. 5.

Anon, 1861. Teignmouth. *Western Times*, 7 September 1861. 2.

Anon, 1861. Teignmouth Petty Sessions. *Supplement to the Western Times*, 21 December 1861. 3.

Anon, 1866. St Austell County Court. *The Shipping and Mercantile Gazette*, 26 October 1866. 2.

Anon, 1867. Plantation House School, Dawlish. *The Western Morning News*, 25 January 1867. 1.

Anon, 1870. In the matter of the Teignmouth and General Shipping Assurance Association. *Torquay Times and South Devon Advertiser*, 1 January 1870. 4.

Anon, 1867. Teignmouth Sea Wall. *Western Times*, 31 December 1867. 5.

Anon, 1870. New Congregational Church at Dawlish. *The Western Times*, 6 May 1870. 3.

Anon, 1871. New Chapel at Dawlish. *The Western Morning News*, 10 March 1871. 2.

Anon, 1882. The Famine in Iceland. *The Globe,* 31 October 1882. 6.

Anon, 1887. Teignmouth Quay Company Limited. *Exeter & Plymouth Gazette*, 6 December 1887. 4.

Anon, 1887. Teignmouth Quay Extension Scheme. *Western Times,* 12 December 1887. 3.

Anon, 1895. Grimsby Trawlers Seized Off Iceland. *The Lincolnshire Echo*, 11 July 1895. 3.

Anon, 1896. Aberdeen Trawlers at Iceland. *The Dundee Courier*, 1 May 1896. 3.

Anon, 1896. Iceland and the Trawlers. *The Aberdeen Press and Journal*, 3 August 1896. 4.

Anon, 1898. Iceland "Catches". Recent Seizures by Gunboat Under Danish Rule. *The Hull Daily Mail,* 3 June 1898. 3.

Anon, 1898. Iceland and Great Britain. *The Aberdeen Press and Journal*, 3 January 1898. 4.

Anon, 1898. Iceland's Freed Fishing. *The Aberdeen Press and Journal*, 4 January 1898. 6.

Anon, 1899. News from Iceland. *The Aberdeen Press and Journal*, 27 September 1899. 8.

Anon, 1900. Illegal Fishing off Iceland. *The Morning Post*. 22 January 1900. 3.

Anon, 1900. The Trade of Iceland. *The Dundee Evening Post*. 8 November 1900. 2.

Anon, 1900. Icelanders for Canada. *The Dundee Evening Post*. 15 November 1900. 2.

Anon, 1900. Progress in Iceland. *Pall Mall Gazette*, 7 November 1900. 8.

Anon, 1901. A Chat About Iceland. *The South Bucks Standard*. 8 March, 1901. 5.

Anon, 1902. Auglýsing. *Austri*, 28 February 1902. 23

Anon, 1902. Icelanders and Liquor. *The Northern Whig*. 18 August, 1902. 5.

Anon, 1902. Exeter Day by Day. *The Western Times*, 10 September 1902. 3.

Anon, 1902. Baldwin's Polar Dash. *Dundee Courier*, 22 September 1902. 5.

Anon, 1903. Telegraphic Communication with Iceland. The Aberdeen Press and Journal, 7 March, 1903. 5.

Anon, 1903. Wards fiskverzluni, ný peningalind. *Austri*, 5 October 1903. 122.

Anon, A, 1903. Wardsfiskur. *Gjallarhorn*, 13 November 1903. 124.

Anon, 1904. Vatnsleiðlsurnáið. *Reykjavík*, 5 (23), 90-91.

Anon, 1904. The Iceland Cable. *The London Evening Standard*, 27 September, 1904. 3.

Anon, 1906. Björgunarbátur. *Frækorn*, 16, 126.

Anon, 1906. Samskot. *Norðri,* 20, 80.

Anon, 1906. Earthquake and fire: San Francisco in ruins. *Call-Chronicle-Examiner*, 19 April 1906. 1.

Anon, 1906. News of the West: Teignmouth. *Western Times*, 24 April 1906. 2.

Anon, 1906. Drama in Iceland. *The Exeter and Plymouth Gazette*. 26 July, 1906. 4.

Anon, 1906. The Iceland Fishing Industry. *The Aberdeen Press and Journal*. 31 August 1906. 6.

Anon, 1906. The Telegraph Cable to Iceland. *The Lichfield Mercury*, 31 August 1906. 8.

Anon, 1906. The Herring Fishing at Iceland; Very Successful Season. *The Shields Daily News*, 15 September 1906. 3.

Anon, 1906. Some Impressions of Iceland. The Barnet Press. 27 October 1906. 7.

Anon, 1909. Uppboðsauglýsing. *Ísafold*, 20 March 1909. 63.

Anon, 1909. Skip. *Austri*, 18 September 1909. 125.

Anon, 1910. Skip. *Austri*, 21 May 1910. 69.

Anon, 1910. Skip. *Austri*, 14 October 1910. 131.

Anon, 1911. Skip. *Austri*, 15 July 1911. 107.

Anon, 1911. Skip. *Austri*, 7 November 1911. 161.

Anon, 1912 Skip. *Austri*, 31 August 1912. 129

Anon, 1913. Skip. *Austri*, 3 May 1913. 62.

Anon, 1913. Pike Ward fiskikaupmaður. *Óðinn*, 1 August 1913. 1.

Anon, 1917. Jóhannes Pétursson, kaupmaður. *Morgunblaðið*, 12 July 1917. 3.

Anon, 1919. Dr. Björn M. Ólsen. *Morgunblaðið*, 17 January 1919. 1.

Anon, 1924. Friðrik Ferdinand Wathne. *Hænir*, 9 February 1924. 23.

Anon, 1929. Dagbók: Björgunarbátur. *Morgunblaðið*, 14 April 1929. 8.

Anon, 1929. Famous Schooner to Be Broken Up. *The Northern Whig and Belfast Post*, 19 September 1929. 10.

Anon, 1929. Slysavarnafjelag Íslands. *Lesbók Morgunblaðsins*, 13, 98-99.

Anon, 1932. Deaths: Sigurdsson. *The Scotsman*, 20 October 1932. 16.

Anon, 1935. Asgeir Sigurðsson, konsúll, látinn. *Morgunblaðið*, 27 September 1935. 3.

Anon, 1935. Deaths: Sigurdsson. *The Scotsman*, 28 September 1935. 24.

Anon, 1937. Íslandsvinur látinn. *Morgunblaðið*, 16 April 1937. 4.

Anon, 1937. Pike Ward. *Ægir*, 1 July 1937. 138.

Anon, 1945. Louis Zöllner konsúll látinn. *Morgunblaðið*, 23 January 1945. 12.

Anon, 1949. Dr. phil. Helgi Péturss minningarord. *Morgunblaðið*, 5 February 1949. 11.

Anon, 1950. Borgarsafn Exeter gefur Þjóðminjasafninu á fjórða hundrað muni. *Morgunblaðið*, 8 March 1950. 9.

Anon, 1950. Gull í Vatnsmýrinni. *Lesbók Morgunblaðsins*, 26 March 1950. 1.

Anon, 1981. Endalaus auðnin og ógnþrunginn hvítur jökull. *Morgunblaðið*, 24 January 1981. 13.

Anon, 1987. Sjötíu manns farast á Faxaflóa, þar af 20 fyrir augum Reykvíkinga—engum vörnum við komid. *Morgunblaðið*, 18 October 1987. 5.

Anon, A, 1998. Bragi Halldórsson aðalféhirðir látinn. *Víkurfréttir*, 20 August 1998. 7.

Atkinson, G.L. and Doughty, G, 1897. The Icelandic Fisheries. *The Hull Daily Mail*, 31 March 1897. 3.

Benediktsson, Kristin, 2006. Á um 30 hús á Austurlandi. *Morgunblaðið*, 27 March 2006. 1.

Congregational Federation. 2017. *A Century of Women's Ordination*. [ONLINE] Available at: https://www.congregational.org.uk/the-congregationalist/a-century-of-womenas-ordination. [Accessed 10 November 2017].

Cook, F.A, 1909. *Through the First Antarctic Night, 1898-1899.* New York: Doubleday, Page & Co.

Crangle, R., Herbert S. and Robinson, D., 2001. *Encyclopaedia of the Magic Lantern.* Exeter: Magic Lantern Society.

Daníelsson, Daníel, 1937. *Í Áföngum.* Reykjavík: Steindórsprent.

Devonshire Association. 2017. *The Devon-Newfoundland Story.* [ONLINE] Available at: http://devonassoc.org.uk/the-devon-newfoundland-story/. [Accessed 12 November 2017].

Edinborg menningarmiðstöð. 2007. *Saga hússins.* [ONLINE] Available at: http://www.edinborg.is/index.asp?lang=is&cat=31&page=576. [Accessed 28 August 2017].

Einar Jónsson Museum. 2017. *Outlaws.* [ONLINE] Available at: http://www.lej.is/news/21/80/Outlaws-1901/d,nodate/. [Accessed 27 October 2017].

Eldon, 1945. Northern Outlook. *Newcastle Evening Chronicle,* 22 January 1945. 3.

'Eliza Ward', 1902. England, Wales & Scotland Census return for Teign St, West Teignmouth. [ONLINE] Available at: http://www.findmypast.co.uk/. [Accessed 6 November 2017].

'Eliza Ward', England & Wales Deaths 1837-2007, Newton Abbot, Devon. 5B, 193. [ONLINE] Available at: http://www.findmypast.co.uk/. [Accessed 6 November 2017].

Fjelagið Bjólfur, 1910. *Til Mr Pike Ward.* Private collection.

'George Perkins Ward', England & Wales Deaths 1837-2007, Newton Abbot, Devon. 5B, 83. [ONLINE] Available at: http://www.findmypast.co.uk/. [Accessed 9 November 2017].

'George Perkins Ward and Eliza Pike', Exeter: All Hallows on the Walls Parish Registers, Marriages 1837-1912. 2739A/PR/1/7. Devon Heritage Centre, Exeter.

Gunnlaugsson, Gísli Ágúst, 1980. Fiskveiðideila íslendinga og Breta 1896 og 1897, mynd 4: W. G. Spence Paterson. *Saga tímarit sögufélags,* 18, 108.

G.V. Turnball and Co., 1906. Iceland, Iceland. Advertisement in *The London Evening Standard.* 2 June, 1906. 1.

Hall Caine, T.H., 1905. *The Works of Hall Caine Volume 10: The Prodigal Son*. London: Heinemann.

Hall Caine, T.H., 1905. Letter to Pike Ward, 13 July 1905. In *Pike Ward's Icelandic Scrapbook,* volume 8. PKW/1/8. Devon Heritage Centre, Exeter

Helgi Pjeturss Institute. 2017. *Helgi Pjeturss Studies in Cosmobiology.* [ONLINE] Available at: http://www.helgipjeturss.is/?lang=en. [Accessed 30 September 2017].

Higgins, J. 2007. *19th Century Cod Fisheries*. [ONLINE] Available at: http://www.heritage.nf.ca/articles/economy/19th-century-cod.php. [Accessed 12 November 2017].

Huff, C. 1988. Diaries and Diarists. In: Mitchell, S. ed. *Victorian Britain: An Encyclopedia*. London: Routledge.

Ingólfsson, Ólafur. 2008. *Icelandic Glaciers*. [ONLINE] Available at: https://notendur.hi.is/oi/icelandic_glaciers.htm. [Accessed 20 October 2017].

Joensen,Tómas and Þórhallsson, Baldur, 2015. Iceland's external affairs from the Napoleonic era to the occupation of Denmark: Danish and British shelter. *Icelandic Review of Politics and Administration*, 11, No 2, 187-204.

Jónsson, Hannes, 1982. *Friends in Conflict: The Anglo-Icelandic Cod Wars and the Law of the Sea*. London: C. Hurst & Co.

Jónsson, Jón Auðunn, 1936. Letter to Pike Ward, 28 February 1936. Private collection.

Jónsson, Jón Auðunn, 1972. Mr. Pike Ward og fyrstu fiskkaup hans við Ísafjarðardjúp. *Ársrit Sögufélags Ísfirðinga*, XVI.

JSBlog—Journal of a Southern Bookreader. 2015. *Labrador Bay and its Tea Gardens*. [ONLINE] Available at: http://jsbookreader.blogspot.co.uk/2015/01/labrador-bay-and-its-tea-gardens.html. [Accessed 30 September 2017].

Karlsson, Gunnar, 2000. *The History of Iceland*. Minneapolis: University of Minnesota Press.

Kiernan, K. et al, 1998. *Lone Motherhood in Twentieth-century Britain*. Oxford: Clarendon Press.

Kristjánsson, Lúðvík, 1944. Þættir úr sögu íslenzkrar togaraútgerðar. *Ægir*, 1 November 1944. 220.

Magnússon, Sigurður Gylfi, 2010. *Wasteland with Words*. London: Reaktion Books.

Marconi Wireless Telegraph Co., Correspondence about a possible wireless installation in Iceland, 1905-6, MS. Marconi 213. Bodleian Library, University of Oxford.

'Margaret Anne Sarah Vening', 1911. Census for England & Wales return for 50 Bitton Avenue, Teignmouth. [ONLINE] Available at: http://www.findmypast.co.uk/. [Accessed 6 November 2017].

'Margaret Anne Sarah Vening', 1939. National Register return for Upper Hermosa Road, Teignmouth. [ONLINE] Available at: http://www.findmypast.co.uk/. [Accessed 6 November 2017].

'Margaret Anne Sarah Vening', England & Wales Deaths 1837-2007, Newton Abbot, Devon. 21, 1622. [ONLINE] Available at: http://www.findmypast.co.uk/. [Accessed 6 November 2017].

Morris, M, 1937. Funeral of Mr Pike Ward: An Appreciation. *The Teignmouth Gazette*, 17 February 1937. 2.

Ólafsdóttir, Hildigunnur, 2000. *Alcoholics Anonymous in Iceland: From Marginality to Mainstream Culture*. Reykjavík: University of Iceland Press.

Ólafsson, Jón Þ., 1990. Saltfiskur við sundin blá. *Ægir*, 1 October 1990. 510.

Ólafsson, Matthías, 1914. Fiskverkunin á Íslandi. *Lögrétta*, 14 October 1914. 69.

Östlund, D, 1904. Ferðapistlar 1. Skotland. *Frækorn*, 5 (14), 110-112.

'Pike Ward', 1861. England, Wales & Scotland Census return for the Strand, East Teignmouth. [ONLINE] Available at: http://www.findmypast.co.uk/. [Accessed 6 November 2017].

'Pike Ward', 1864. East Teignmouth Parish Registers, Baptisms 1834-1886. 3231A/PR/1/4. Devon Heritage Centre, Exeter.

'Pike Ward', 1871 and 1881. England, Wales & Scotland Census returns for Northumberland Place, East Teignmouth. [ONLINE] Available at: http://www.findmypast.co.uk/. [Accessed 6 November 2017].

'Pike Ward', 1891. England Wales & Scotland census return for Teign St, West Teignmouth. [ONLINE] Available at: http://www.findmypast.co.uk/. [Accessed 6 November 2017].

'Pike Ward', 1911. Census for England & Wales return for 25 Teign St, West Teignmouth. [ONLINE] Available at: http://www. findmypast.co.uk/. [Accessed 6 November 2017].

'Pike Ward and Grace Agnes Wollacott', 1896. Certified copy of the marriage certificate of Pike Ward and Grace Agnes Wollocott, 20 April 1896. Application number 8302157-1. General Register Office.

'Pike Ward',1936. Certificate of stórriddarakrossi conferred by King Christian X. Private collection.

Pike Ward Ltd. 2016. *About us.* [ONLINE] Available at: http://www. pikeward.co.uk/. [Accessed 29 October 2017].

Plantation House, Dawlish,1824- 1916, title collection, 5843F/T. Devon Heritage Centre, Exeter.

Redding Ware, J. 1909. *Passing English of the Victorian Era: A Dictionary of Heterodox English, Slang and Phrase.* London: Routledge.

Statistics Iceland. 2017. *Live births by marital status and age of mother 1853-2016.* [ONLINE] Available at: https://www.statice.is/. [Accessed 17 August 2017].

Thomsen, S, 1988. Thomsensverslun í þrjár kynslóðir. *Morgunblaðið*, 2 October 1988. 10-11.

'Thorarin Ward' 1901. Certified copy of death certificate of Thorarin Ward, 5 October 1901. Application number 8302146-1. General Register Office.

Thoroddsen, G, 1953. Knud Zimsen fyrrverandi borgarstjóri. *Morgunblaðið*, 21 April 1953. 7.

US National Archives. 2017. *San Francisco Earthquake 1906.* [ONLINE] Available at: https://www.archives.gov/legislative/features/sf. [Accessed 6 August 2017].

Vestberg, J, 1944. Thor E. Tulinius in *Danish Biographical Reading* , 3rd edition. Gyldendal 1979-84. Accessed August 25, 2017 from http://denstoredanske.dk/index.php?sideId=298597

Ward, P. 1898. *A Voyage from Liverpool to Labrador, August 1898.* Private collection.

Ward, P. 1936. Draft of letter to J.Sveinbjörnsson, 10 April 1936. Private collection.

Ward, P. Date unknown. *Pike Ward's Icelandic Scrapbook,* volumes 1-8. PKW/1/1 to PKW/1/8. Devon Heritage Centre, Exeter.

Watts, Blake, Bearne & Co., 1868-1929. Letter books nos.20-321. Devon Ball Clay Heritage Society Archive, Newton Abbot.

Wreck Site. 2010. *SS Ceres (+1917)*. [ONLINE] Available at: https://www.wrecksite.eu/wreck.aspx?132059 [Accessed 10 December 2017].

Wreck Site. 2011. *SS Kong Inge (+1906)*. [ONLINE] Available at: https://www.wrecksite.eu/wreck.aspx?202863. [Accessed 10 December 2017].

Wreck Site. 2013. *SS Vesta (+1917)*. [ONLINE] Available at: https://www.wrecksite.eu/wreck.aspx?134834. [Accessed 10 December 2017].

Wreck Site. 2014. *SS Laura (+1910)*. [ONLINE] Available at: https://www.wrecksite.eu/wreck.aspx?217518. [Accessed 10 December 2017].

Þórðardóttir, Hjálmfríður. 2009. *Vatnsveitan 100 ára*. [ONLINE] Available at: https://efling.is/2009/11/26/vatnsveitan-100-ara/. [Accessed 4 August 2017].

Þorvaldsson, Ólafur, 1950. Fólk glápti hissa á fyrsta vagn inn sem fór Hafnarfjarðarveg. *Lesbók Morgunblaðsins*, 7 May 1950. 1.

Þorvaldsson, Ólafur, 1951. *Harðsporar*. Reykjavík: Prentsmiðja Austurlands.